An Illustrated Handbook of
HORSE & PONY
CARE

An Illustrated Handbook of
HORSE & PONY
CARE

TIM HAWCROFT B.V.Sc(Hons) M.A.C.V.Sc
Consultant   Jane Kidd

Crescent Books
NEW YORK

A SALAMANDER BOOK

First English edition published by Salamander Books Ltd by arrangement with Merehurst Ltd, 5 Great James Street, London WC1N 3DA.

This 1987 edition is published by Crescent Books, distributed by Crown Publishers, Inc., 225 Park Avenue South, New York, New York 10003.

ISBN 0-517-62829-5

CREDITS

Editor: Jocelyn Finnis
Colour Reproductions: York House Graphics Ltd, London, England
Typeset by AKM Associates (UK) Ltd, Southall, London
Printed in Belgium by Proost International Book Production, Turnhout, Belgium

AUTHOR

Tim Hawcroft was born in Sydney, Australia, in 1946. He has been involved with horses from early childhood, learning how to handle horses and riding in gymkhanas. He graduated from the University of Sydney as a veterinary surgeon in 1968. Since then, he has been in private veterinary practice, specialising in the problems of racehorses. He has also been involved in stud work and general horse and pony practice as well as working with race clubs, checking the fitness of racehorses. As a Member of the Australian College of Veterinary Scientists, he has presented many papers to the leading Australian equine bodies, such as the Australian Equine Research Foundation and the Australian Equine Veterinary Association.

CONSULTANT

Jane Kidd has ridden internationally in show jumping and dressage and has many books on equestrian subjects to her credit. Among others, she has written *The Better Horse, Horsemanship in Europe* and *Festival of Dressage*. For Salamander Books, she has written *Horse Breeds and Breeding*, and has compiled *The Complete Horse Encyclopaedia, The Horse and Pony Manual* and *An Illustrated Guide to Horse and Pony Care*. She has also extensively revised *The New Observer's Book of Horses and Ponies* and is a regular contributor to leading equestrian magazines, including *Horse and Hound*.

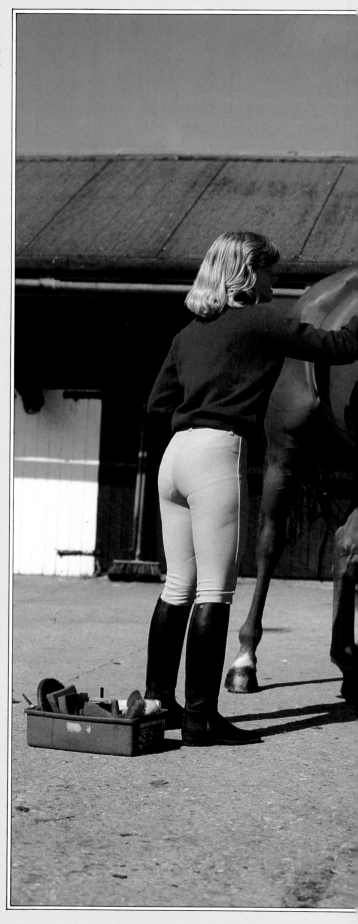

CONTENTS

INTRODUCTION

For horse owners, breeders, riders, trainers, stud masters and others who are closely interested in and active with horses, there are rich and rewarding experiences. Observing and helping with the birth of a foal, grooming a horse's coat till it gleams, riding a disciplined yet fresh and willing colt, participating in a pony club or gymkhana, and feeling companionship and closeness with the horse in the daily management of feeding, grooming and handling; these are only a few of the many experiences that can give great satisfaction.

The healthy, well-behaved and well-disciplined horse may be regarded as normal, and the purpose of horse care is to maintain that state. But at times there are problems, and these may cause worry, work, a degree of sacrifice, additional expense and even an increase in danger.

Some problems are inherent in the nature of the horse, such as lameness due to poor conformation. Others are manmade because of the environment that is provided: fractures caused by reckless galloping over uneven ground, haemorrhage and wounds due to the horse being frightened when tethered to a barbed wire fence, and colic caused by a haphazard worming programme. Such problems as these and others may be alleviated, reduced or even avoided if proper preventative and corrective measures are taken. The information in this book, based as it is on sound veterinary knowledge and experience, will help if conscientiously applied; it will also help to discourage many unsound practices in horse care that have been carried out through lack of proper scientific information.

No matter how complete a book may purport to be, it cannot hope to give information that will be universally applicable. If in any doubt, seek advice from a recognised authority. Always keep in mind that horses, like humans, are individuals and must be treated as such. Good selection, good housing, good feeding, good training and loving care usually lead to a healthy horse, a fruitful owner-horse relationship and hours of pleasurable relaxation.

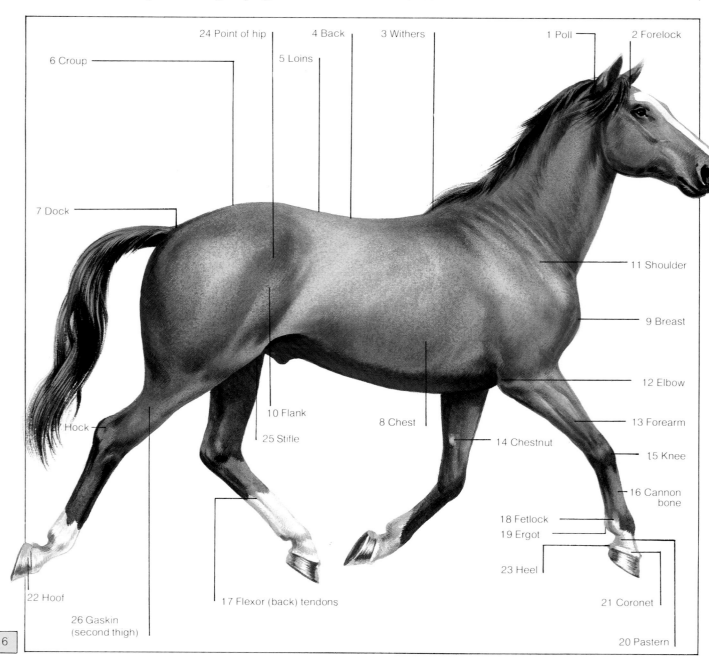

24 Point of hip — 4 Back — 3 Withers — 1 Poll — 2 Forelock
6 Croup
5 Loins
7 Dock
11 Shoulder
9 Breast
12 Elbow
10 Flank
8 Chest
13 Forearm
Hock
25 Stifle
14 Chestnut
15 Knee
16 Cannon bone
18 Fetlock
19 Ergot
23 Heel
22 Hoof
17 Flexor (back) tendons
21 Coronet
26 Gaskin (second thigh)
20 Pastern

POINTS OF A HORSE

1 The poll is the bony prominence lying beween the ears. Except for the ears, it is the highest point on the horse's body when it is standing with its head up.

2 The forelock is the hair that covers the forehead and that grows from the poll area. It must not be confused with the fetlock.

3 The withers is the prominent ridge where the neck and back join. At this ridge, powerful muscles of the neck and shoulder attach to elongated spines of the second to the 6th thoracic vertebrae. The height of the horse is measured vertically from the withers to the ground, because the withers is the horse's highest constant point.

4 The back extends from the base of the withers to where the last rib is attached.

5 The loin or coupling is the short area joining the back to the powerful muscular croup (rump).

6 The croup (rump) lies between the loin and the tail. When one is looking from the side or back, it is the highest point of the hindquarters.

7 The dock is the bony portion of the tail that tapers to a point about one-third of the way down the tail.

8 The chest is encased by the ribs, extending from between the forelegs to the flanks.

9 The breast is a muscle mass between the forelegs, covering the front of the chest.

10 The flank is the area below the loin, between the last rib and the massive muscles of the thigh.

11 The point of the shoulder is a hard, bony prominence surrounded by heavy muscle masses. It is approximately level with the intersection of the lower line of the neck and the body.

12 The elbow is a bony prominence lying against the chest at the beginning of the forearm.

13 The forearm extends from the elbow to the knee.

14 The chestnuts are horny growths on the insides of the legs, located approximately halfway down.

15 The knee is the joint between the forearm and the cannon bone.

16 The cannon bone or shin, as it is called when in the foreleg, lies between the knee and the fetlock, and is visible from the front.

17 The flexor (back) tendons run from the knee to the fetlock and can be seen lying behind the cannon bone.

18 The fetlock is the joint between the cannon bone and the pastern.

19 The ergot is a horny growth at the back of the fetlock, hidden by a tuft of hair.

20 The pastern extends from the fetlock to the top of the hoof (coronet).

21 The coronet is a band around the top of the hoof from which the hoof wall grows.

22 The hoof refers to the horny wall and sole of the foot. The foot includes the horny structure and the pedal and navicular bones, as well as other connective tissues.

23 The heels are the bulbs at the back of the hoof and, while horny in texture, they are softer than the normal hoof wall.

24 The point of the hip is a bony prominence lying just forward and below the croup. This is not the hip joint.

25 The stifle is a joint at the end of the thigh corresponding to the human knee.

26 The gaskin (second thigh) is the region between the stifle and the hock.

27 The hock is the joint between the gaskin and the cannon bone. The bony protuberance at the back is called the point of the hock. It may be easily injured, especially when the horse kicks.

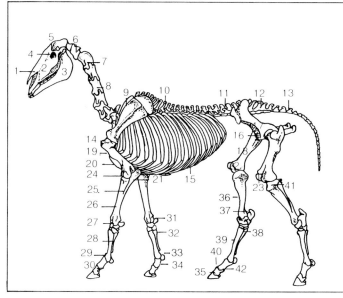

1 Nasal bone		**22** Stifle joint	
2 Maxillary bone		**23** Patella	
3 Mandible		**24** Elbow joint	
4 Orbit		**25** Ulna	
5 Frontal bone		**26** Radius	
6 Atlas		**27** Carpus	
7 Axis		**28** Cannon (metacarpal) bone	
8 Cervical vertebrae		**29** Fetlock joint	
9 Scapula		**30** Coffin joint	
10 Thoracic vertebrae		**31** Accessory carpal bone	
11 Lumbar vertebrae		**32** Splint bone	
12 Sacral vertebrae		**33** Sesamoid bone	
13 Coccygeal vertebrae		**34** First phalanx	
14 Shoulder joint		**35** Pedal bone	
15 Ribs — 18 in number		**36** Tibia	
16 Pelvis		**37** Tarsal bones	
17 Hip joint		**38** Splint bone	
18 Femur		**39** Cannon bone	
19 Humerus		**40** Pastern joint	
20 Sternum		**41** Fibula	
21 Olecranon		**42** Navicular bone	

BUYING A HORSE

In buying a horse, you should first consider what it will be used for. This will dictate the importance that should be given to such characteristics as conformation, temperament, breed, fertility, soundness, age and size when making a selection. For example, if you intend to buy a horse for breeding, you will concentrate on examining the reproductive system, as well as generally checking conformation, temperament and other characteristics. The selection of a horse for racing places emphasis on conformation, pedigree, soundness and ability to gallop; when buying a first horse for a child, you will give particular attention to the horse's temperament and size. A veterinary surgeon should then be engaged to evaluate the horse's health in greater detail. This examination would include checking the horse's sexuality, its eyes for blindness, its heart for abnormalities and its respiratory tract for 'roaring'. Of course, the emphasis during the examination will vary according to such factors as the age of the horse, its previous history and the kind of work that the intending buyer expects it to perform. This section focuses in turn on every aspect to be considered when choosing a horse.

CONFORMATION

Conformation is the name given to the overall size and shape of the body and the limbs, and the relationship of the limbs with one another and with the body. It is the product of genetic and environmental factors; genetic factors include good heredity (a sire and a dam with good conformation are likely to produce a foal with good conformation) and environmental factors include good nutrition and disease control.

The mare plays an important environmental role in good conformation through her influence on the foetus in her uterus and on the young foal by her side up to the time of weaning. Another important environmental influence in the development of the horse's conformation is the stud manager, who determines nutrition and parasite and disease control.

Poor conformation can produce abnormal strain on a particular part of the body or legs. Depending on the severity of the conformation defect, the tissues in the area can be stretched, torn or broken, thus leading to lameness. If this is permanent and renders the horse incapable of performing to the best of its ability, the animal is unsound.

Even a horse with perfect conformation can go lame because of trauma, fatigue, nutritional deficiencies, forced training, improper shoeing, performing on bad ground and other external factors. At least if you select a horse with near-perfect conformation, you can reduce the risk of lameness, which could result in an unsound horse.

In examining a horse's conformation, look at it standing still a short distance away to ascertain its overall balance. Then examine it more closely for body detail, the detail of each limb, and the relationship of the limbs to each other. The horse should then be observed in motion to evaluate its co-ordination.

Conformation is an important factor in determining whether or not all parts of the body work together harmoniously while the horse is in motion.

Above: Horses with near-perfect conformation are rare. This horse's back is rather straight, but he has a good front with an intelligent elegant head and a bold outlook.

Above: The body should be well-proportioned so that every section is in balance. This horse's neck is of a good length for the body. The back is neither too long nor too short.

Body Conformation

The relationship between conformation of the body and the limbs is more important than body conformation itself. The body should be well-proportioned and in balance with the limbs. Size varies between different breeds, and this should be taken into account when evaluating the horse. However, certain conformation characteristics such as the angle and length of the pastern are common to all breeds.

Horses with near-perfect conformation are rare, so when buying a horse you have to weigh up the good points against the bad, taking into account the purpose for which the horse will be used. However, even with this knowledge in the back of your mind, don't lower your standards and always aim to purchase a horse with perfect conformation.

The head should be neither too big nor too small; it should be intelligent-looking and well set on the neck. The forehead should be broad, with the eyes set well apart, and the nostrils should be large with well-defined edges. The carriage of the head should not be too high or too low, otherwise it will interfere with the horse's sight and balance.

The neck can be a very attractive feature. It should be of ample length (ie, in the right proportion to the head and body) with an arch, a curved top line and a straight bottom line.

The muscles of the shoulders should be well-developed. A long, sloping shoulder allows greater flexibility of the joint, permitting a longer stride and giving a smoother

Above: This horse has a sway back. It is very hollow which will make the back weak, and such horses rarely stand up to hard work.

ride. Straight, upright shoulders can increase concussion and give a rough, unpleasant ride.

The chest should be rounded and have plenty of depth (a good girth). The width of the chest between the forelegs should be sufficient to eliminate any friction between the forelimbs.

Normal forelimb confromation

1   2   3

Normal hindlimb conformation

4

Located at the base of the neck, the withers are the high point of the horse's back and it is from this point that a horse's height is measured. The width, height and length of the withers should be sufficient to provide a good anchor for the saddle. Thin, over-prominent withers are prone to damage from the saddle.

The back should be strong because it bears the weight of the rider. Long backs are weaker than shorter ones, and they predispose the horse to back strain. Short backs, on the other hand, predispose the horse to interference between hind and front limbs when it is in motion. The line of the back should not be too concave (sway back) nor in any way convex (roach back).

The quarters should be powerful (well-muscled) but in proportion with the rest of the body. It is from this region of the body that the horse gets most of its forward thrust for such movements as galloping and jumping. The top of the hindquarters should be rounded, not falling away too sharply.

Limb Conformation

To assess this aspect of a horse's conformation, the horse should be standing squarely on a flat, hard surface, bearing its weight equally on all four legs.

The amount of weight taken on the forelimbs can vary according to overall conformation. The forelimbs not only bear some 60 to 65 per cent of the body weight at certain times when the horse is in motion, but also aid the hindlimbs in propelling the body forward. The forelimbs are subject to more injuries than the hindlimbs because of the extra concussion and stress placed upon them, as well as their structure. Ideal conformation does not put excess strain on any single structure of the limb.

When the horse is seen from the front, the chest appear to be well-developed and well-muscled and the legs should be straight. An imaginary line from the point of the shoulder to the foot should divide the leg into two equal parts. The toes of the feet should point straight forward and the feet should be as wide apart on the ground as the origin of the legs at the chest. The knees should be flat, not deviating towards or away from one another. The cannon bone should be centred under the knee.

From the side, an imaginary line from the spinous process of the shoulder blade should divide the leg into two equal parts down to the fetlock joint and continue to ground level to a point just behind the heel.

The muscles of the forearm should be well-developed and should balance the limb. The knee should not bend forward (standing over at the knee) or backward (back at the knee). The cannon bone should not give the impression of being tied-in below the knee. The pastern should be of correct length (ie, in proportion to the total length of the leg) and the hoof wall should slope at the same angle as the pastern. The angle between the sloping hoof wall and the ground surface of the foot should be between 45 and 50 degrees.

When the horse is studied from behind, an imaginary line drawn from the point of the pelvis should divide the leg into two equal parts. The hocks should be large, strong, clean and well-defined.

When the horse is viewed from the side, a line drawn from the point of the pelvis should touch the point of the hock, run down the rear aspect of the cannon and touch the ground 7–10 cm behind the heels. The angle of the stifle and hock should be neither too straight nor too acute.

The forefoot should be round at the toe and wide at the heels. The wall should be thickest at the toe, thinning at the quarter and thicker at the heel. The sole should be moderately concave and the ideal angle made by the face of the wall and the sole at the toe is 45 to 50 degrees.

The frog should divide the sole into halves. It should be well-developed and rubbery in consistency. When the horse is bearing weight on the foot, the frog should be touching the ground.

The hindfoot is more pointed at the toe and the sole is more concave than the forefoot. The angle made by the face of the wall and the sole at the toe is between 50 and 55 degrees.

11

CONFORMATION FAULTS

There are several conformation faults in combination, such as base-wide with the feet turning out, or base-wide with the feet turning in. Irrespective of whether the feet turn in or out, this fault places abnormal stress on the medial (inside) part of the leg because the horse tends to land on the inside wall of the hoof. The horse is thus more likely to suffer from medial sidebone, ringbone and wind galls of the fetlock joint.

The base-narrow conformation results in the outside edge of the foot hitting the ground first, placing stress on the lateral (outside) aspect of the limb. Lateral sidebone, ringbone, and wind galls of the fetlock joint are related to this type of fault.

If the horse has short or long upright pasterns, the concussion on the fetlock joint, pastern and navicular bone may predispose the front of the fetlock to osselet formation. A short pastern may lead to ringbone and concussion on the navicular bone may lead to navicular disease.

If a horse has long, sloping pasterns, instead of the concussion being distributed between the bones and the tendons when the horse is in motion, most of it is placed on the flexor tendons, suspensory ligament and sesamoid bones. This predisposes the flexor tendon and suspensory ligament to sprain and the sesamoid bone to inflammation and fracture.

When the cannon bone is offset, ie, when it deviates laterally from under the knee, the upper medial (inside) area of the cannon is placed under excessive strain, predisposing it to splint formation. This condition is known as bench knees.

Knee problems can range from joint capsule strain to ligament strain, arthritis, chip fractures and slab fractures. Slight forward deviation of the knees (over at the knees) is not necessarily a bad thing. Backward deviation of the knees (behind at the knees, medial deviation of the knees or knock knees) and lateral deviation of the knees (bow legs) are all serious conformation faults. They can give rise to one or more of the above-mentioned problems.

A hindlimb fault is cow hocks. When the horse is studied from the rear, the hocks are close together and point toward one another and the feet are widely separated with the toes pointing outwards, causing strain on the inside of the hock. This predisposes the horse to bog and bone spavin.

Another hock fault is known as sickle hocks. The angle of the hock joint is greater than ideal, placing stress on the ligament just below the point of the hock and predisposing the horse to curb.

The fault of being straight behind occurs when too little angle in the stifle can result in upward fixation of the patella (locked stifle). Too little angle in the hock may give rise to knee problems.

A common foot fault is flat sole, in which the soles of the front feet in particular may be flat, rather than

Above: Young foals often suffer with medial deviation of the knees (knock knees) which can be successfully treated by hoof trimming.

concave as they should be. In the heavy breeds, the incidence of flat sole is higher than it is in the lighter breeds. Flat sole predisposes the horse to bruising, pedal osteitis and lameness.

The sole may be convex or flat, instead of being concave (dropped sole). This condition is often due to rotation downwards of the pedal bone as a result of chronic founder. Horses with dropped soles are often chronically lame.

Contracted heels is a condition that occurs when the frog does not touch the ground.

Rings on the hoof wall can be normal, or they may indicate some previous upset of the horse's well-being such as an infection, malnutrition (perhaps due to drought) or founder. There is no need for concern if rings only are present in the foot, but if a closer examination reveals other abnormalities such as flat sole, dropped sole, contracted heels or club foot, the owner may have reason for concern. You can probably find the causes of rings in the horse's history.

A horse may suffer from a club foot. This is a foot that is very upright and is associated with a short toe and long heels that are often contracted. It can be caused by injury, disease, malnutrition or improper trimming and shoeing. Horses with this condition are susceptible to suspensory ligament trouble and invariably have a rough gait.

After you are satisfied that your horse has good body and limb conformation, the next step is to evaluate the horse's co-ordination. To do this, it is necessary to see the horse in motion.

Below: Various shapes of pastern, all of which have weaknesses apart from the far left.

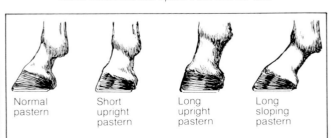

Normal pastern

Short upright pastern

Long upright pastern

Long sloping pastern

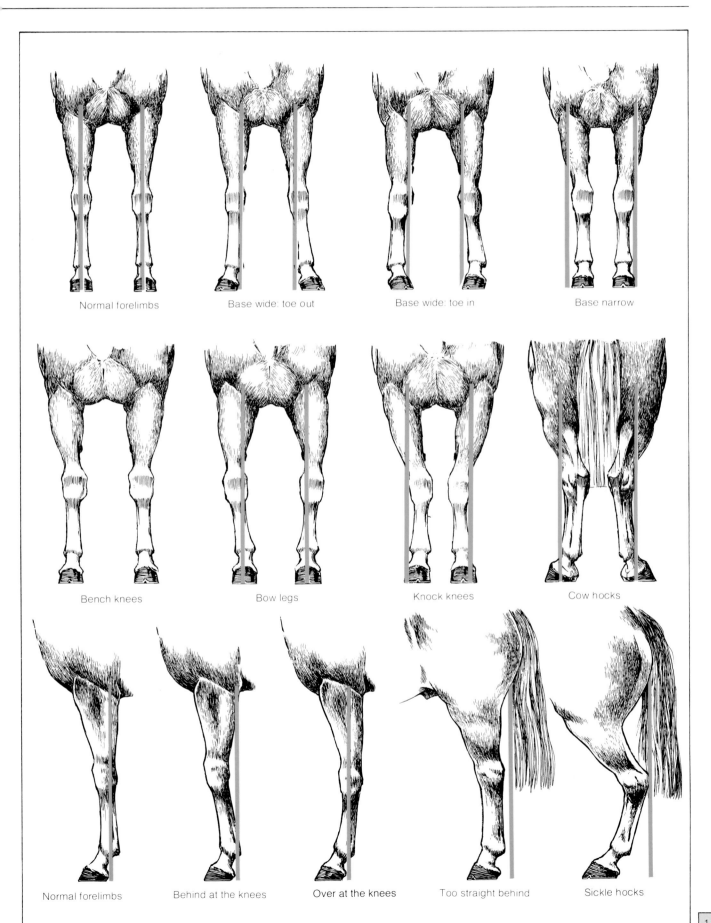

Normal forelimbs

Base wide: toe out

Base wide: toe in

Base narrow

Bench knees

Bow legs

Knock knees

Cow hocks

Normal forelimbs

Behind at the knees

Over at the knees

Too straight behind

Sickle hocks

THE GAITS

The ideal surface on which to see a horse walk and trot is a smooth, hard one such as bitumen. The feet should be studied as they leave the ground, during their flight through the air and as they land; uneven soft surfaces make these observations difficult. On a hard surface you can also hear the sounds of the feet as they land, which aids in evaluating the rhythm of the gait.

The horse on a lead should be walked briskly in a straight line away from you for 50 m (50 yd), then turned and walked straight back towards you. As the horse approaches, step on one side and observe it from the side as it passes by. This should be done a number of times until you have made a satisfactory evaluation. Then carry out the same procedure with the horse at the trot.

You are watching to see if the limbs all move in a straight line. Any deviation is wasted effort, with the risk of one limb interfering with another and undue strain being placed on a section of the limb. The stride should be long and free with a certain rhythm in the 'way of going' of all four legs. The horse should negotiate all turns freely; shuffling around them is undesirable and could indicate soreness or restricted flexibility in a joint.

You should also observe the horse's action, the term used to describe the amount of flexion of the knees and hocks. Horses used for different purposes have different actions: the hackney has a high knee and hock action and the racehorse has a free-moving, long-striding, 'daisy-cutting' action.

Brief descriptions of horses' natural gaits are given above (see also diagrams below, and photographs opposite), but real understanding of the terms will only come if you read about horses, listen to them and watch them, as well as riding and driving them.

The walk is an even 4-beat gait with at least two feet in contact with the ground at any one time. The sequence of footfalls is: left hind, left fore, right hind, right fore.

The trot is a 2-beat gait where the forelimb on one side moves in unison with the hindlimb on the other side, ie, the limbs move in diagonal pairs with a moment of suspension in between.

The pace is a 2-beat gait in which the forelimb and hindlimb on the same side leave and strike the ground at the same time. It may be a natural or artificial gait. It is a faster gait than the trot because, two legs on the same side being off the ground, the horse becomes unbalanced and would fall if it failed to bring the legs through quickly to recover.

The canter is a 3-beat gait in which two of the diagonal legs are paired and the other fore and hind leg act independently. The horse can lead with the left fore when the sequence is right hind, left hind, right fore, left fore, followed by a moment of suspension when all the limbs are in the air. With the right lead, the left hind starts the sequence followed by the right hind and left fore together, then the right fore and finally the moment of suspension. When cantering in a straight line, the horse may change the lead foreleg as it fatigues more quickly than the legs that are working diagonally together. When turning to the left, the horse will naturally lead with the left foreleg and will do the opposite when turning to the right.

The gallop is a 4-beat gait. The sequence is the same as that in the canter, except that the diagonal pair do not move together. So for the right lead it is left hind, right hind, left fore, right fore, then the moment of suspension. It is the horse's fastest gait with the head and neck extended and the stride reaching its maximum length.

The Gaits of the Horse

Sequence of steps at the walk

Sequence of steps at the trot

Sequence of steps at the canter

Above: A horse walking. This is a marching 4-time gait with equal intervals between each hoofbeat. When the gait is correct the horse will at one stage in the stride form a V with his lateral pairs as shown in this picture.

Above: A horse trotting. This is a 2-time gait. The horse moves his limbs in diagonal pairs with a moment of suspension between. This horse is trotting correctly. moving his near foreleg and off hind simultaneously.

Above: A horse cantering. This is a 3-time gait and. like the trot. has a moment of suspension. One pair of diagonals move as a pair - in this case the near hind and off foreleg. He can lead either with the near or off foreleg. depending which comes further forward each stride. In this case it is the near foreleg which comes further forward. The diagonal pair of the leading leg - in this case the off hind leg - will move independently of its pair. This will then start the sequence when the horse takes its first canter stride. The horse may change the lead foreleg as it tires more quickly than the legs that are working diagonally.

TEMPERAMENT

When buying a horse, especially a first horse, temperament is often overlooked or dominated by the horse's conformation, coat colour, way of going or some other factor.

The horse's temperament should be considered with regard to the purpose for which the horse will be used and the personality and ability of the rider or driver.

Temperament would be given a different emphasis if one were choosing a child's pony for the experienced and adventurous rider as compared to an inexperienced, nervous rider. The latter requires a horse with a placid, understanding nature, one that requires urging rather than restraint.

Temperament is better evaluated by a stranger than by someone familiar with the horse. When approached by an unfamiliar person, the good-natured horse will take little notice or may even walk up to the stranger to investigate and allow itself to be touched and handled. A nervous horse will try to get as far away from the person as possible, jamming itself into a corner with muscles tensed.

A bad-tempered horse will often lay its ears back, extend its head and bare the teeth, or put the head in a corner and present the hind-quarters, half raising a leg as a warning not to come any closer.

The horse with a good temperament should be easily caught and allow you to put a head collar or bridle on without objection, especially when handling it around the ears. You should also be able to run your hands all over the horse and pick up its legs without its objection.

Tie the horse up and move about near it. You may spend a great deal of time in catching a horse that pulls back, and repairing the broken gear can be costly. Horses that pull back can also be dangerous. It is a vice associated with nervousness and poor training.

Lead the horse around to see if it rears. Rearing is a dangerous vice because of the risk of the handler being struck with flaying legs. With the aid of a rearing bit, an experienced handler can prevent the horse from rearing; however, some horses may never be cured.

Striking is a natural act of aggression or defence for the horse, and it is very dangerous to the person leading or holding it. Horses that habitually strike are undesirable.

If the horse has been educated to the saddle and to riding, put on the saddle and observe its reaction, especially when tightening the girth. Ask the owner or handler to ride the horse, watching its reaction as the rider mounts and moves off. The horse should be observed at the walk, trot, canter and gallop for such vices as bucking, bolting, shying and head tossing or for such good points as being responsive and calm. If you are still considering the horse for purchase, it is a good idea to take it for a ride yourself.

On returning the horse to its stable or yard, you should observe it from a distance for various vices.

Crib biting is a common vice, in which the horse grasps a solid object with the incisor teeth, arches the neck and swallows air. This can cause gastritis (irritation of the stomach), poor appetite and loss of weight. It is a vice related to boredom.

The boredom may be alleviated by putting a hay net in the horse box, or a hen or small goat in the box as a companion. Put the horse out in a yard or paddock. Eliminate as many objects as possible that the horse can grasp with the incisor teeth. Commercially available straps put tightly around the neck can be effective.

The horse may sway its head from side to side, alternating the weight on each front leg as the head and neck swing. This is known as weaving and can cause stress on the legs as well as physical exhaustion. It is a

Above: Crib biting is a vice. The horse catches hold of an object, as in the picture, and sucks in air. Ways of stopping crib biting are discussed here. A horse sucking in air without catching hold of an object is windsucking.

Above: A horse fitted with a strap around his neck to stop him windsucking or crib biting.

vice associated with nervous, highly strung horses and may be aggravated by boredom. Alleviate the boredom in the same way as suggested for the crib biter. Hanging objects from the roof rafters, especially in doorways, or specially made grids, may physically prevent the horse from weaving.

Stall walking is closely related to weaving. The horse constantly walks in circles around the stable, causing fatigue and strain on the legs. This vice is associated with bored, nervous horses.

Place the horse in a yard with another of a placid

Above: Diagram of a horse weaving when he swings his head and neck from side to side.

Below: Many horses will chew at wood. Wood areas can be covered with metal or unpleasant tasting substances to prevent this.

nature. Tying up the horse in a stable or placing such objects as bales of straw in the stable help prevent stall walking.

Wood chewing is a vice that can be costly as horses chew through stable doors or paddock fences. The cause of this vandalism is boredom, although some people attribute it to a nutritional deficiency.

A hay net can keep horses with this vice occupied to a certain extent. Capping doorways and exposed timber edges with metal strips can be helpful. Painting the timber with creosote or other commercially available unpalatable products sometimes proves a satisfactory restraint. Replacing timber in stable doors and door jambs with metal, and timber rails in fences with wire serves the same purpose.

Pawing occurs mostly near doorways and could be associated with the horse not wanting to be confined in a stable or by itself. In the process of digging large holes in the ground, it wears away the toe of the hoof.

Put the horse in a stable with a concrete floor and an attached yard so that it does not feel so confined. Shoe the horse to stop the toe wearing away.

Kicking stable walls and gates can cause the horse to sustain injury (eg, capped hocks), as well as expensive damage to the surroundings. Kicking deliberately at a handler is dangerous and is associated mainly with vicious or nervous horses.

In their natural environment, horses roamed freely in herds with continual access to natural pasture. Many of the vices outlined here occur because of solitary confinement in a stable. No matter how large the stable, it is small and lonely compared to the open range.

IDENTIFICATION

Every intending buyer of a horse should be able to identify it specifically and so should every horse owner. This advice is given to guard horse owners against problems associated with mistaken identity. It applies particularly to owners who enter their horses in competition, who have lost or found a horse, who export or import horses, who are involved in a lawsuit about a horse or who sometimes send their horse away for training, veterinary care, lease or for some other reason. Specific identification is a requirement if a horse is to be registered in a recognised stud book.

Colour, shape and size are not sufficient for identification as many horses would fit the same description in relation to these three features and any such identification would be worthless in law. The identification is based on brands, sex, age, colour, natural markings, acquired markings, whorls and congenital peculiarities, as described below. Most identity forms require that a veterinary surgeon fills them in.

Brands

Brands are permanent marks that identify horses. They refer to the owner-breeder, year of foaling or a coded reference number, entered in a particular breed's stud

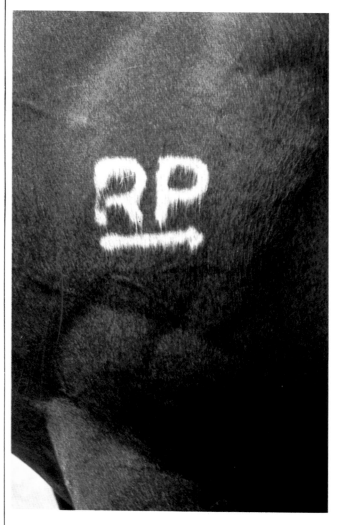

A freeze brand. This is a permanent mark which identifies the horse. In England, it is usual to put the brand in the area under the saddle.

book. Lip tattoos are a form of permanent marking used for positive identification in some areas of the world so that the horse's coat is not blemished.

Look for brands on the right or left shoulder, thigh and neck and on the left jaw. If the brand is indistinct, the hair should be clipped off the site so that the brand can be more easily read.

Sex

The best way of identifying a horse's sex is by observing its genitalia. The following terms are used in relation to a horse's sex and age.

A colt is an uncastrated male up to and including the age of 3 years.

A stallion is an uncastrated male, 4 years of age and over.

A gelding is a castrated male.

A filly is a female up to and including the age of 3 years.

A mare is a female, 4 years of age and over.

Age

There are several points of reference if you wish to find out the age of a horse. The first is the use of the stud book, but this is risky; the horse's age would only be found in a stud book if it has been registered at birth.

Brands are sometimes used in Australia to indicate age by showing the year of foaling. The reference number 2 over 1 appearing in the brand would indicate that it was the second foal born on the stud in 1981. If a horse is branded with a reference number, it may be seen on the right or left shoulder.

The teeth are a good guide to a horse's age. The incisor teeth, ie, the front ones, are the most significant, and several features about them are considered. These are: the time of the eruption of temporary teeth, distinguishing the temporary teeth from the permanent ones, the time of eruption of the permanent teeth and the amount of wear that the permanent teeth have undergone.

The temporary teeth are whiter, smaller, and cup-shaped, while the permanent ones are larger, off-white, and more rectangular.

If the incisors are milk or temporary teeth and only the two central ones have erupted, you know that the foal is up to 4 weeks old. If the two lateral ones have also erupted, the foal is from 4–6 weeks old. Finally, if the two corner incisors have erupted, the weanling is 6–9 months old or older.

At 2½ years old, the permanent central incisors erupt. When the horse is 3½ years old, the permanent lateral incisors appear and finally at 4½, the permanent corner incisors have fully erupted. In erupting, it is customary for the incisors to push out the temporary teeth.

In all these teeth, the infundibulum, which appears as a black cavity in the centre of the table of the tooth, is evident. At 6 years old, it disappears from the table of the lower central incisors due to wear; it disappears from the lower lateral incisors at 7 years old and from the lower corner incisors at 8 years.

When the horse is about 10 years old, a groove known as Galvayne's groove appears on the outside of the corner incisors of the upper jaw. It will reach one third of the way down the tooth by the time the horse is 13.

From 13 years onwards, the estimation of a horse's age is based on the length of Galvayne's groove, the development of the triangular shape of the tables and the angle at which the incisors project outwards.

Above: This mare is about eight years old. At this age, a mare is fully mature, and she can be said to be at the prime of her life.

Above: This horse is about twenty years old. At this stage of his life, he will be too old and probably too stiff in the joints to do much, if any, work.

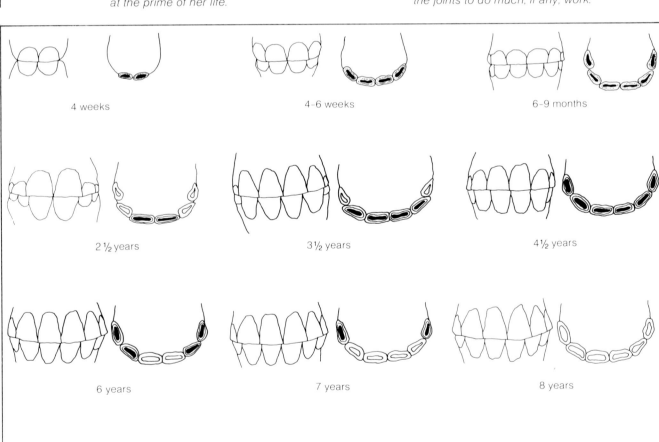

4 weeks

4–6 weeks

6–9 months

2½ years

3½ years

4½ years

6 years

7 years

8 years

These diagrams show the development of the horse's teeth at various stages of its life. The teeth are seen from the front of the mouth and the lower jaw from above, or the upper jaw from below.

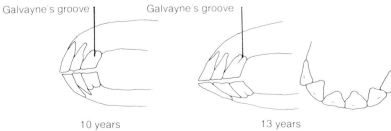

Galvayne's groove

Galvayne's groove

10 years

13 years

COLOUR

There are 4 basic coat colours: black, brown, bay and chestnut. These are genetically modified to produce white, grey, cream, dun, roan, piebald and skewbald.

Black: the body, head, limbs, mane and tail are all black.

Brown: the body colour is brown and the mane, tail and lower parts of the legs are black.

Bay: the body colour may vary from a yellowish colour to red to light brown, with the mane, tail and lower parts of the legs being black.

Chestnut: the body colour ranges from a light golden red to a dark chocolate shade, often described as liver chestnut. The legs, mane and tail may be a shade lighter or darker than the body colour, but they are never black.

White: the foals are born white, and in some cases the eyes are blue. Most white horses are greys that have become whiter with age.

Grey: the body colour of the foal at birth shows one of the basic colours, ie, black, brown, bay or chestnut. As previously stated, the grey horse becomes whiter with age since white hairs develop in the same way as they do in the ageing human being. The white hairs usually appear first on the face.

Grey may appear in combination with other colours: black, brown, bay and chestnut. The mane, tail and points keep their basic colour.

Roan: the foal is born a roan colour, and this remains constant throughout life. The head, neck, mane, tail and lower parts of the limbs are fairly free of white hairs.

The different combinations of white hairs with the four basic colours give the different types of roan: black (blue) roan, brown roan, bay (red) roan and chestnut (strawberry) roan.

Dun: the body colour ranges from a light yellowish to a dark brown. The mane, tail and points are dark. Duns have a stripe down the back and may have transverse stripes on the knees and hocks.

Piebald: the body coat colour shows large white areas alternating with black.

Skewbald: large white areas alternating with any colour but black.

Cream: the body coat, mane and tail are cream. Palomino, a variation, is a body colour varying from light to dark gold, with a light mane and tail.

NATURAL MARKINGS

The most common natural markings on a horse's head and legs are usually formed by white hair assuming a particular shape, irregular but recognisable.

Face Markings

Star: a solid, white mark on the forehead, varying in size and shape.

Stripe: a narrow band of white running down the face, approximately from the eyes to the nostrils. It may be joined to a star or separate from it.

Bay   Black   Chestnut (Sorrel)   Claybank (Red roan/Red dun)

Blue roan   Brown   Cream   Dapple Grey

Above: A dun coloured horse. This is a colour typical of many of the oldest breeds of horses. There are quite a range of colours covered by dun, from pale yellow to dark brown.

Below: Illustrations of the most common colours of horses found in the numerous breeds scattered all over the world. The most numerous colours are chestnut and bay.

Dun (Buckskin)   Liver chestnut   Piebald (Pinto. Calico)   Strawberry roan

Flea-bitten grey   Grey   Palomino   Skewbald (Pinto. Calico)

Above: A strawberry roan horse, or roan chestnut. It is one of the more unusual colours.

*Above: A grey horse. These are usually born
quite dark with the darker rings of hair known as
dapples, but lighten with age.*

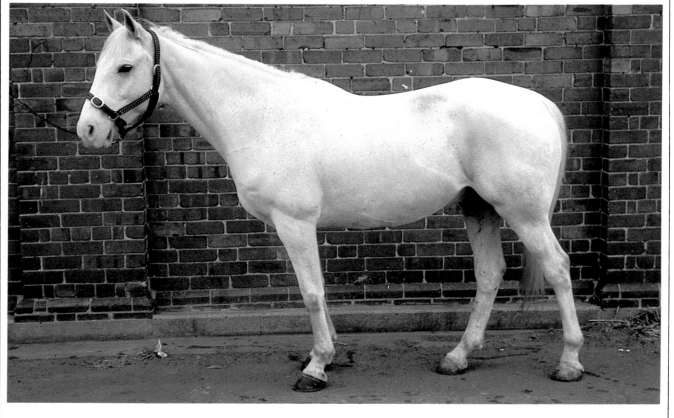

*Above: A white horse. It is rare to be born this
colour, but many grey horses go white with age.*

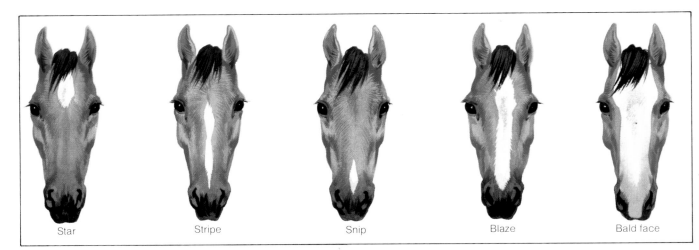

Star   Stripe   Snip   Blaze   Bald face

Snip: a white mark situated between or in the region of the nostrils.

Lip: a white mark on the upper and/or lower lip(s).

Blaze: a solid white mark from the position of the star to the snip, covering the full width of the nasal bones.

Bald (White) face: a broader extension of the blaze, usually involving both eyes.

Leg Markings

Heel: a white area above the heel.

Coronet: a white strip of hair just above the hoof.

Pastern: white hair in the area extending from the top of the hoof (coronet) to just below the fetlock joint.

Sock: white hair in the region from the top of the hoof (coronet) to the top of the fetlock joint.

Stocking: white hair extending from the top of the hoof (coronet) to immediately below the knee in the foreleg, or the hock in the hindleg.

Knee or hock: white hair from the top of the hoof (coronet) up to and including the knee or hock.

Arrangements of Hairs

Whorls are spiral twists of hair about 1 cm wide. Their position is unique to each horse so are a useful form of identification.

There are numerous other natural distinguishing marks, such as flecks, black spots and black stripes which, if present, should be included in the identification description.

The horse may also have acquired markings which, apart from brands, may be scars, firing marks and other acquired blemishes.

Right: Diagrams of various types of markings on the horses' limbs recognised officially. The traditional names of stocking and sock are used for the larger areas of white, but the more 'modern' terms describing the area covered, pastern, heel, coronet, are used for the smaller areas.

Above: The various recognised types of markings found on the horse's face.

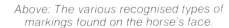

Below: This chestnut horse has a star marking on his forehead.

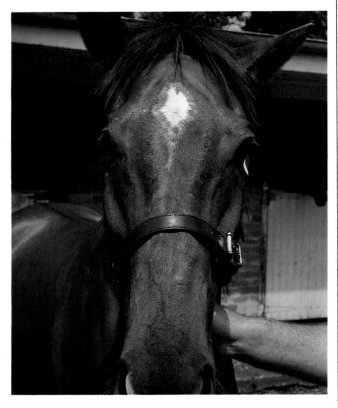

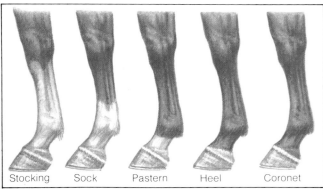

Stocking   Sock   Pastern   Heel   Coronet

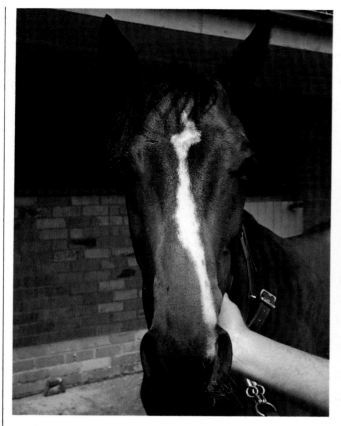

Above: A horse with a stripe on his face, which is a long thin white marking.

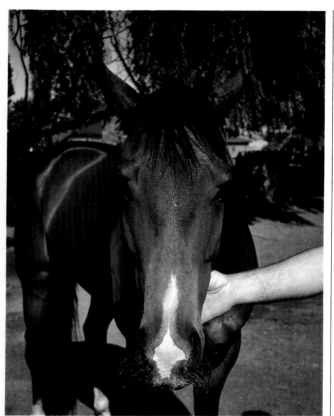

Above: A horse with a snip, which is white hair on the lower part of his face.

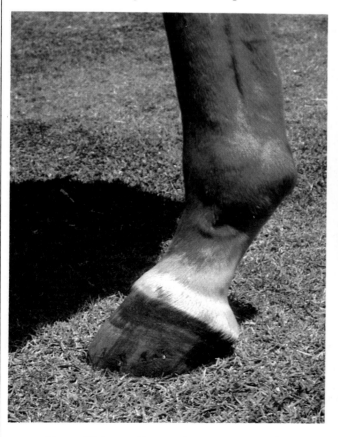

Above: White marking on the pastern area of a limb is known as a Pastern.

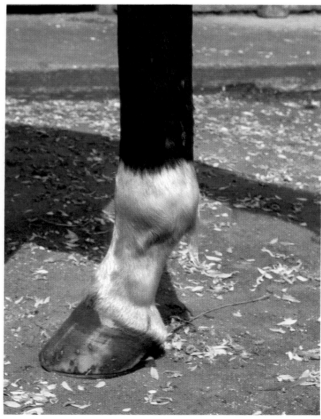

Above: White marking stretching up over the fetlock is known as a Fetlock.

CONGENITAL PECULIARITIES

The horse may have peculiarities that have existed from birth. Where the upper jaw protrudes further than the lower jaw, causing the lower incisors to bite the palate behind the upper incisors, this is known as parrot mouth. In contrast, the normal jaws are so structured that the lower incisors meet the upper incisors on the bite.

Prophet's thumb is a muscle impression mainly found on the neck. It is a cavity that resembles the impression left by the thumb when it is pressed into soft clay or putty. Old horsemen say it is a sign of a good horse; in reality, prophet's thumb is caused by pressure on the developing muscle while the foal is in its mother's uterus.

In the congenital marking known as wall eye, the iris lacks the normal pigment; it is either white or faintly blue in colour.

Below: This horse has a Parrot mouth when the upper and lower jaw do not meet but overlap. This can make eating difficult. There is a further disadvantage in that the teeth tend to wear unevenly so need regular checking and filing.

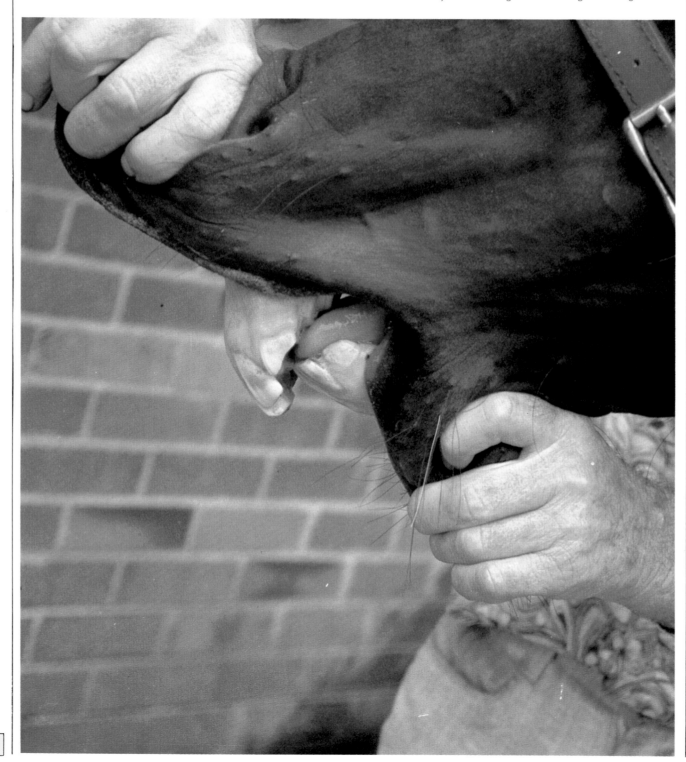

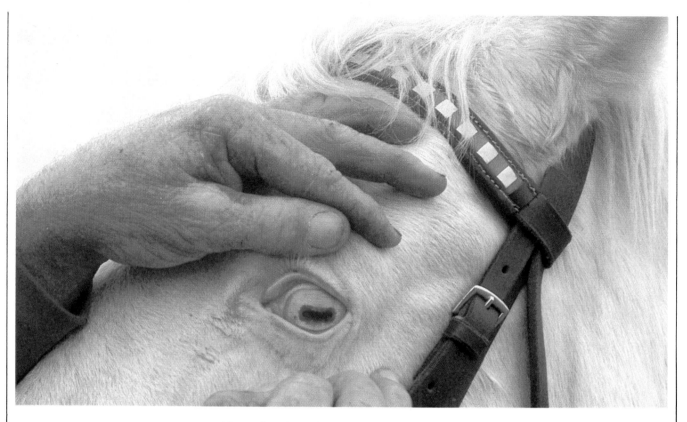

Above: A wall eye is a congenital marking. The iris does not have the normal pigment, and is much lighter in colour.

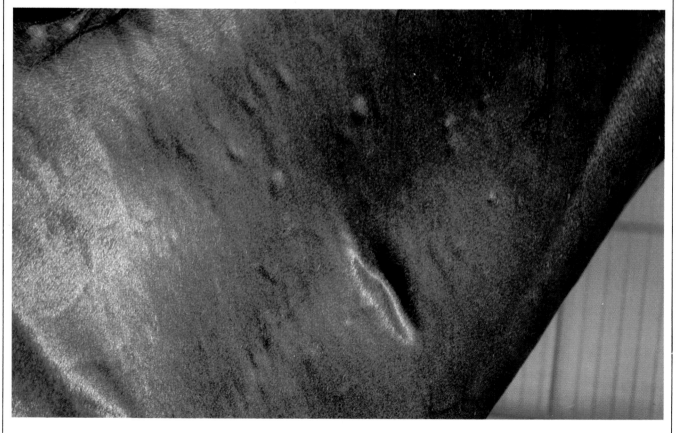

Above: A prophet's thumb mark on the neck, considered by many to be a sign of good luck.

HANDLING THE HORSE

The handling of the horse on the ground is just as important as learning how to control it when ridden. The horse must learn to trust and respect the human if full use is to be made of his talents, and this begins with how he is treated in the stable, when being led, caught in the field, transported and restrained. He is a very powerful creature, with much greater strength than the human, so the latter must use his brain in order to become his master.

If the horse learns to obey and be relaxed with people when they are looking after him on the ground, then not only will he also be easier to look after but will be much more trainable and amenable when ridden.

The first part of this section deals with the various aspects of handling the horse from the ground.

The second part looks at the tack; exactly what is required for each aspect of riding; step-by-step instructions with accompanying photographs showing how to put on the tack; how to clean and store this valuable equipment; bandages, boots and rugs — their uses and how to put them on.

APPROACHING AND CATCHING

When catching a horse, always take a lead and head collar with you so that you can lead it back to the stable or to some appropriate place. It is unwise to catch the horse with the idea of leading it back with your hands, unless you know its temperament so well that there is no question of its pulling away from you or resisting your attempt to lead it.

You should approach the horse from the left hand side. Avoid approaching it directly from the front or the rear; it has been trained since birth to accept the approach from the left side as natural.

As you walk up to the horse, hold out your hand, talk to it gently, do not hurry and be confident. If the horse looks tentative or moves away a little, stop or withdraw until the horse, by its demeanour, seems secure. Then move towards it again.

When you are close enough, do not grab at the horse, but with the hand outstretched, rub it gently on the neck, talking to it. Then quietly but calmly slip the lead around its neck and, when the horse is ready, put the head collar on and clip the lead to it.

When you approach the horse and it allows you to rub its neck gently with the hand, the fact that you speak quietly to it is a form of reward; another form is giving it a small piece of bread or some other titbit. The reward is actually reinforcing its behaviour of allowing itself to be caught and this reinforcement ensures that next time, in a similar situation, it is more likely to allow itself to be caught.

Because of their previous poor education or their innate cussedness, some horses are difficult to catch. In this situation, patience, a reward and keeping any gear such as the lead out of sight, as well as containing the horse in a relatively small yard, should all be tried.

LEADING THE HORSE

Always lead the horse from the left, ie, the near side. The handler should walk on the near side of the horse halfway between its head and shoulder. The excess lead is looped and held in the left hand and the right hand holds the lead about 30 cm (1 ft) from the head. If the horse has too much lead and attempts to break away, it can develop a fine turn of speed before you have a chance to check its progress.

The horse should be trained to walk alongside the handler, neither pulling out in front nor dragging behind. Make sure that gateways or doors are fully opened and secured. Approach the opening at right angles and step through quickly, keeping to the side and ahead of the horse.

Make sure you are well into the stable or paddock before releasing the horse. Let it go, facing away from the entrance, and walk away rather than having it pull and run away from you.

RESTRAINT

An important requirement of anyone in charge of a horse is the ability to restrain, ie, to hold it in a controlled manner under various conditions. The degree and type of restraint vary with the horse's level of education, maturity, temperament and function.

Always begin with minimal restraint and, if the horse does not respond, progress from there. Keep in mind that some horses with severe restraint will become uncontrollable to the point where sedation by a veterinary surgeon will be necessary to achieve your purpose.

Using Head Collar and Lead

If you control a horse's head, you basically control the rest of its body and limbs. If you have no control over the horse's head, dealing with it is almost impossible. A rearing bit in the horse's mouth or a chain shank over the muzzle or through the mouth can give extra control over the head.

Someone, preferably an experienced person, should hold the horse's head when you want to do something to the horse, such as removing a loose shoe or checking its temperature. This person should stand on the same side as the operator. He can thus observe the operator's position in relation to the horse. If the operator hurts or frightens the horse, it will tend to jump away from him as well as away from the person holding the horse (as both are standing on the same side). The experienced person holding the horse can pull its head towards himself, thus causing the hindquarters to swing away from the operator, who might otherwise be kicked by the hindleg of the horse. He can distract the horse by jiggling the lead attached to the head collar, by rubbing its head with the free hand and by talking to it.

Gripping the Neck

If the horse will not co-operate in beng handled and the procedure (such as removing a bandage from a hindleg) takes very little time, a handful of loose skin on the side of the neck towards the base can be gripped and squeezed as tightly as possible. This must be quickly done because the hand soon tires and the pressure

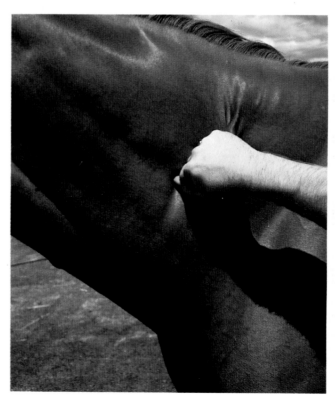

Above: A useful form of restraint is to grip a section of the loose skin on the horse's neck in the hand. This takes his attention and will usually stop him from playing around without causing him any discomfort.

Above: Holding the head collar and rope in one hand, approach from the near side.

Above: Take your time, move slowly and if necessary talk to the horse to keep him calm.

Above: Slip the rope gently and slowly around the horse's neck.

Above: Keeping the rope around his neck, slip the head collar forward to his nose.

Above: Put his head through the head collar and secure it at the top.

Above: Lead him by walking on the near side, halfway between his head and his shoulder.

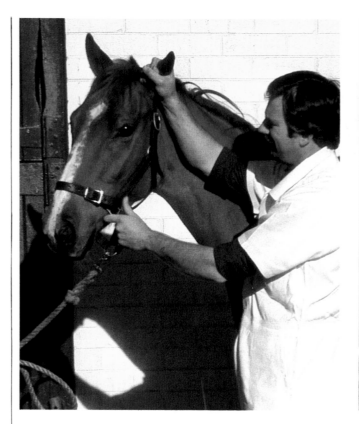

Above: Twisting the ear is a simple method of restraint that can be quickly applied.

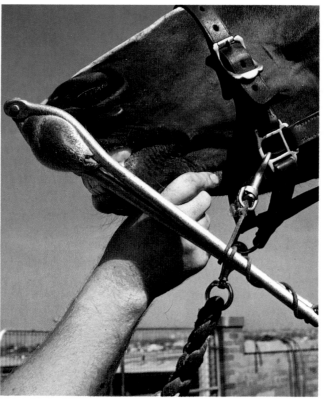

Above: These shaped metal bars are a commercial modern form of twitch.

weakens to the point where it no longer restrains the horse. This is a very good technique to use on horses that prove difficult when touched around the head.

Twisting the Ear

Starting at the neck, rub your hand upwards to the base of the ear and gently wrap your hand completely around it before applying pressure. Do not make a quick grab at the ear; this frightens the horse, often causing it to half rear and jump away. You can twist and squeeze the ear with your hand as hard as you like without doing any damage. Apply just enough pressure to provide the restraint that enables you to carry out the procedure.

Take care when you use this restraint technique. If used too much with excessive pressure, the horse may become head shy.

Applying the Twitch

There are numerous types of twitches with various positions of attachment to the horse. The oldest type is a wooden handle about a metre (3 ft) in length with a rope loop fixed to the end, large enough in size to accommodate a horse's muzzle plus the handler's hand.

The twitch should be applied to the upper lip. If this is difficult because of the horse's resistance, an assistant may grip the skin of the horse's neck or ear. If this is impossible, the twitch may be applied to the lower third of the ear. Applying the twitch to the lower lip is not recommended because the lip may be torn at its point of attachment to the gum if the horse rears suddenly.

When putting the twitch on and holding it, always

stand to the *side* of the horse, *never in front*, because it may strike out with its forelegs, severely injuring the operator and/or the assistant.

The rope loop is applied over as much of the upper lip as can be gathered into it. Twist the handle of the twitch to tighten the loop only to the point where there is firm pressure on the lip and so the loop will not slip off. Do not twist the handle so quickly that the loop snaps tightly on the nose; this may cause the horse to rear suddenly and to strike with the foreleg.

Immediately the twitch is tightened, two half hitch knots with the lead clipped to the head collar should be put on the handle of the twitch. This precaution is taken in case the horse rears and pulls the twitch out of your hands. If it does, you will still be holding the lead and will stop the twitch handle from flaying around in the air, with the risk of seriously injuring anybody near the horse.

A good horse handler always maintains control of the twitch. The long-handled twitch is more readily controlled because it can be gripped with both hands and it allows the handler to stand at a safer distance from the horse than the short-handled twitch.

If the horse resists this procedure, the twitch can be tightened. The person holding the twitch can help by jiggling it, talking to the horse, rubbing its neck with one hand and generally by distracting it.

An attempt by the horse to strike with the foreleg can be anticipated if it starts to become restless. In this case, the pressure on the twitch should be released.

If the twitch has been on tightly for some time, some horses will start to object and may suddenly strike out. There is no need to have a twitch on tightly for a lengthy period; relax it when the operator is resting and tighten it when he is proceeding.

Above: The traditional type of twitch with its wooden handle is still used extensively.

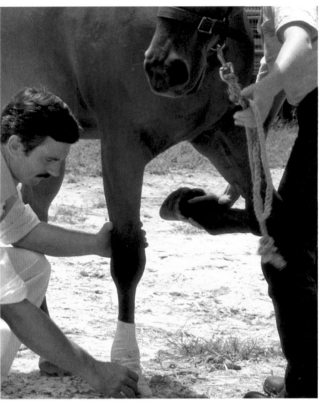

Above: Holding up the near side foreleg to allow the off side foreleg to be bandaged.

Some twitches do not have a handle: these include ring twitches and commercially available clamps. These types can be applied and secured to the head collar, leaving one hand free, and if the horse pulls free there is no danger that the handler will be hit. Their disadvantages are that they are slower to apply and release and they can only exert a certain amount of pressure, which can be crucial when dealing with a fractious horse.

A twitch that is safe for the holder and effective on the horse is one with a handle made of stiff, heavy rubber hosing.

Holding up a Front Leg

Restraining the horse by this method is useful only with horses that have been well-handled and are familiar with having their feet picked up. Position the horse so that it is standing squarely on all four feet, bearing its weight equally, thus making it easier to pick up a foot.

If held off the ground, the front foot prevents the horse from kicking with the hindleg on the same side. The person holding up the foot should therefore be working on the same side as the operator. When holding the leg up, do not allow the horse to lean on you to the point where you bear most of the weight. With you as support it can kick with the hindleg on the same side, using enough force to hurt.

A Single Sideline

This is a good method of restraining either hindlimb. Using good, strong, solid rope, a loop is passed over the horse's head and round the neck. The free end of the rope is passed down to and through the ring in the hobble (a solid leather strap around one pastern) and back up through the loop of rope around the neck. By pulling on the rope, the hindlimb is raised off the ground. If a hobble is not available, bandage the pastern to prevent the rope burning the skin if the horse resists and struggles.

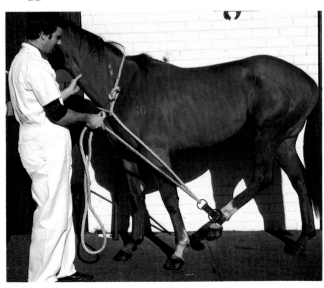

Right: This single sideline is an effective means of restraining either hindlimb. By pulling on the rope, the hindlimb is raised off the ground. This provides a useful way of ensuring a horse cannot kick with a hindleg.

FOALS AND WEANLINGS

When held around the head, young foals tend to rear backwards. They often strike the head, and may thus suffer concussion or a fracture that sometimes results in death. Instead of rearing backwards, they may rush backwards, lose balance and fall over.

The foal is best handled in close proximity to its mother, where it feels more secure. Approach the foal slowly, cupping one arm under and around the neck and the other around the rump and forming a cradle so that it cannot rush forwards or backwards.

Weanlings tend to rear and flip over backwards. Make sure the weanling is backed up against a wall or fence, with someone holding the tail to stop it sitting down.

The person at the head restrains the weanling by rubbing a hand on the neck and working gradually up to the ear, cupping a hand around it and squeezing hard. If further restraint is required, the other ear is gripped in the same manner.

N.B. Normal handling and leading of the foal is covered on Page **154**.

Alternative Approaches

When restraining horses, bear in mind that there is always the exception to the rule. The horse may not always respond to the accepted methods of restraint. For example, the author was once asked to examine a horse's eye. Whenever the author came close to its eye it would rear, no matter what method of restraint was applied. An old horseman suggested that the horse be led into a shed with an iron roof. This was done; the roof was about 10 cm above the horse's head so that the tips of its ears were just touching the iron. The horse then allowed the author to examine its eye without so much as blinking. Horses that fail to respond to accepted methods sometimes respond to the unconventional restraint.

Above: Gripping both ears tightly is a useful means of restraining foals.

Below: Supporting the tail helps to prevent the foal sitting down and even going over backwards.

Above: Foals and weanlings can often be difficult to restrain.

Below: These are a simple version of hobbles preventing the horse from striking out.

Below: Restraining youngsters must be done with great care as rough handling can frighten them for life. This foal is well held, with one arm under and around the neck and the other around the rump.

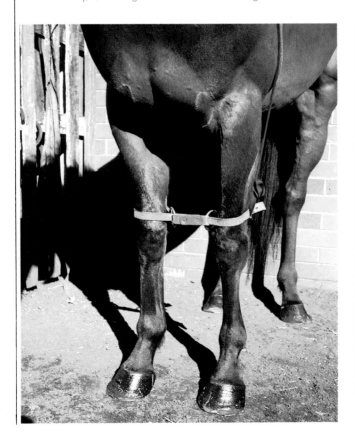

TRANSPORTATION

Horses are moved short and long distances within a country and overseas for numerous reasons such as riding, exhibiting and breeding. It is important for the horse to travel quickly and to arrive at its destination in good condition.

Before attempting to move a horse overseas, you should contact the local or national authorities to find out about quarantine laws and regulations. If a horse is travelling a great distance it is more likely to be exposed to injury and stress that may lead to travel sickness pneumonia. It is wise to prepare all horses for long-distance travel by attending to their feet, diet, worming, exercise and general health, so that the risks of injury and illness are minimal. It is also wise to insure the horse against injury or death.

A strong, well-fitting head collar and a lead rope are essential equipment for the horse. Groom it before putting on a rug, leg bandages or boots, a tail bandage and knee boots. On a difficult journey, or if the horse kicks, hock boots are advisable, but the horse should have been accustomed to these before travelling. If the weather is cold, a woollen rug will provide warmth, whereas if it is hot, a summer sheet is sufficient. If the horse is a nervous traveller, then a sweat sheet under the rug is a good idea as horses sweat more freely when excited and confined.

A horse should be fed and watered approximately 2 hours before the journey. If the journey is a long one, a hay net should be provided for nutrition and to alleviate the boredom of travelling. Also the grain in the diet should be markedly reduced 48 hours prior to travelling. This will help to prevent swelling of the legs which is associated with standing and confinement for long periods of time.

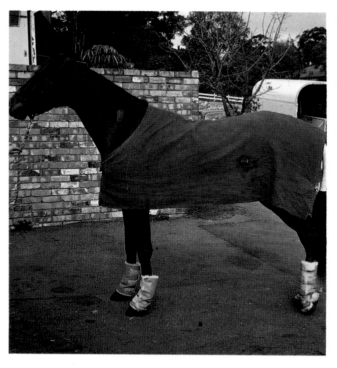

Above: Wearing a headcollar, tail bandage, boots and a rug this horse is ready for travel.

Below: A pony wearing travelling bandages over gamgee being led into a horsebox. He should be wearing a tail bandage.

Transport by Road

Horses that travel frequently should not present any problems when loading. If your horse is a shy loader or has rarely been placed in a trailer or horsebox, allow plenty of time for loading in case of refusal.

The ramp should be as level as possible; horses often baulk at a steep ramp. Select a place where the ramp can be lowered onto a raised mound of earth. The ramp should be covered with a non-slip rubber matting. The rubber deadens the noise of the horse's hooves as it walks up. Clatter and banging from the hooves on the ramp will often frighten the horse and make it shy away.

Allow the horse time to become familiar with the box and ramp before leading it on. If the horse refuses to walk into the box, it will often follow another horse that walks on quietly. A handful of oats will tempt some; a blindfold will work with others.

If a horse refuses to load, a long rope looped around the hind-quarters and pulled by the person leading it is often successful. A hit on the rump with a long-handled whip will often encourage an obstinate horse to walk up the ramp and into the box. The author recalls an incident where a person hit a horse on the rump with his hand to encourage it to go up the ramp. The horse kicked out, severely injuring the person. Take care to be well out of kicking range.

Always put a horse that is nervous and travels badly last on a multi-horsebox. If trouble develops while in transit, the horse is within easy reach and can be removed quickly if necessary.

In transit, all horses should be securely tied with a quick-release knot. The author recalls an incident that

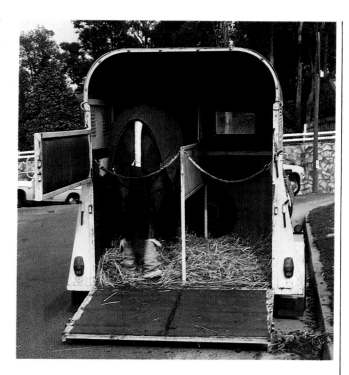

Above: This horse is ready to travel in comfort with a good straw bed on which to stand.

Below: With horses and riders spending much time travelling, horseboxes are becoming more and more large and luxurious.

Above left: Horse's foreleg being bandaged with a travelling bandage and special fibre for protection.

Above: Air transportation is used particularly for Thoroughbreds who travel to different continents to race and to be bred. These horses are being elevated to the aircraft door.

occurred when a horse was travelling in a two-horse trailer without being tied up or confined by a central partition. The horse got under a bar in the trailer, severely injuring its spine. When the driver stopped and lowered the ramp, the horse fell out onto the road, paralysed in the hindlegs. Euthanasia was the only answer.

Well-padded partitions should be placed between horses. These offer support against sudden movements of the vehicle or protection from a nearby fractious horse.

When a very nervous horse is in a box with other horses, it is sometimes a good idea to use partitions for leaving an empty space between horses to minimise injury and feelings of claustrophobia.

A hay net or nose bag is useful on long journeys to provide nutrition and to act as a source of comfort. If the journey is lengthy, at some stage the horses should be removed from the box to alleviate stiffness and swelling of the legs, and to be watered.

Transport by Air

Transport of horses by air within a country or to and from other countries has become more popular in the last 10 years, mainly because of the speed and efficiency of jet aircraft. Some of these aircraft can carry up to 50 horses at a time.

Horses may be loaded in boxes; these are elevated to the aeroplane door and the horse walks into the plane. The development of walk-on, walk-off ramps has reduced the risk of loading as well as making it faster.

Air travel is a safe and efficient method of transport for most horses. The main disadvantage is the cost; the main advantage is the saving in time.

Transport by Sea

The legs of horses travelling long distances by ship are prone to swell and this can be very difficult to control with limited space for exercise. Other problems include digestive disturbances, colic and travel stress sickness (pneumonia). Mares more than 8 months pregnant are not permitted to travel by sea.

An inspection by a government veterinary surgeon is made before horses undertake sea travel.

Above: The horse in this picture is tied to a sturdy object. He has been correctly secured with a quick-release knot. However, most experts think it is dangerous to attach a horse to an immovable object. This is because he may run back. It is safer to tie him to a loop of breakable string which is also around the post or ring.

SAFETY

A horse can be a wonderful friend and companion but, unless certain safety precautions are observed when dealing with it, the handler, the rider, or someone else may be injured or property may be damaged. Even when proper precautions are taken, accidents still happen. However, most accidents occur because simple safety precautions have been ignored, are unknown or are practised without sufficient care.

The following precautions are simple to carry out and should never be ignored.

Approaching and Handling

Move about a horse confidently, quietly and slowly, speaking firmly but kindly to it.

Brush your horse with your hand rather than patting it; a brush soothes a horse, but a pat often frightens it.

Always approach, lead, mount and dismount from the near (left) side of the horse. Stay out of kicking range if you can. When you are within kicking range, it is always safer to walk close to the hind-quarters so that you do not receive the full force of the blow if the horse does happen to kick.

When handling a horse, make sure that no-one is standing behind you blocking any quick movement backwards away from the horse and danger.

Shoeing and grooming equipment should be placed at a reasonable distance away when you are working on the horse to prevent yourself from accidentally stepping on them and overbalancing. When picking up a horse's foot, always begin by touching the horse's shoulder or hip. Keeping in contact with it all the time, run the hand down the horse's leg to the pastern, then lift the foot.

Above all, familiarise yourself with each horse, and treat it as an individual. When the horse needs some form of discipline, deal it out immediately so that it associates the punishment with the 'crime'.

Leading and Tying Up

Lead from the near side (left), in a position halfway between the horse's head and shoulder. When leading a horse through narrow openings, quickly step through first and move to one side.

Tie the horse with a lead rope by a quick-release knot to a sturdy object at wither height, out of kicking and biting range of other horses. This can however lead to the horse hurting itself if it pulls back, and it is more usual to tie a piece of string (which can break) to the sturdy object and the rope to the string. Make sure the rope is not too long as the horse is likely to become tangled. Do not use the reins to tie it.

Mounting and Riding

A horse should stand still when the rider is mounting and dismounting. Avoid mounting and dismounting near protruding or overhanging objects. Check saddle girth for tightness before mounting. Ask an assistant to hold the horse if he is nervous and likely to move off, or if the rider is a novice.

Become familiar with a strange horse by riding in an enclosed, safe area before venturing into the open country. In rough country, allow your horse to pick its way, especially up or down steep inclines. Always maintain control, whatever the gait may be.

Avoid galloping past other horses moving at a slower gait.

When going out for a ride, walk the horse for the first $\frac{1}{2}$ mile or so (or kilometre) and for the last $\frac{1}{2}$ mile home.

When riding or driving on the road, national or local traffic laws must be observed. In Britain, for example, you would have to ride or drive as close as possible to the appropriate side of the roadway, avoid riding on foot-paths or median strips, obey stop and give way signs and traffic lights, and signal when pulling out from the kerb, changing direction, stopping, or to slow a car down as it approaches the horse.

When there is more than one horse, ride in pairs and if one is nervous or ridden by an inexperienced person, it should be kept on the inside. In heavy traffic, or if a car wants to overtake on a narrow road, ride in single file. It may be a legal requirement for motorists to give way to a restive horse if the rider requests or signals to the motorist to do so.

If possible, avoid main roads with heavy traffic and do not ride at night on a road carrying traffic. If it is necessary wear reflective (not fluorescent) materials, and fix a light on the stirrup, or carry it with white to the front and red to the rear.

Tack and Clothing

Check the girth and reins regularly for signs of brittle-ness, wear and tear. This is best done when cleaning the tack.

Around the stable, wear boots to protect your feet from nails and other foreign material, as well as from the weight of the horse's hoof, if it accidentally treads on you. When riding, wear boots, preferably with a good heel and a tapered toe so that the boot can slide in and out of the stirrup freely. The surface of the heel and toe should be smooth so it does not catch on the stirrup.

Wearing protective headgear at all times when riding a horse is most important.

Never smoke, light a match or hold any naked light within the stable where bedding, particularly straw, could easily catch fire.

Transportation

Be careful when leading a horse into a trailer or horsebox. Some horses scramble up the ramp, with the risk of the handler being trampled or crushed against the side of the trailer.

Always tie the horse securely in the trailer or box using a quick-release knot. Allow sufficient rope for head movement, but not so much that the horse becomes tangled in it.

When unloading, always untie the horse first before lowering the tail gate or ramp.

Check the trailer frequently for roadworthiness.

Drive with caution, looking ahead to avoid sudden stopping or change of direction and do not swing the vehicles around corners.

THE TACK

SADDLERY

Good-quality, well-cared-for tack is an essential part of any efficiently run stable. For the sake of safety, appearance, durability and comfort, it is advisable to buy the best leather and metalwork, and to make sure you keep it in good condition.

The Saddle

The framework is known as the 'tree', and was traditionally made of beech wood, but laminated wood or metal is more usual today. A 'spring tree' is used in most modern saddles. This has two pieces of tempered steel running lengthwise along the tree from the front arch to the cantle. This makes the seat more resilient and so more comfortable for the rider, who can feel and follow the horse's movements more closely. The seat is built on

the tree, and is usually made of pigskin. The flaps are attached to the seat.

The panels are stuffed with wool or shaped felt, and act as a cushion between the tree and the horse. There is a channel (gullet) running through the centre, which ensures that weight is not placed on the horse's spine. The panels may be full (reaching almost to the bottom of the saddle flap) or half (reaching only halfway down).

The Types of Saddle

Variation in the design of the tree, panels, etc, are made because the best place for the rider's weight is as near as possible to the centre of gravity of the horse. This varies with changes in the posture and speed of the horse: for

Below: Diagrams showing the various sections which make up a saddle.

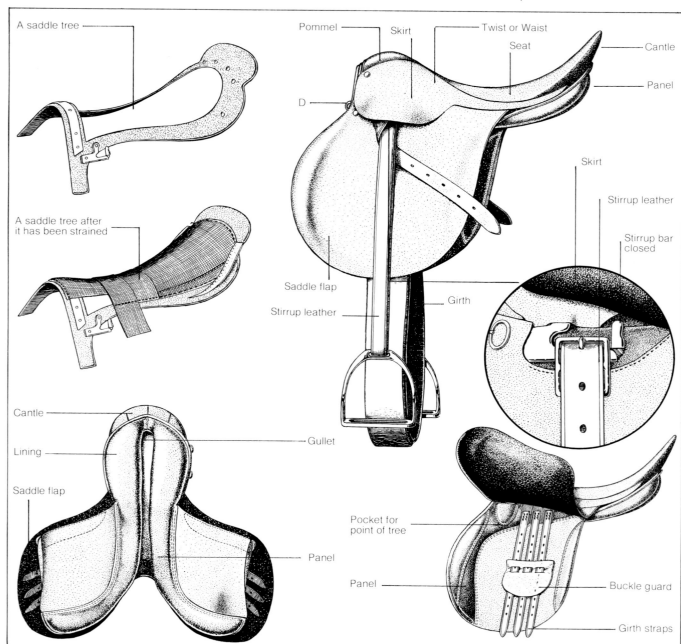

A saddle tree

A saddle tree after it has been strained

Cantle

Lining

Saddle flap

Gullet

Panel

Pommel

Skirt

D

Saddle flap

Stirrup leather

Twist or Waist

Seat

Cantle

Panel

Skirt

Stirrup leather

Stirrup bar closed

Girth

Pocket for point of tree

Panel

Buckle guard

Girth straps

example, in racing, the horse is extended and the rider's weight needs to be well forward. In dressage, the horse is collected and the weight needs to be further back.

The jumping saddle has to bring the rider's weight well forward. To do this the bars for the stirrup irons are placed forward, the panel is extended and forward cut with rolls to support knee and thigh, and the tree is deep (ie, concave).

The all-purpose saddle is a modification of the above, with panel and flap less forward cut, thus making it possible to ride with longer stirrups.

The dressage saddle, in which the rider has to use very long stirrups and to have a deep seat, is straighter cut, the roll for lower thigh is on the forward edge of the panel, and the dip in the tree is deep, positioning the rider well back.

The show saddle is designed to show the front of the horse to its best advantage. It is therefore excessively straight cut and it fits as closely as possible to the horse's back with normally a half panel used, having little padding and no knee rolls.

The racing saddle is rarely sat in by the rider so the seat is unimportant. Its outstanding feature is that it is very light, weighing about 0.5–1kg (1–2lb). Light materials are used, such as kangaroo-skin and aluminium, the panels are cut to a minimum and the stirrup bars are usually omitted, leathers passing over side bars of the tree.

The stock saddle is used for the Western style of riding and has a high pommel with horn in front for securing a lasso when roping. The cantle is also high. Fenders (like long narrow saddle flaps) on each side protect the rider's legs from sweat. There are leather thongs along the back on which to tie lassos, saddlebags and other gear, and the cinch (girth) is secured by two thongs in cloverleaf knots. The stirrups are wide and made of solid wood.

Below: Diagrams showing the wide range of types of saddles used for different forms of riding.

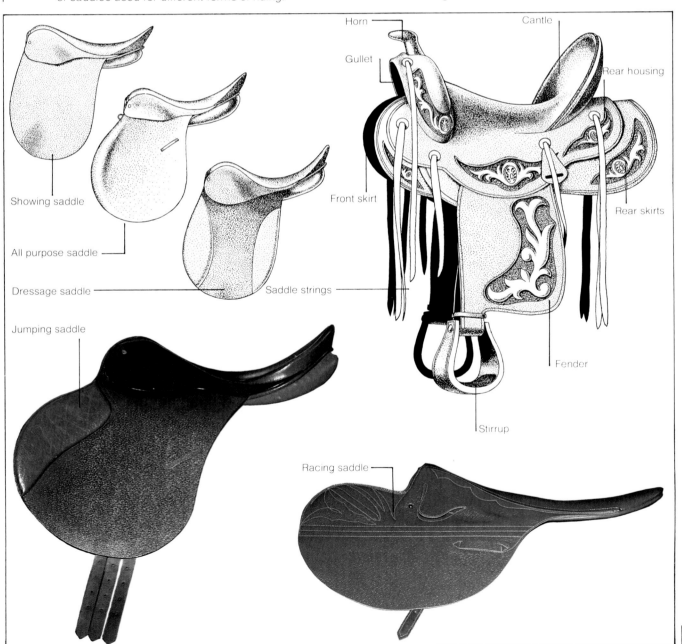

To Fit a Saddle

An ill-fitting saddle can make both horse and rider sore, and make it difficult for the rider to get into the correct position. It is important to check the saddle carefully, bearing the following points in mind.

The weight must not be concentrated on a particular point but distributed evenly over the back muscles. None must fall on the loin muscles or on the spine. The withers must not be restricted: the front arch of the saddle should be high and wide enough to prevent them from being pinched or pressed upon. The horse's shoulder blades must be able to move freely. Panels must be stuffed so that the rider sits in the correct position. Too much or too little stuffing, or wrong tilting, can result in the rider's seat not being in contact with the horse and/or sliding backwards. It is possible for a tree to break in a fall, or if the saddle itself is dropped. The saddle with a broken tree must not be used, because it would hurt the horse.

To ensure that the saddle fits correctly, it is advisable for the saddler to carry out an annual check-up.

Care of the Saddle

When placing the saddle on the ground, rest it on the front arch (not flat), taking care that the leather is not scratched. When carrying, place the front arch in the crook of the elbow. Clean regularly in accordance with general instructions (see below).

To clean the lining, take care to use the appropriate materials. A leather lining should be sponged off, ensuring that water does not run under the lining to dampen the stuffing. Dry with chamois leather, and finally soap. If the lining is made of linen, sponge or scrub it first, and dry away from direct heat with the saddle standing on its arch. A serge or wool lining should be dried and brushed. Do not scrub it unless it is very dirty.

To wash leather, make sure that the small black spots of grease found under the flap are removed: a small pad of horse-hair is the best means of doing this.

Saddle Accessories

The pad or numnah is worn underneath the saddle. It helps to protect the horse's back. It is made in many types of material, the most common being leather, felt, sponge rubber, synthetic fibres and sheepskin.

It is usually held in place by straps attached to the girth straps. Correctly fitted, it should be large enough to project about 2 cm (1 in) all round the saddle. Before the girths are tightened, the forward part of the numnah should be pulled up in order not to put pressure on the withers or spine.

Cleaning a numnah depends on the material from which it is made. Leather should be washed with pure soap; felt and sheepskin should be dried and brushed (scrub only when necessary). A synthetic fibre pad may be washed in a machine.

The girth secures the saddle and there are a number of types:

Web girths wear out more quickly than other types and can snap. Always use two. Leather girths are excellent as long as they are kept supple and used with caution on soft, unfit horses, when the leather can cause girth galls. They may be shaped, straight, cross-over or three-fold. The last-mentioned should have an oiled flannel inside the fold to keep it soft. Balding girths are narrow in the centre and reduce the chance of rubbing. They allow air to circulate. They are easy to clean with a brush, although an occasional wash is advisable.

Stirrup irons are best made of hand-forged stainless steel. Rubber treads are a useful addition as they help to prevent the rider's foot from slipping. Safety irons are used by many children and these have a rubber band on one side of the stirrup, allowing the foot to come free in a fall. (The rubber is worn on the outside.) This iron does have disadvantages, as it does not hang straight and the rubber often breaks.

A well-fitting stirrup iron should leave the rider's foot with 13 mm (½in) on either side, between it and the iron. Less space means the foot might be wedged in a fall, and more can cause the entire foot to slip through.

THE BRIDLE

The major purpose of the bridle is to hold the bit in the mouth. The snaffle bridle provides attachments for one bit and the double bridle for two bits.

The Snaffle Bridle

This, the simpler of the two bridles, consists of the following:
the headpiece and throat lash are in one piece, with the throat lash preventing the bridle from slipping forwards;
the brow band prevents the bridle from slipping backwards;
the two cheek pieces are attached at one end to the headpiece and at the other to the bit. The noseband is on its own headpiece. There are 4 basic types of noseband.

The cavesson fastens below the projecting cheek bone and normally serves no purpose other than providing an attachment for the standing martingale. A dropped noseband is fastened under the bit and prevents the horse from evading the bit by opening his mouth. The flash noseband is a cavesson noseband with a small loop at the front through which a strap runs to under the bit and is then fastened close to the loop. The grackle noseband has two crossed straps fastening above and below the bit. The pressure preventing the mouth from opening and the jaws from crossing is higher with the grackle than with the dropped noseband.

The bit is attached to the cheek pieces and the rein by either stitches (neater), studs (convenient for bit changes) or buckles (convenient, but clumsy in appearance).

The reins have a central buckle. They can be plain, plaited or laced leather (the last two are less likely to slip), covered in a rubber grip (which is the best means of preventing slipping), or plaited or plain linen or nylon.

The Double Bridle

The double bridle has the same constituents as the snaffle bridle, plus the following:
the bridoon headpiece and one cheek piece;
two bits, comprising a bridoon (thin snaffle) and a curb bit (usually called 'the bit');
an additional pair of reins of which both are of plain leather, but the bridoon rein is wider than the curb bit rein;
the curb chain, which is attached to hooks on either side of the curb bit;
and the lip strap, which is attached to the small 'D's on the curb bit and runs through the fly link of the curb chain.

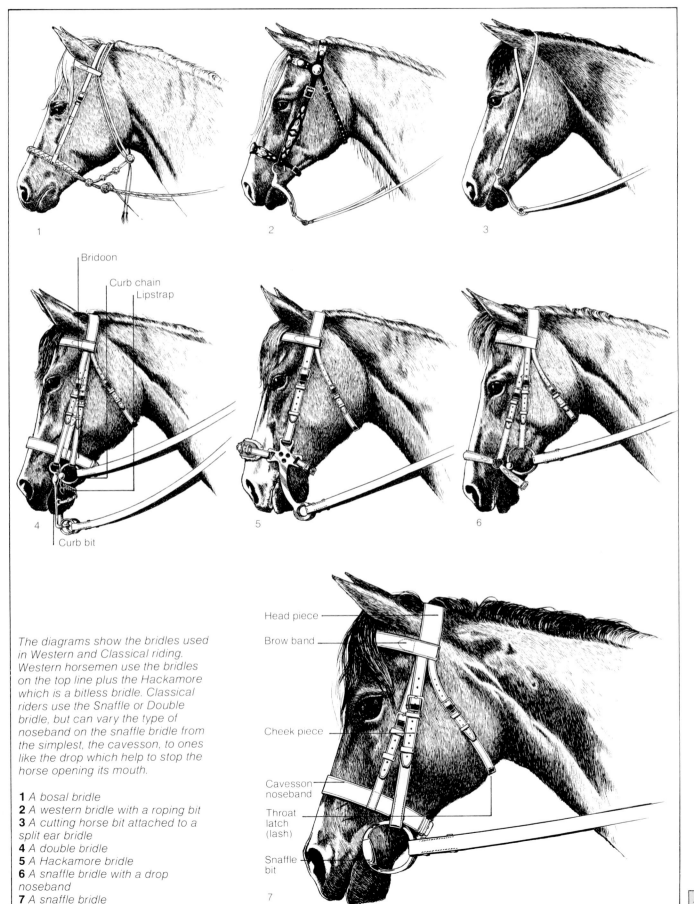

Bridoon
Curb chain
Lipstrap

Curb bit

Head piece
Brow band

Cheek piece

Cavesson noseband

Throat latch (lash)

Snaffle bit

The diagrams show the bridles used in Western and Classical riding. Western horsemen use the bridles on the top line plus the Hackamore which is a bitless bridle. Classical riders use the Snaffle or Double bridle, but can vary the type of noseband on the snaffle bridle from the simplest, the cavesson, to ones like the drop which help to stop the horse opening its mouth.

1 A bosal bridle
2 A western bridle with a roping bit
3 A cutting horse bit attached to a split ear bridle
4 A double bridle
5 A Hackamore bridle
6 A snaffle bridle with a drop noseband
7 A snaffle bridle

To Fit the Bridle

The throat lash should be loose enough to allow an adult's fist to be placed between it and the jawbone (if too tight, it restricts the breathing and flexion; if too loose, it will not serve its purpose of preventing the bridle from coming over the horse's head, which could lead to a serious accident).

The brow band prevents the bridle from slipping back too far, but must not be so tight that it touches the ears or pulls on the headpiece. The fit of the noseband varies a great deal according to the type.

A cavesson should lie halfway between the projecting cheek bone and the corners of the mouth. Normally, it should be loose enough to allow two fingers between it and the horse's nose but if done up tightly it can help to prevent the mouth from opening.

A dropped noseband is the normal way of preventing the mouth from opening, but it can be used only with a snaffle bridle and it must be very carefully fitted if it is not to pinch or restrict breathing. The front piece must be well above the nostrils and the back strap should lie in the chin groove, firmly but not tightly fastened.

The bit must be of the right width and attached so that it hangs in the correct position. If it is too narrow or too high, it will wrinkle or pinch the horse's lips. Too wide or low, it will fall on the teeth. In a double bridle, the bridoon should be higher than the curb bit.

The curb chain is attached to the hook on the offside of the bit, twisted until flat and then attached to the nearside. The length should be such that it comes into play when the bit is drawn back to an angle of 45 degrees.

The lip strap is attached to one side of the curb bit, passed through the fly link of the curb chain and buckled to the other side of the curb bit.

THE BIT

Bits can be made of various materials. Nickel has a yellow appearance. It is relatively cheap but tends to wear badly, resulting in rough edges, and it may bend or break. Plated steel is stronger than nickel but tends to chip. Hand-forged steel is the strongest but also the most expensive material. Mouthpieces of rubber, rubber-coated metal or vulcanite are comparatively soft, producing a very mild bit.

The bit is used in conjunction with the rider's seat and legs to control the horse. The pressure of the bit on the mouth conveys a message to the horse. With good training, the horse will react by relaxing his jaw and will not resist. He will obey, not out of fear or pain, but because he has learned to understand and trust his rider. Consequently the key to any horse's mouth does not lie among the numerous types of bits that apply varying degrees of pressure to different parts of the mouth and chin, but in good training, and reliance on a rider with a strong seat and good hands. Mechanical contrivances should be resorted to only if the horse has already been spoilt.

The Snaffle

This has a single mouthpiece, which acts upwards against the corners of the lips, particularly when the horse's head is low, on the bars of the lower jaw, particularly when the horse's head is high, and on the tongue. There are many different types and shapes.

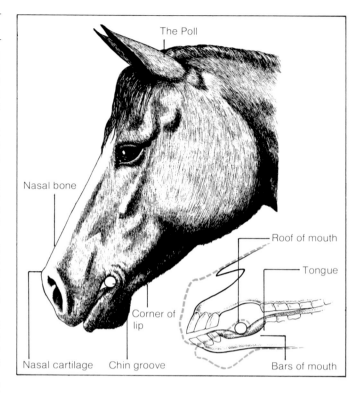

Above: Diagrams showing the areas of the head on which the bit and bridle can act. The cross section of the jaw shows where the bit lies in the mouth.

Right: The basic types of bridle correctly hung.

The half-moon (slightly curved) or straight bar snaffle is a very mild bit, especially if made of rubber, and can be used on young, sensitive horses or those with injured mouths. The single-jointed snaffle has a joint in the centre of the mouthpiece. This creates a 'nutcracker' action causing more pressure to be applied than with the half-moon. It is the most common type of snaffle and has a number of variations.

The thickness of the mouthpiece alters the severity of the bit. The thinner the mouthpiece, the more severe the bit becomes, because the pressure is more concentrated. The thin version is known as a racing snaffle, and the thick one as a German snaffle. The latter is a gentle bit and most riders use it on their young horses.

The rings can be large, small, fixed to the mouthpiece or loose (traversing rings). The two most common types are the egg-butt snaffle (in which the rings are fixed to the mouthpiece and are straight where attached, so that they are less likely to pinch the lips) and the loose ring snaffle in which the rings are the traversing type.

The texture of the mouthpiece also varies. A rough texture helps to prevent the horse or pony from leaning on the bit. The most common variation is the twisted snaffle, in which the mouthpiece is twisted, sharpening the pressure on the horse's mouth. It is a severe bit and should be used only on hard-mouthed horses. Other variations are ridged or square mouthpieces and those with chains and rollers. These are all hard on a mouth and should be used only with caution.

The method of attaching the bit to the leather cheek piece can affect the severity of the bit. The cheek pieces are normally looped on to the rings of the bit, but in the gag-bit they are rounded and pass through holes at the

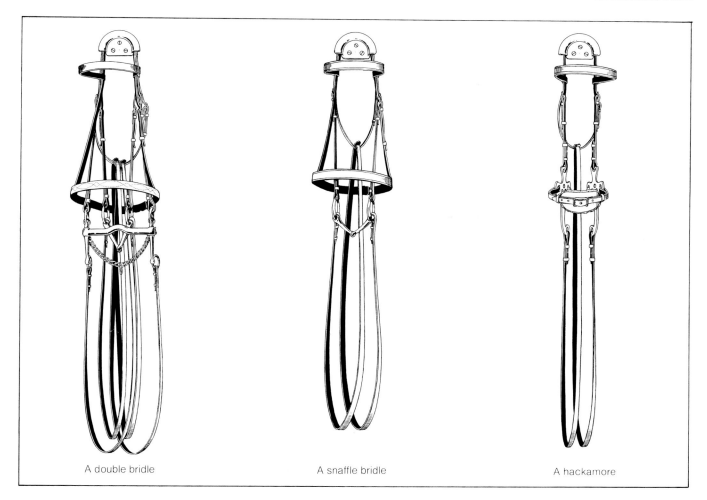

| A double bridle | A snaffle bridle | A hackamore |

top and bottom of the ring so that the rein is attached directly to the cheek piece. A pull on the rein results in the bit rising against the corners of the horse's mouth. It has a very severe action and the gag-bit should be used only in the last resort.

A double-jointed snaffle has two joints, thus reducing the 'nutcracker' action. Furthermore, the bit will not rest so low and gives the horse more freedom to move its tongue. Sensitive horses and those that put their tongue over the bit are often more relaxed in this snaffle.

The Bits of the Double Bridle

These give a more precise control, and a double bridle, therefore, should not be used until the horse accepts a snaffle bit. To use it before a horse or pony has learned to relax will tend to frighten him, and get him to stiffen against it, so he will obey only because of its severity. The result of this is that he develops resistances in order to try to avoid the action of the bits.

The double bridle has two bits. The bridoon is a snaffle that is usually thinner than the simple snaffle. The curb bit provides additional control and makes possible more refined aids. It acts partly on the tongue, and the pressure is greatest when the mouthpiece is straight. If there is a port (upward curve) in the centre of the curb bit, then there is more room for the tongue to move.

Pressure is also felt on the bars of the mouth (area of gum between the incisor and molar teeth) through the action of the metal cheek piece, which may be fixed (action more direct) or movable; in either case, it has a lever effect.

The third area of pressure is on the curb groove, for, as the metal cheek pieces are pulled back, they cause the curb chain to apply pressure on the curb groove. The greater the length of the cheek piece, the greater the leverage and the severity of it and the curb chain.

The fourth area of pressure is on the poll; when the metal cheeks are pulled back, the eye (the ring of the bit to which the leather cheek pieces are attached) goes forward and, as it is connected to the bridle, exerts a downward pressure on the poll.

The Pelham

This aims to combine the effect of a snaffle and a curb bit in one. Two reins are normally used. The bridoon rein is attached to rings level with the mouthpiece, and the curb rein to the bottom of the metal cheek piece, thus obtaining the lever and curb chain effect. The mouthpiece may be vulcanite and straight or half-moon, with a port or even jointed. A 'Pelham converter' or leather roundings are curved couplings that join the bridoon and curb rings on a Pelham bit, so that only one rein need be used. Having only one rein reduces the variations in pressure that can be applied, but it is simpler for the rider to handle.

The Kimblewick

Using the same principle of roundings, it consists of a single, large metal 'D' running from the mouthpiece to the bottom of the cheek piece. It is a severe bit, and must be used with caution.

The Bitless Bridle

This bridle has no mouthpiece; pressure is placed on the nose and chin. The hackamore is the best-known type; it has two long metal cheeks that are curved so that their leather attachments act across the nose and behind the chin when the rider pulls on the reins. The hackamore is sometimes called a bosal.

The Principles of Bitting

Whenever possible, use the mildest bit. A severe bit can often worry a horse so much that he becomes more excitable and more difficult to control. If the horse resists the bit or is too strong, always consider other possible causes before selecting another bit. These could include bad riding, rough teeth, too much energy-giving food, an injured mouth, a badly fitting bit or bridle, or simply that the horse is too inexperienced to do what is asked.

If none of these applies, the next step is to analyse the form of resistance before making a selection. If the horse or pony is too strong and has the experience and temperament to accept a stronger bit then try one, but with caution and good hands. If the resistance takes the form of the horse crossing his jaw and opening his mouth, a dropped or crossed noseband should be used. If the tongue is brought over the bit, then the bit is acting only on the bars of the mouth and not on the tongue. To prevent this from occurring, make sure the bit is high in the mouth, use a dropped or crossed noseband (as the horse needs to open his mouth to get its tongue over) or try a mouthpiece that has a port or is double-jointed (as these give more freedom for the tongue to lie beneath the bit). If all else fails then a device to prevent the tongue from getting over the bit can be used.

The most common forms of resistance are going behind the bit when the head is tucked in, or going above the bit when the head is raised. In the former case, a less severe bit is needed, so that the horse will not be frightened to take hold of it. The latter might be due to a lack of training or fear of a severe bit (shown by nervous jerks of the head), and only if the mouth is hard can a curb bit help.

Below: Some of the variations in the types of bit used for riding. Clockwise from the top:
1 *Jointed Pelham. A single mouthpiece with rings at both ends in addition to those at the top and bottom ends of the cheekpiece.*
2 *Bit and Bridoon. A combination of 2 bits for a double bridle.*
3 *Jointed Curb.*
4 *Jointed Egg-butt Snaffle. The smooth sides prevent rubbing.*
5 *Rearing Bit. Used when a horse proves to be playful or wayward.*

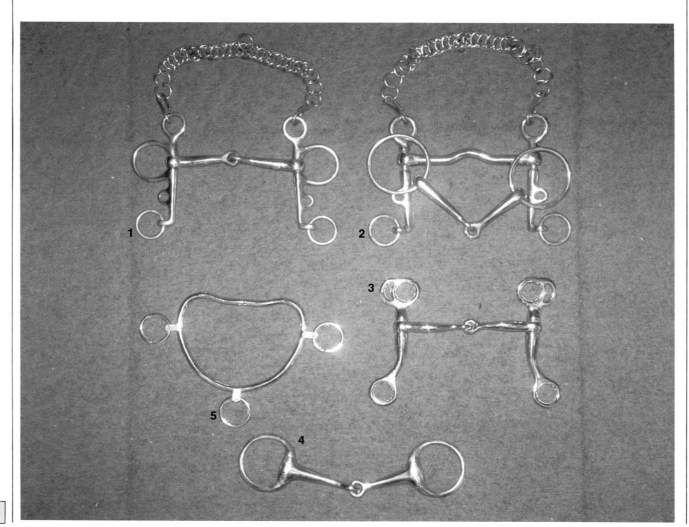

ACCESSORIES

The Halter

There are two types of halter, both used to tie up or lead a horse. One is made of hemp or cotton and usually has no throat lash or buckles. The more expensive variety is made of leather or nylon and fitted with buckles and a throat lash. In the USA the term halter still applies, but in the UK this type is known as a headcollar or headstall.

Martingales

These are used to control the position of the horse's head. There are various types:

The standing martingale, consisting of a strap running from the girth to a cavesson noseband (never to a dropped noseband, as this can restrict breathing), it prevents a horse from throwing his head in the air. The running martingale is a strap that runs from the girth, divides in two and ends in rings running along the reins. The effect of this martingale is thus felt on the bit, and a very short running martingale has a severe lever action on the mouth. It should be fitted so that the rings are in line with the withers, thus discouraging the horse from raising his head above this level. The neck strap must not be too tight, as this would rub the animal. Leather or rubber stoppers should be used on the reins to prevent the rings from getting caught on the buckles of the veins. The Irish martingale is used to stop the reins from going over the head.

The Chambon

This is a strap which runs from the girth through the bit to rings on an attachment over the poll.

It is advisable to use the Chambon only on the lunge. It is harmful if used too tightly and is useful only in the hands of an expert.

Above: This picture shows a running martingale, which helps to stop the horse from putting his head too high in the air.

Below: Draw reins which also help to control the position of the head, but are a stronger aid and should be used only by experts.

The Draw Rein

This runs from the girth through the rings of the bit to the rider's hands, giving him greater control over the horse's head position. It is frequently used by top show-jumpers but can do much damage in the hands of a rider with limited experience or rough hands.

The Breastplate

This a neck strap with attachments to two 'D's of the saddle and to the girth, which prevents the saddle from slipping back. To fit the breastplate, ensure the neck strap is not too tight and that the attachments are not strained.

PUTTING ON THE SADDLE

Above: First, put on the saddle cloth. This should be used when pleasure riding as it protects the horse's back, absorbs sweat and also helps to protect the saddle.

Above: Approach the horse with the saddle. It should be carried as shown, with the front arch in the crook of the elbow, and the stirrup irons in the up position.

Above: With the left hand on the front arch and the right hand on the cantle, approach the horse from the nearside and carefully swing the saddle onto the back of the horse.

Above: Put the saddle down well forward of the withers, and then slide it back into place. Make sure the saddle sits comfortably in the deeper part of the back.

Tie up the horse on the halter or headcollar before collecting the saddlery from the tack room. The saddle should be carried with the front arch in the crook of the elbow, with the irons run up, the girth attached on the offside lying over the seat and the pad/numnah (if being used) underneath them all. The bridle and martingale can be hung over the shoulder of the same arm.

The martingale and the saddle are put on first, so the bridle can be hung up nearby. Check that there is no mud or dirt on the horse where the saddle will lie. Unfasten the neck strap of the martingale and put around the neck so that the buckle is close up on the nearside.

With the left hand on the front arch and the right hand on the cantle, approach the nearside and place the saddle well forward of the withers. Slide it back so that it sits in the deep part of the back. Check to see that the

flaps are straight and, if a numnah is used, that it too is flat, pulled well up into the arch of the saddle and protruding evenly around the entire rim of the saddle.

Go to the offside, let down the girth and check that it is straight. Return to the nearside, take the girth, put it through the martingale, if using one, and buckle up. Ensure that the girth is not pinching the skin and that there are enough holes left to be able to tighten it later. Where two webbing girths are used the two should overlap, with the underneath one attached to the forward buckles on either side. Make sure, whichever the girth, that it is done up tightly before mounting.

Right: The saddle is incorrectly placed (a) too far forward, and (b) resting on the withers. The inset shows the correct position.

Above: When you have made sure the saddle is in the correct position, go to the offside, let down the girth and check that it is straight and not twisted. Return to the nearside..

Above: Take hold of the girth and then pull it under the chest of the horse. Put it through the martingale, if you are using one. The next step is to buckle up the girth.

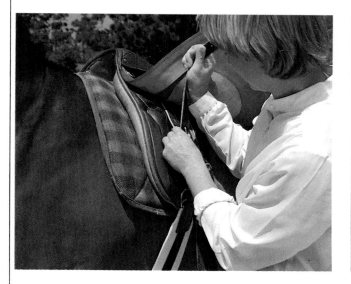

Above: Gently put the saddle straps through the girth, tightening it a few holes at a time so that you can just put a finger or two under it, until the saddle is held firmly in place.

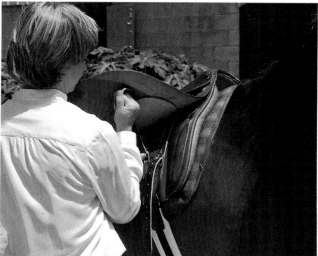

Above: If necessary, tighten the girth on the right side. To ensure the girth is not pinching the skin, take hold of a foreleg and bring it forward to stretch the skin under the girth.

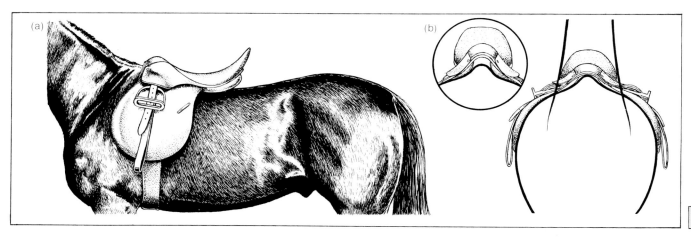

(a)

(b)

Putting on the Bridle

Untie the horse and put the reins over his head. Still holding the bridle, remove the halter and hang it up. With the right hand take the headpiece of the bridle and let the bit rest against the left hand, which is then positioned under the muzzle. Insert the thumb or first finger where there is a gap between the horse's teeth and gently prise the mouth open. The bridle can then be lifted with the right hand while the left hand guides the bit into the horse's mouth. Use both hands to ease the headpiece over the ears, ensuring that no skin or hair is pinched and that the leather is not twisted.

The buckles can then be done up, starting with the throat lash and followed by the noseband, which must lie inside the cheek pieces. All the keepers have to be checked to ensure that the flaps are held in place. With a curb bit, the curb chain must be fastened, twisting it until straight, followed by the lip strap (if there is one).

Check that the bridle is on straight and that the bit is level (ie, that the buckles on both cheek pieces are in matching holes).

With a running martingale, the reins should then be undone and put through its rings. With a standing martingale, the loop should be hooked to the noseband before the latter is buckled up.

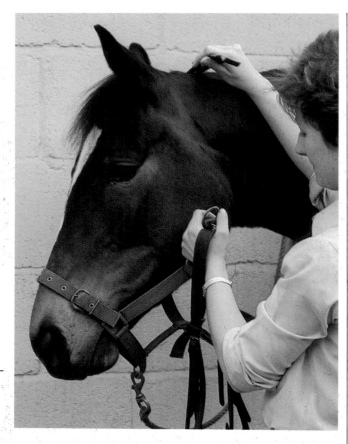

Right: The first stage is to hold the bridle in the left hand and then take the reins over the horse's neck. The next step is to undo the headcollar.

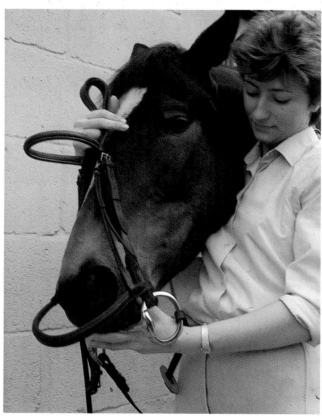

Above: Taking the headpiece of the bridle in the right hand, lift the bridle so that the bit, held in the left hand, is brought towards the mouth.

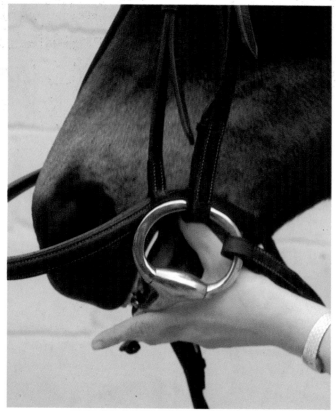

Above: With the thumb of the left hand gently prise open the mouth by putting the thumb into the mouth in the area where there are no teeth.

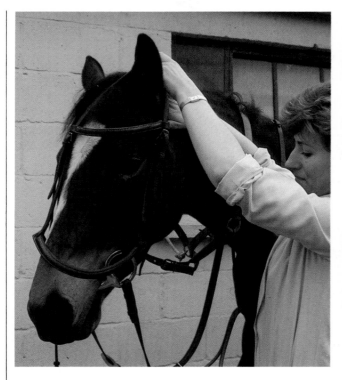

Above: Lift the bit up into the mouth with the left hand and raise the headpiece with the right hand until it can be lifted over the ears, taking care not to pinch them.

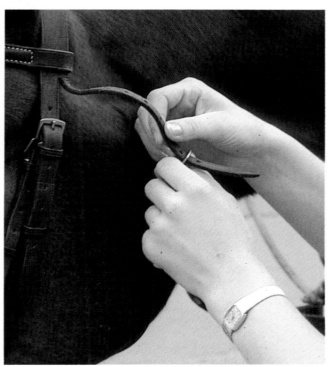

Above: Once the bridle is in place, the first buckle to be done up is the throat lash. It should be possible to put a fist between the lash and the horse's jaw.

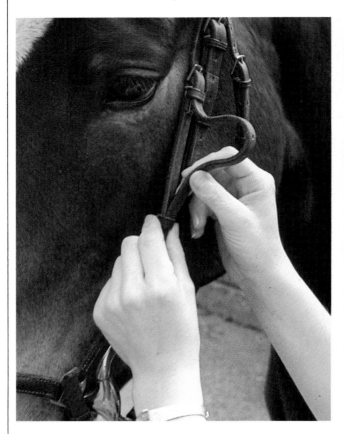

Above: It is now time to tuck any of the straps not yet tucked into their appropriate keepers. This prevents the straps from flapping about and looking untidy.

Above: The noseband should be fastened. As this one is a drop it should be around the bottom of the bit and enough room left so that two fingers can be placed between it and the horse.

CARE OF TACK

Regular inspections are essential, because it is safer and cheaper to replace rotting stitches or repair cracked leather in the early stages of deterioration. Tack should always be hung up or stored carefully so that air can circulate around it and prevent mildew. It must be kept clean and the leather pliant.

Equipment for Cleaning Tack

In order to clean tack efficiently, the following equipment is needed: a towel for washing; sponge for saddle soap, chamois leather for drying; saddle soap; metal polish and several soft cloths; rubber for drying metal work; dandy brush for removing mud from girths, lining, etc; nail for cleaning out curb hooks, etc; glycerine for covering tack to be stored; a bucket; a hook on which to hang bridles; and a saddle horse.

The Do's of Tack Cleaning

Hang bridle and leather accessories on a tack-cleaning hook, and place the saddle on a saddle horse. Undo all buckles and remove fittings (bit, stirrup leathers, irons, etc). Wash leather and metal with lukewarm water and dry with chamois leather. Apply saddle soap to leather with a sponge, using as little water as possible. If using bar soap, it is best to dampen the soap and not the sponge. Apply metal polish to metal and then thoroughly clean off. On any parts of the tack that need washing (eg, girths, pads) use pure soap, not detergent. When cleaning is finished put all the parts together again.

The Don'ts of Tack Cleaning

Never wash leather with washing soda or hot water, or saturate it with water. Never let it dry too close to a strong heat.
   Never use linseed, or mineral oils; use saddle soap, glycerine, neatsfoot oil or a proprietory brand of leather preservative to keep leather soft.

Storing the Tack

The bridle should be hung up by placing the rein or reins through the throat lash and the noseband outside cheek pieces. There is no need to buckle, but the end of the strap should be put through the keepers. Put the bridle on a wide bridle rack so that the leather keeps its shape and does not crack. Do not use a nail or coat hook. If there is no special hanger, an empty round saddle soap or coffee can, nailed to the wall, makes a good substitute.

The Saddle

Place the saddle on a bracket about 45 cm (18 in) long attached to the wall. The accessories can be hung beside the saddle.

BOOTS

Brushing Boots
These can be made of many types of material (felt,

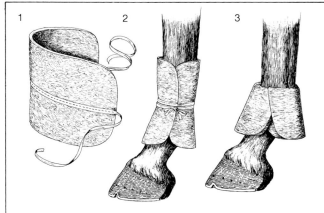

Above: How to put on Yorkshire boots.
1 A boot before it is fitted on the horse.
2 It is wrapped around the fetlock and tied.
3 The boot is then folded over to give extra protection to the fetlock joint.

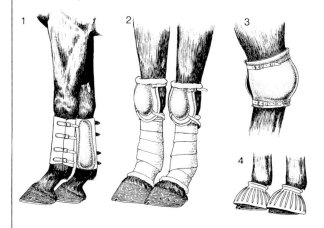

Above: Illustrations of various types of boot.
1 Brushing boots, showing the leather protection pads inside.
2 Knee caps in place, with travelling bandages also fitted.
3 A hock boot made of heavy wool protects the horse when travelling.
4 Protective over-reach boots.

leather, etc). They are worn around the cannon bone and the upper half of the fetlock joint, and help to stop damage from blows and brushing when the horse is ridden.

Over-Reach Boots
These are bell-shaped and fit over the hoof to protect the heels of the forelegs.

Knee Caps
Horses' knees can be protected when travelling by the use of knee caps. It is also advisable to use them when exercising on hard roads, in case of a fall.

Hock Boots
Worn over the hock, they are made of heavy wool and protect the horse when travelling or, in the stable, if he is a kicker.

Yorkshire Boots
These are worn to protect the hind fetlocks and/or coronet.

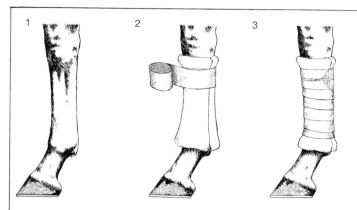

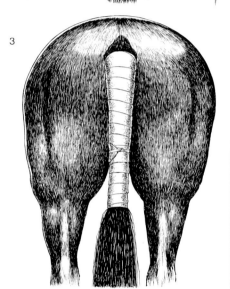

Above: How to put on an exercise bandage.
1 *The area covered, from below the knee to the centre of the fetlock.*
2 *How the bandage is begun over the gamgee.*
3 *The finished bandage, tied below the knee.*

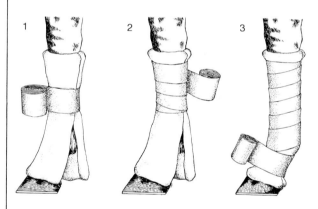

Above: How to put on a travelling bandage.
1 *The bandage is started about the centre of the canon bone.*
2 *The bandage is taken up to below the knee.*
3 *It is taken down to cover the pastern.*
4 *It is then taken back to the knee and tied. This completes the bandage.*

Above: How to put on a tail bandage.
1 *The bandage is started from the top of the dampened tail.*
2 *It should be kept as tight as possible at this stage to ensure it stays firmly in place.*
3 *The bandage is taken down to the end of the tail bone and is then finished by securing the strings a quarter of the way up the bandaged area.*

BANDAGES

Exercise Bandages
Made of stockinette or crepe, 65–75 mm (2 ½–3 in) wide, they are used for support and protection. They cover the legs below the knee or hock and above the fetlock joint.

Stable or Travelling Bandages
These are made of flannel or wool and are about 10 cm x 2.5 m (4 in x 7–8 ft). They are used to keep the horse warm, and for protection when travelling. They should cover as much of the leg as possible, from the knee or hock down to the coronet. They should be firmly, but not too tightly, applied over gamgee or cotton wool. Start at the top and wind it around the leg until the fetlock is covered then work upward until the starting point is reached.

Tail Bandages
Made of stockinette or crepe, 65–75 mm (2½–3 in) wide, these are used to protect the tail when travelling and/or to improve its appearance by getting the hairs to lie flat. To apply, dampen the tail. Unroll 15 cm (6 in) of the bandage and hold the end under the tail. Make two turns, to secure the bandage, and then two above, to cover the highest part of the tail; then wind downward around the tail to the end of the tail-bone, where the tapes should be tied. To remove, slide off, grasping bandage at the top of the tail.

Surgical Bandages
Surgical bandages cover wounds, cuts, abrasions and partially immobilise sprained joints. They are plaster bandages with an adhesive surface 75 mm (3 in) wide.

To Roll Up Bandages

Tapes should be tucked in on the side where they are sewn in. They should then be rolled up with the sewn side facing inward.

The Stable Blanket or Rug

This is made of heavy jute, hemp or sail canvas and is lined with wool blanketing. It is used in the stable to keep the horse warm.

The Day Blanket or Rug

A wool rug, often decorated with braid, it is used to keep the horse warm when travelling, and on any occasion when he needs to look smart.

The Woollen Blankets

Worn under rugs to give extra warmth when it is cold. It is not shaped, but oblong or square.

The Roller

This is used to keep rugs in place and is made of leather, web or jute, padded on either side where it passes over the backbone so that pressure does not fall on the spine (a pad is often used in addition to give further protection against pressure on the spine). Surcingles, which have no padding, should be used with caution; they often cause sore backs.

The Anti-Cast Roller

Two pads are joined by a metal hoop which prevents the horse from rolling over and getting cast.

The Summer Sheet

Made of cotton, this is used instead of a rug in hot weather. It provides some warmth and is a protection against flies and dust in the summer months.

The Cooler or Anti-Sweat Sheet

The holes in this sheet made of open cotton mesh allow ventilation; it is therefore used for cooling off horses that have sweated. If worn under a rug, it provides a layer of insulation against heat and cold, and helps to prevent a horse from 'breaking out' (sweating) after heavy work or other strain.

The New Zealand Rug

This is made of waterproof canvas, partly lined with wool, and has special straps to stop it from slipping. It is used to keep horses warm when turned out to grass. For a horse with a full coat, this is unnecessary, but for stabled horses, who may be turned out for a few hours during the day, New Zealand rugs are advisable, in cold weather.

Rugging Up

This is necessay in all but the hottest weather for the horse kept in a stall or stable. To put it on, tie the horse up, take the blanket (rug) at the front and gently swing it

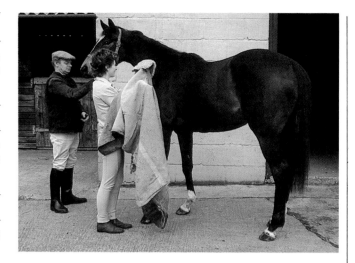

Above: The front of the rug is held and then it is thrown gently over the horse.

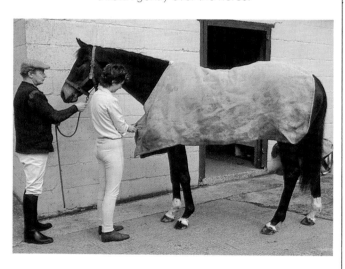

Above: The buckle at the front of the rug is first done up as shown here.

over the horse to lie centrally along the back but high up on the neck. Buckle up the front and then slide back into position, but not so far that it drags on the shoulders.

If there is no surcingle attached to the blanket (rug), use a roller pad under a roller. Position this pad behind the withers and put the roller over it, ensuring that there are no twists (see photographs). Buckle up the roller so that it is firm, but not squeezing the horse. Run the fingers between the roller and the rug to ensure that there are no lumps. Check that the rug is not too small, and is not pulling on the shoulders and withers, as this can make the animal sore.

In cold weather, a clipped horse may need an additional blanket for warmth. This is put on first, again well forward, and slid back so that it nearly touches the root of the tail at the back. The blanket (rug) is then added, the roller done up and the free portion of the under blanket, at the front, folded back over the rug, to make it neat and stop it slipping back.

To take the blanket (rug) off, remove the roller and unfasten the front buckle. With the left hand, grasp the part of the rug that is over the withers, and with the right hand the part over the back. Slide it off in the direction of the hair and fold it up four-square.

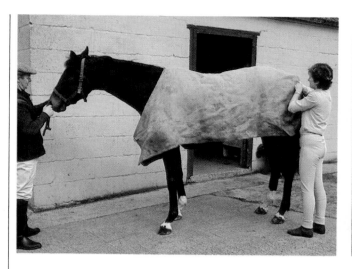

Above: The rug is then pulled back with the lie of the hair.

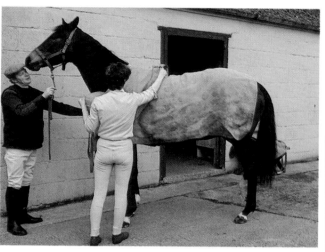

Above: The roller is taken and placed with the buckle on the near side.

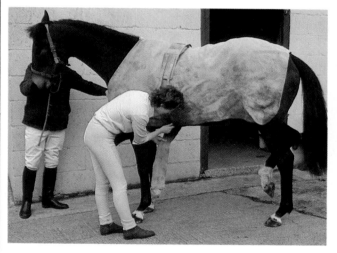

Above: The far side of the roller is then taken and brought towards the buckle.

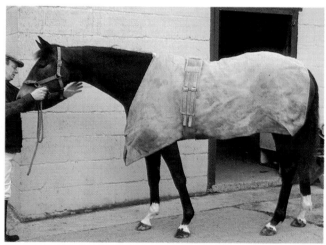

Above: This shows the horse with the rug and the roller in place.

Above: A pony wearing a sweat sheet which helps him to dry off after sweating.

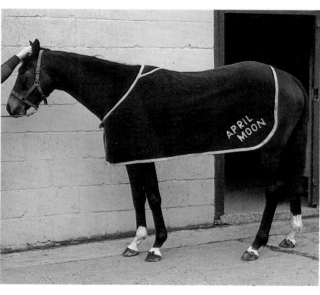

Above: Here, a horse is wearing a day rug but without a roller.

THE HEALTHY HORSE

The old adage 'Prevention is better than cure' applies just as well to horses as to human beings. For humanitarian, utilitarian and financial reasons, owners, trainers and breeders should take appropriate steps to maintain and consolidate their horses' health. This involves establishing certain routines in healthy horse care. In this section, these routines are set out in two parts: those to be carried out on a daily basis, and those to be followed periodically.

But however comprehensive your preventative programme of health care, it cannot entirely eradicate the risks of injury. It is important, therefore, to be well-organised in advance to cope with any emergency. This section deals with first-aid techniques and the administration of medication, to enable you to minimise the horse's pain and fear when hurt and to prevent further injury until the veterinary surgeon arrives. When illness does strike, the close contact you have with your horse day to day should enable you to detect symptoms early on, and to take appropriate action. The A-Z of specific diseases and problems in this section details causes, signs and treatment for each ailment.

DAILY CARE

FEEDING AND DIET

The little documented research that has been done points out some glaring faults in the feeding of horses.

The nutritional requirements of horses vary according to individual needs and are determined by such factors as maintenance, growth, work, pregnancy or lactation. The basic ingredients of any sound nutrition programme are proteins (amino acids), carbohydrates, fibre, fats, vitamins and minerals.

Compared with other animals, the horse has the smallest stomach relative to body size, and it can hold only a limited quantity of food at any one time. Since the horse's digestion requires a certain amount of roughage, the remainder of its diet must be high in energy yield and protein concentrates.

However, no matter what the quality or balance is in the diet, if the horse has poor teeth or is infected with worms, little or no benefit will be derived.

Types of Feed

Grains

Various types of grain are a good source of energy. The more common types are discussed here.

Oats This grain is the one most widely used to feed horses, but every effort should be made to secure the best quality. Make sure that the grain is full and of good colour. Oats may be given to the horse either as whole grain or as processed grain that may be crushed, rolled or bruised. The processed grain is no more digestible than whole grain and if kept for longer than 2–3 weeks, it will lose some of its nutritional value.
Corn (maize) This grain has a greater energy content than most others. It is best used as a supplement to oats rather than as the main source of energy. It can be fed whole to the horse but it is more beneficial if cracked.
Barley This grain has a greater energy content than oats but less than corn. It is of greater value if boiled before being fed to the horse. Often this grain is used to improve a horse's general condition, including weight and coat.
Milo This is a hard, small grain and to be of value it should be ground, rolled or boiled; otherwise, it cannot be properly digested.
Soya bean If this grain is made into a meal by removing the hull or husk, its digestibility is improved and it becomes an excellent source of protein.

Wheat This grain is not recommended. If fed, it should be crushed or boiled and given in small quantities only.

Hays

Good quality hays can completely satisfy a horse's nutritional requirements, provided that there is no additional demand such as that arising from growth in foals and work by competition and racehorses. Broadly speaking, hay is a good source of protein, energy, fibre, calcium and vitamins. Any of the well-known hays can be fed to horses, but keep in mind that it is the quality of the hay, not the type, which is the most important consideration. The characteristics of good quality hay are that it should be leafy without too much stem, free from weeds, dust and mould, greenish in colour (yellow or black should be rejected), succulent without being too damp or even too dry and sweet smelling. It should be more than 6 months old and less than 18 months old. (The age of the hay at harvesting time is important, as young plants contain more nutrient and less fibre.)

Additives

Bran has limited nutritional value. It can be fed dry or damp as a mash. It has a laxative effect and if the horse is fed the right quantity (see diet chart), bran will maintain the horse's droppings (manure) at the right consistency (ie, they break up as they hit the ground).

Molasses, being raw sugar, is a good source of energy. It also serves to make the feed more palatable.

Nuts/cubes can be used as a complete diet, depending on their formulation. They are recommended for use as an additive or supplement to avoid the possibility of some deficiency developing.

Vitamin and mineral supplements are valuable, especially for the performance horse. It is important that they contain the whole range of vitamins, minerals and trace elements in correct balance. When purchasing these supplements, read the label carefully. It is not sufficient for the label to list what is included in the contents of the container; the precise quantity of each vitamin, mineral and trace element should also be included. Only then can you evaluate the quality and economic value of the product.

Below: A feed bin containing the various feedstuffs which are being mixed for an individual feed for a horse.

Above: The picture shows various types of horse feed. Top left (in bucket): oats; top row, left to right: chaff, salt; second row: soya bean meal, cotton seed meal, sunflower seed; third row, left to right: vitamin and mineral supplement, calcium, bran; bottom (in bucket): barley.

Chaff

Chaff is usually made from finely chopped hay or oat straw. In the process, nutrients in the hay and straw are destroyed to some extent. Lucerne hay chaff has greater nutritional value than the others whereas other hays and straw contain more roughage and bulk.

Meals

Linseed meal is high in fibre and low in digestibility. It is often fed to improve the appearance of the coat, but its value is doubtful.

Cotton seed meal can be used as a source of protein. It need not be de-gossypoled.

Soya bean meal as a source of protein is superior to the others because of its high digestibility and high quality protein.

Pasture

Pastures can vary greatly for many reasons, including season, management and soil suitability.

Good quality pasture is adequate for mature horses that only require food for maintenance. If possible, all horses, expecially those being fed in stables, should have access to pasture for at least 2 hours every day. Not only is the fresh pasture nutritionally valuable, but the exercise that the horse takes while foraging in the paddock aids digestion.

Horses without access to pasture benefit if given a daily sheaf of freshly cut grass.

Water

Water should be freely available at all times except immediately after the horse has taken strenuous exercise. It should be fresh, clean and cool.

Feeding Routine

Small feeds should be give at regular intervals 3–4 times a day. The horse should be fed by weight, not by volume, and the weight and type of food should be varied according to exercise or work done. Changes in the type and weight of food should be made gradually.

Keep the feed tin clean and avoid using old, stale, mouldy food. Bear in mind that exercise aids digestion and that fresh, clean, cool water should always be freely available.

PERFORMANCE HORSES

Above: Good quality pasture such as this is vital for the maintenance of condition.

Below: This foal is getting plenty of sunshine, to produce vitamin D naturally in the skin.

Energy, Calcium-Phosphorus Balance

Work denotes the expenditure of more energy. Grain is a very good source of energy; the most common grain being fed to horses is oats. All cereal grains contain high phosphorus levels, so that an increased grain diet increases the phosphorus level. Because the amount of grain in the diet is increased with a corresponding decrease in the amount of roughage, there is a resultant decrease in the calcium level, for hay is a source of calcium. Young horses that have not reached their maturity need food for energy as well as for growth, so that if their energy food upsets their calcium requirements for growth, they need a calcium supplement. It is most important that the calcium supplement does not contain any phosphorus such as calcium phosphate because the imbalance is not rectified.

'Tying-Up' and Lactic Acid

High-grain diets also lead to a storage of glycogen in the body. Glycogen is used by the muscles when work is being performed, and the waste product from the chemical change that takes place is lactic acid. If the lactic acid accumulates and is not expelled from the muscle tissue, it damages the muscle fibres, producing a condition called tying-up or, if large areas of muscle fibre are damaged or destroyed, azoturia (see page **98**).

In any case, this condition adversely affects a horse's training programme and performance.

Often if a blood count is taken, certain enzyme tests can be done to confirm the diagnosis of tying-up. In work with race horses, the author has often found that, if serum enzyme levels in a horse's blood are very high just prior to racing, in most cases performances are disappointing, although in track work before the race there has been no sign of stiffness or soreness in their action. Serum enzyme tests are discussed further on page **77**.

Some horses that are not on high-grain diets tie-up because they are hypersensitive to lactic acid or have little ability to metabolise the by-product. These horses require medical treatment both orally and by injection to prevent tying-up ruining their career. Prevention also involves reducing the grain level when there is a reduction in the workload and, in some cases, keeping the grain level at a minimum all the time.

Founder

Founder, ie, laminitis or inflammation of the sensitive laminae in the hoof (see page **107**), occurs in all classes of horses. However, it is most often observed in overfed (high-grain diet or lush, highly palatable pasture grass diets) and underworked horses, especially confined ponies that have little or no exercise.

Hydration

Work is associated with sweat which is made up fluids and electrolytes. If the fluid and electrolytes are not replaced, dehydration sets in and a poor performance results.

Electrolyte loss and imbalance can be evaluated on a blood count and treated accordingly. The usual method is to restore the electrolytes through the feed, a stomach tube or an intravenous injection.

Stress

Continual hard exercise leads to stress that depresses erythropoesis (red blood cell production). Exacerbating this problem is an increase in red blood cell fragility and destruction. Horses that cannot cope with stress become anaemic.

It is important to have a blood count done to determine the type of anaemia so that the appropriate treatment can be carried out.

As a rule, all high performance horses should be on a selected vitamin and mineral supplement that is balanced, and the concentration of vitamins and minerals should be fully stated on the container. An iron supplement that will directly influence the haemoglobin levels is also recommended. You will need to be careful, as some irons are not readily absorbed.

Loss of Weight

Decrease in protein intake due to poor appetite associated with hard work can cause weight loss. A more subtle cause of weight loss can be the increased amount of grain being fed to provide energy for hard work. Grains, eg oats, are a poor source of protein. Hard work causes muscle fibre fatigue which, if prolonged, leads to muscle fibre breakdown. This puts the horse in a negative nitrogen balance.

Serum protein levels evaluated on the blood count can determine whether a high protein feed additive such as soya bean meal, cotton seed meal or dried powdered milk, is required. Beware of some high protein feeds such as linseed meal which is very low in digestibility.

Certain anabolic steroids that can be used to stimulate appetite assist in efficiently converting protein in the diet to muscle and other kinds of tissue, offsetting the muscle fibre breakdown and putting the horse into a positive nitrogen balance.

Stallions

Stallions are often overfed and under-exercised. Poor quality diet leads to testicular degeneration and atrophy, diminished sexual drive, decreased number of spermatozoa and increased abnormal forms of spermatozoa. If the poor diet is prolonged, these changes can be irreversible.

Vitamin A is essential for sperm production. Green pasture is a source of carotene which is converted to Vitamin A. Exposure of lucerne hay, clover and green herbage to sunlight and air, as well as the physical destruction of leaves during drying, destroys carotene, the source of Vitamin A. Good hay is a source of Vitamin A for 6–12 months only.

Vitamin A can be stored in the liver for 6–12 months. A stallion's requirements are 2000 to 5000 I.U. vitamin A per 50 kg (1 cwt) body weight. Ten times the amount mentioned can be toxic.

It has been claimed that vitamin E is important for increased libido and semen quality, the requirement being 20 I.U. per 50 kg (1 cwt) body weight. There is no scientific evidence to support this claim.

Feeding Brood Mares

A mare's chances of becoming pregnant are better on a rising plane of nutrition when her condition is being built up. It is not desirable for a non-pregnant mare approaching the stud season to be overfat, as she has less chance of becoming pregnant. Allow the non-pregnant mares to lighten off during winter and restore them to a gaining weight phase as they approach the stud season.

The volume of food given during the first two thirds of pregnancy does not have to be markedly increased. It is important to make sure that ample quality feed is available in the last 3 months of pregnancy to satisfy the demands of the rapidly growing foetus. The environment 3 months before birth often coincides with very poor pasture so the diet needs to be supplemented.

For good early foetal development, it is important that there should be no nutritional deficiencies. A well-balanced vitamin-mineral supplement in a good nutrition programme is essential for early foetal formation.

There is an increased demand for protein during lactation. Good sources of protein are lucerne hay and soya bean meal. To raise the total protein level of the diet by adding a high protein supplement, one must be aware of the existing amino acid deficiency in the basic diet. For example, milk is high in the amino acid lysine whilst grain is low in that amino acid, so that the addition of skin milk improves the protein value of grain feed.

There is an increased demand for calcium, phosphorus and magnesium. Lucerne and molasses have high calcium levels. As already mentioned, grains are an important source of phosphorus.

One has to contend with the 9th day of foaling heat. If

the nutrition is poor, coupled with the stress of lactation and the effect of parturition (birth) on the mare's metabolism, she may not come on heat at the normal 9 to 10–day post-foaling heat period or in some cases for months afterwards.

Food for Foals and Yearlings

Foals and yearlings need to grow in terms of muscle and bone development. This growth phase is concerned with protein and calcium, phosphorus and vitamin D. The quality and quantity of mare's milk are not adequate to satisfy the nutritional requirements of the foal. For rapid development, foals should be fed with high quality grains and hay.

Adequate levels of calcium and phosphorus are very important, as well as the ratio of calcium to phosphorus.

An imbalance of calcium and phosphorus associated with bone disorders has been recognised for a long time.

Yearlings stabled in dark barns without adequate direct sunlight are susceptible to vitamin D deficiency. Vitamin D is important for calcium absorption and utilisation. Exposure of the skin to direct sunlight brings about natural production of vitamin D.

Some geographical areas are deficient in iodine, an element that is important for the function of the thyroid gland which plays a role in the horse's overall metabolism. Deficiency results in goitre (hypothyroidism). The symtoms are weak foals, contracted tendons, poor muscular development, delayed ossification of the bones and leg fractures. Iodised salt licks are a good form of therapy.

If in doubt, a well-balanced, quality-controlled vitamin-mineral supplement will ensure that the diet is not deficient in vitamins, minerals or trace elements.

DIET CHART

Type of Horse	8 am	12 Noon	5 pm
In hard work Racehorse Endurance horse	4½ lb (2 kg) oats 2 lb (1 kg) corn 1 lb (500 g) oaten chaff 4½ lb (2 kg) hay	4½ lb (2 kg) oats Sheaf of fresh-cut grass or ten-minute pick	4½ lb (2 kg) oats 2 lb (1 kg) corn 1 lb (500 g) oaten chaff 4½ lb (2 kg) hay ½ lb (250 g) soya bean meal 1 lb (500 g) bran 1½ oz (40 g) calcium 4 oz (120 g) vitamin-mineral supplement 2 oz (60 g) electrolyte salts
In hard work Event horse Hunter Polo pony	4½ lb (2 kg) oats 1 lb (500 g) chaff 4½ lb (2 kg) hay	4½ lb (2 kg) oats Sheaf of fresh-cut grass or ten-minute pick	4½ lb (2 kg) oats 1 lb (500 g) chaff 4½ lb (2 kg) hay ½ lb (250 g) soya bean meal 1 lb (500 g) bran 1½ oz (40 g) vitamin-mineral supplement 2 oz (60 g) electrolyte salts
In hard work Show jumper Dressage horse	4½ lb (2 kg) oats 1 lb (500 g) chaff 4½ lb (2 kg) hay	2 lb (1 kg) oats 4½ lb (2 kg) hay Sheaf of fresh-cut grass or ten minute pick	4½ lb (2 kg) oats 1 lb (500 g) chaff 4½ lb (2 kg) hay ½ lb (250 g) soya bean meal 1 lb (500 g) bran 1½ oz (40 g) vitamin-mineral supplement
Out of work Racehorse Endurance horse Event horse Dressage horse Show jumper	2 lb (1 kg) oats 6½ lb (3 kg) hay 1 lb (500 g) oaten chaff	2 lb (1 kg) oats 4½ lb (2 kg) hay Sheaf of fresh-cut grass or ten-minute pick	2 lb (1 kg) oats 6½ lb (3 kg) hay 1 lb (500 g) bran
In work Riding horse	2 lb (1 kg) oats 4½ lb (2 kg) hay	4½ (2 kg) hay Allow to pick during day	2 lb (1 kg) oats 4½ lb (2 kg) cubes 1 lb (500 g) chaff 1 lb (500 g) bran 1½ oz (40 g) calcium 4 oz (120 g) vitamin-mineral supplement 2 oz (60 g) electrolyte salts
In work Child's pony	2 lb (1 kg) oats/1 kg cubes 2 lb (1 kg) hay	2 lb (1 kg) hay Allow to pick during day	2 lb (1 kg) hay 3½ lb (1.5 kg) cubes 1 lb (500 g) chaff 1 lb (500 g) bran 1½ oz (40 g) calcium 4 oz (120 g) vitamin-mineral supplement

CLEANING THE STABLE

Your horse's health, feeling of well-being and appearance are partially dependent on a good, regular stable routine.

Bedding impregnated with urine and dung (faeces) is an excellent environment for infectious diseases and worms (parasites) to multiply and grow.

Mucking Out

This is a daily routine best done in the early morning when the horse is out of the stable exercising or grazing in a paddock. If the horse is in the stable it is essential that you tie it up. With a horse loose in the box, it is in danger of being stabbed with a pitchfork, and the person of being accidentally kicked or bitten. When tied up, the horse should be trained to stand on one side along the wall of the stable, giving plenty of room to work.

The horse should be taught that when gently touched on the rump and told, 'Move over' it moves over to the other wall, allowing you to clean the area where it was standing.

The most common form of bedding is wheat straw, although some people prefer wood shavings or sawdust, depending on availability and cost. Furthermore, some horses eat the wheat straw but not the shavings or sawdust.

With the use of a pitchfork (3 or 4-pronged for straw, multi-pronged or a rake for shavings) the clean bedding is heaped up into one corner or along one wall so that the floor is exposed. Any soiled or wet bedding is discarded into the wheelbarrow and taken to the manure pit; the clean bedding is used again.

The floor is vigorously brushed with a hard broom and the bedding left up, if the floor is damp, to allow it to dry. Otherwise, the bedding is spread evenly over the floor, with any excess stacked around the walls.

The feed bin should be emptied of any feed left over from the night before. Scrub out any food that may stick to the bin, especially in the corners. Empty the water tin and fill it with clean water.

During the day when you go into the stable, the first thing you should do is look at the bedding for any fresh droppings. If there are any, pick them up and put them in a heap in the corner or directly into a skip or wheelbarrow. Otherwise, when you and the horse move about in the stable, the dung will be trodden in, spreading it and soiling more of the bedding.

In the afternoon, any dung in the stable should be removed to the manure pit. Fluff up the bedding with a pitchford so that it is soft and springy for the horse to stand or to lie on during the night. Fill the water bucket with clean water.

Intensive Clean Up

When the stable is not in use or a new horse is coming into the stable, all the bedding should be removed and disposed of and the stable itself should be given a thorough cleaning.

The floor and walls should be swept thoroughly. Cobwebs and dust from the roof rafters or ceiling should be removed. Hose the walls and floor and, while still damp, disinfect them with chlorhexidine or a similar product. Open the doors and windows to dry out the stable. While waiting, give the feed bin and water container a thorough scrubbing with hot water and disinfect. Rinse and tip them upside down, and allow them to dry in the sun.

When the floor is dry, lightly sprinkle lime over it, then put in fresh bedding and replace the feed and water containers.

Below: A stable in which the straw bed is being mucked out directly into a wheelbarrow.

GROOMING

The Purpose of Grooming

First and foremost, grooming keeps a horse clean. It also massages, stimulates circulation of the blood and lymph, and tones up the muscles. Thus grooming is a means of preventing disease (especially of the skin), of maintaining condition, and of improving appearance. For the horse in the stable, deprived of a natural life, daily grooming is essential to its well-being.

The Grooming Routine

Brief grooming, or quartering, is a 15-or-10-minute grooming before a stable horse is worked. The feet are picked out and stable marks removed with a dandy brush or, if necessary, a damp sponge. The mane and tail are brushed with a body brush and put in place with a water brush. The eyes, muzzle and docks are sponged.

Grooming After Exercise

When the horse returns to the stable after exercise the feet, if muddy, should be washed and then picked out. Any dry sweat marks may be removed with a dandy or body brush, but not until the coat is completely dry. If the horse is hot or wet, he may need to be sponged down before being dried off.

Thorough Grooming (Strapping)

Thorough grooming is the hardest part of the grooming routine; the best effects will be achieved only by 'elbow grease'.

Start with the dandy brush, to remove mud and sweat marks. This can be done only if the dirt has dried. Although it is possible to sponge marks off, it can lead to chapping and sores unless the area is dried adequately afterwards.

The field-kept horse stimulates his circulation by moving around, and the grease in his coat acts as a natural waterproofing agent. Because a horse kept in the stable has lost both these safeguards, it is best to avoid wetting the coat. Brush off dirt wherever possible.

The real hard work starts with application of the body brush. The bristles must be driven through the horse's coat, beginning at the neck on the near side, to remove all the dirt and dried sweat. Stand far enough away from the horse to get your weight behind the brush. More force can be put into the task if the brush is held in the left hand on the nearside and in the right hand on the offside. With a strong, circular motion, work the brush from the neck along the body, occasionally cleaning the brush with the curry comb. The belly, the flank and the area between the forelegs should be covered. When grooming the hind legs, it is best to stand as close as possible at the side (not behind), so as to feel and see more easily if the horse is about to kick or move.

The head, especially around the eyes and ears, is a very sensitive area; use the brush gently but firmly. A dandy brush must never be used on the head. The mane and tail should be groomed into place and the hairs separated with the body brush. A dampened water brush can then be applied to keep the mane lying over. The tail can be bandaged to keep it in the correct shape.

The dock, eyes and nostrils should then be cleaned with the sponge, and the finishing touch is to wipe the horse over with a damp stable rubber.

Finally, all hooves are cleaned and dressed with a hoof oil. There is more about this in the section on hoof care (pages **70-71**).

The curry comb is also used to clean the body brush. The dirt collected in the curry comb is dislodged by banging it on a solid structure such as the wall of the stable.

The Grass-Kept Horse

Only limited grooming is needed for animals living outside. The grease and dandruff in the coat help to waterproof the hair and keep the animal warm; it is inadvisable, therefore, to clean a grass-kept horse too vigorously, in case his natural means of protection is removed.

Grooming should be limited to picking out this feet, removing mud with a dandy brush or rubber curry comb, brushing mane and tail with a body brush, laying the mane with a water brush, and finally sponging the muzzle, eyes and dock.

Hosing

In the warmer months of the year, the horse can be cleaned by this method every day if you prefer it. The horse is tied up in the hosing dock and hosed all over, taking care to keep water out of the ears. Once a week the horse is saturated with water, a horse shampoo (preferably one with antibacterial, antifungal and insecticidal properties), is worked into the wet coat for 2–3 minutes to produce a rich lather. Rinse the coat, mane and tail thoroughly with a horse, making sure that all the

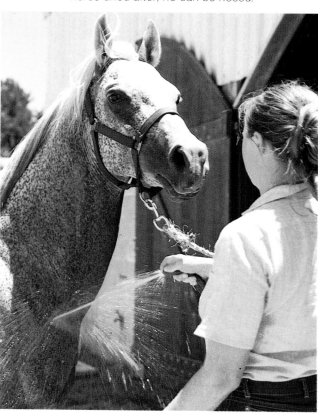

Below: As long as the weather is warm and the horse dried after, he can be hosed.

THE GROOMING KIT

Item	Purpose	Method of Use
Hoof pick	Removal of dirt and stones from feet.	Pick out each foot in turn. Remove stones, mud, bedding, etc, with point of pick. Work from the heel to the toe and take care not to force down on the side, or on the cleft of the frog, too hard.
Dandy brush (stiff)	Removal of caked mud and sweat.	Use with firm 'to and fro' motion on a horse or pony with a thick coat, on legs and under the saddle. It is too hard for the tender regions of a horse with a fine coat. A rubber curry comb is a gentler means of removing mud and sweat marks.
Body brush (soft, with close-set hairs)	Removal of dust and scurf from coat. Also used on mane and tail.	Use short, circular strokes in the direction of the lie of the hair. As much force as possible should be put behind the brush without thumping horse or pony. Mane and tail brushed by separating and brushing a few locks at a time. Head is cleaned after removal of head collar, which is then fastened around the neck.
Curry comb	Removal of dirt from body brush. If made of rubber, comb can be used on horse, to remove hair and dirt.	Curry comb in one hand; body brush in the other. Brush is drawn through it after 4 or 5 strokes. Curry comb is cleaned by being tapped on floor. Do not comb when brushing mane, tail and head; a free hand is needed at these times.
Wisp	Stimulates circulation and massages.	Bring down with a bang in the direction of the lie of the coat. Use on side of neck, quarters and thigh; but not on bony, tender areas.
Water brush (soft)	Dampening of mane and tail, and washing of feet.	Dampen and brush over mane to required position. Wash feet, if dirty.
Sponge	Cleans eyes, lips, nostrils and dock.	Dampen sponge, clean dirt from around eyes, then muzzle. Lift tail and clean dock region. Rinse sponge between cleaning of these areas.
Stable rubber	Gives fine polish after grooming.	Arrange into flat bundle, dampen and wipe coat in direction of lie of hair.
Sweat scraper	Removal of water and/or sweat from coat.	A horse that has been washed or has sweated profusely can have its coat scraped gently but firmly in direction of the lie of the hair.

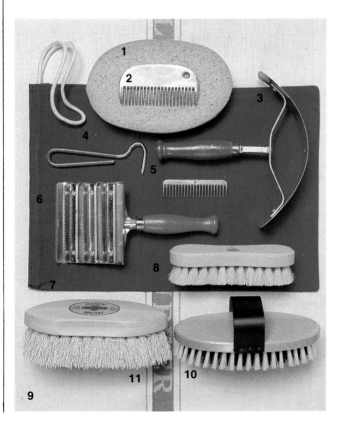

Above: A quick-reference chart, showing the purpose and method of use for each item in your grooming kit.

Left: The picture shows the various items of equipment used for grooming a horse displayed for easy identification.

1 A sponge for cleaning the eyes, lips, nostrils and dock.
2 A large mane comb for removing mud, and untangling and sectioning the hair prior to plaiting.
3 A sweat scraper for removing sweat or water after washing.
4 A hoof pick for removing mud, bedding and stones from the feet.
5 A small mane comb.
6 A grooming kit bag with a draw-string to keep all the grooming equipment together.
7 A curry comb for removing dirt from the body brush.
8 A water brush with soft hairs for dampening the tail and washing the feet.
9 A stable rubber which gives a final polish to the coat after grooming.
10 A body brush with soft, close-set hairs for removing dust and scurf from the coat and for brushing the mane and tail.
11 A dandy brush with stiff hairs to remove caked mud and sweat.

shampoo is removed. The sweat scraper is used to remove excess water from the coat. Start at the neck and follow the direction of the hair.

A cloth washer is used to wipe the horse around the ears, eyes, face and nostrils. A different washer is used to wipe the horse around the anus, tail and genitals.

The horse should be towelled dry, walked or allowed to stand in the sun before being returned to the stable.

A body brush is used to give an even finish to the coat. The mane and tail should be combed to prevent tangling and knotting.

CLIPPING

In the winter months, most horses develop a thick, long winter coat, though some horses that are stabled and heavily rugged do not. If the horse is in full work, it is advisable to clip it to prevent excess sweating, to assist in keeping it clean, and to allow it to dry off quickly after work. Clipping also enhances the horse's appearance.

Electrically operated clippers are the most efficient means of removing the coat. They are quick, easy to use after some practice and, when oiled during the cut and sharpened at intervals, give a satisfactory clip. Hand-operated clippers are good, but their chief disadvantage is that they are rather tiring to use.

Clipping takes time and patience. An assistant should be available to help if required.

The horse's coat should be as dry and well-groomed as possible. The most important factor is not to upset the animal. Before the clip is started, the assistant should hold the horse, talk to it, pat it, and be reassuring; turn on electric clippers, so that the horse becomes accustomed to the noise. If it becomes restless when the ticklish areas (for instance, the belly) are being clipped, the assistant can lift one of its legs to prevent the horse from moving around.

Start clipping in the areas that are least ticklish and sensitive, such as the shoulders — not the head, groin or belly.

Ensure that the clippers do not overheat, and that the blades are sharp and do not pull the hairs; clippers must be run flat along the skin and not dug into the horse, and they should be guided, not pushed, against the lie of the coat.

Do not clip into the sides of the mane or the root of the tail, or inside the ears. The backs of the tendon and fetlock are usually better dealt with by scissors and comb. The comb and scissors should be moved upward against the hair, in the same way as a professional hairdresser trims human hair.

Following the clipping, the horse should be stabled and rugged. It will need an extra blanket to compensate for the loss of this thick coat.

There are numerous types of clips but the full clip, where the long hair is removed from the head, neck, body and legs, is the smartest. A practical type of clip is the hunter clip, where the body is fully clipped and the long hair is left on the legs for protection, or the blanket clip which leaves most of the body hair (in the shape of a blanket) and all the leg hair. The head, neck, belly, part of the thighs and a thin strip up the back of the quarters are clipped. The briefest clip is the trace clip when hair is removed from the belly, chest, part of the thighs, up the back of the quarters and a strip up the underside of the neck.

Often a horse's mane is clipped right back to the neckline. This is known as hogging the mane. It is usually done because the mane looks untidy and spoils the horse's appearance. However, if the horse has a long,

Above: This horse has been clipped out with what is called a hunter clip.

scrawny neck, think twice before clipping its mane as this appearance may be accentuated rather than improved. Other points to consider are that, once hogged, the mane will have to be done again about every 13 weeks. It takes a long time to grow and may end up an unsightly mass of unruly bristles.

Pulling the Mane

Pulling the mane thins out the mane and gives it a uniform appearance and length. Furthermore, it enhances the appearance of the mane and makes plaiting easier.

Pull the mane only when the horse is warm after exercise or on a hot day. Pull the long hair first; if only a few at a time are pulled quickly, the horse will not feel any discomfort. Work from underneath and outwards.

Pulling the Tail

The mane comb can be used, as well as the fingers, for this purpose. The tail may be pulled to thin it out and to improve the appearance of the horse's hindquarters. Before pulling, groom the tail carefully. Begin pulling hairs from underneath, to either side of the tail and as high up the tailbone as possible. Pull only a few hairs at a time, and when the horse is warm, so that the tailbone area is not made sore. Extend the operation over a two-week period, so the chance of the tailbone becoming sore will be minimal. Pull equal numbers of hairs from each side underneath, so that when the task is completed the tail will be uniform, having a slim appearance near the tailbone and showing a gentle flare all the way down.

When a tail is too long, it is wise to cut it because it collects dirt and other foreign material that causes it to mat. Usually the tail is cut square across or to a point, at hock level or about 10 cm below. If you have an assistant to hold the tail in the natural position but just a little out from the horse's legs, the task of cutting the tail is much easier.

Above: A pony with a long pulled mane which has been clipped just on the underside of his neck.

Below: Grooming a horse with the body brush in the right hand and the metal curry comb in the left.

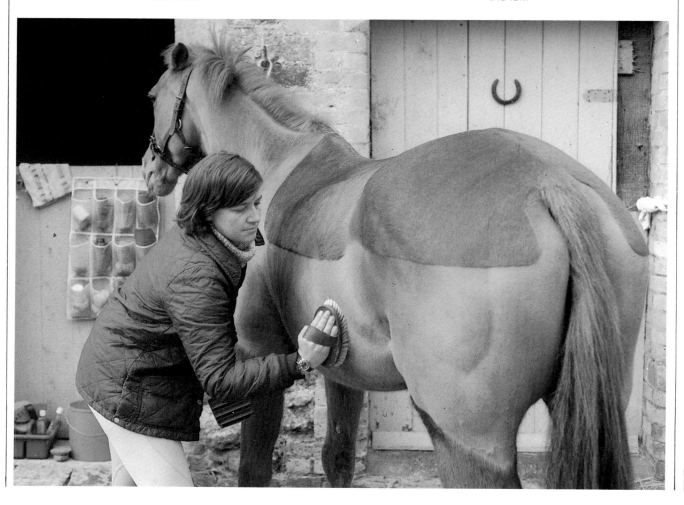

PLAITING

Plaiting or braiding the mane puts the finishing touches to the well-groomed horse. As well as stopping the mane from interfering with the rider, it helps to train a mane to lie on the right side of the horse's neck. Making the plaits smaller can also make the horse's neck look longer or, conversely, the neck can be made to appear shorter by making a few bulky plaits. Plaiting can show off a beautiful neck to full advantage.

Thick manes can be pulled to thin out and shorten the hair, thus making it easier to plait.

To plait a mane, first comb the hair thoroughly. Then dampen the hair and start behind the ears, with a section about 6 cm (2½ in) wide. Divide the section into 3 equal strands and plait them tightly, securing the ends with rubber bands or thread.

The long plait is then folded under and secured to the beginning of the plait at the root of the mane with thread or rubber band. When plaiting the mane, always plait the forelock. The plaits should be an equal distance apart, as well as being firm, neat and of the same size.

Plaiting the tail is more difficult than plaiting the

Right: This picture shows the first stages in plaiting the horse's mane. Plaiting helps to train an unruly mane to lie flat on the correct side. It also has the effect of showing off the neck to full advantage.

Below: Tails which are not pulled are usually plaited for special occasions. This horse has a neatly plaited tail.

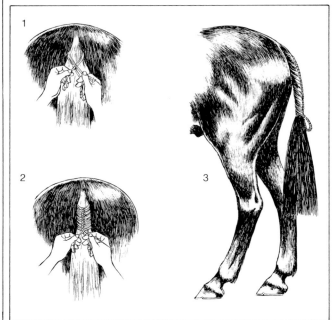

Above: There are many methods of plaiting the horse's mane. These step-by-step diagrams show how it can be done using a needle and thread. Sharp-pointed embroidery scissors are needed to remove the stitches at the end of the day.

Left: These diagrams show the various stages in the plaiting of a horse's tail. When the braid is two-thirds of the way down the tail bone, start leaving out the side hairs. Continue the braid, using only the centre hairs. The end of the braid should be stitched and bound securely with needle and thread, doubled under and attached to where the braiding of the side hairs ends.

mane. Follow the same procedure of brushing it out well and dampening it before plaiting. Start at the root of the tail, underneath, and as high as possible. Plait down the centre, including the hairs on either side. The plait continues almost the full length of the tailbone, ie, about one-third of the way down. The end of the plait is tucked up under the plaited hair above and secured by stitching with needle and thread. The lower two-thirds of the tail is allowed to flow.

HOOF CARE

Structure of the Hoof

When one looks at the horse's hoof planted on the ground, virtually all one can see is the hoof wall. This is made of cells that are keratinised and arranged in tubes that run parallel to each other from the coronary band to the ground border. These cells give the hoof wall its tough, horny properties.

Above the hoof wall is the coronary band, which is the growth source of the hoof wall; any damage to it is reflected in defective wall growth. The wall grows from the coronary band at the rate of about 1 cm per month.

Where the front section of the hoof wall meets the ground, it is known as the toe, the rear section is known as the heel and the section in between is known as the quarter. The hoof wall is thickest at the toe, thins at the quarter and becomes thicker at the heel. At the toe of the forefoot, the angle of the face of the wall with the sole of the foot should be 45 to 50 degrees, and in the hindfoot it should be 50 to 55 degrees.

If one looks at the sole of the foot, it can be seen that the thickness or depth of the hoof wall varies. The white line separates the hoof wall from the sole. The sole is made up of a similar cell structure to the wall. It should always be concave in shape and have no direct contact with the ground, as it is not a weight-bearing structure. Most of the frog is located in the rear half of the sole; it divides the sole into approximately equal halves, with its apex pointing to the centre of the toe. It could be described as a soft, V-shaped, elastic shock absorber that should always have contact with the ground when the foot is bearing weight.

When the horse is moving, no matter with what gait, the heel should meet the ground first, so that the heel and the frog absorb most of the weight. Then the foot rolls forward to the point where, as it leaves the ground, the toe bears the weight as the horse pushes off with that foot and breaks squarely over the centre of the toe.

Cleaning

Horses that are stabled or kept in yards should have their feet cleaned and checked each day.

With a hoof pick, rubbish such as straw, shavings, dirt and manure impacted in the concave sole of the foot should be cleaned out regularly. Always use the hoof pick in a heel-to-toe direction, ie, away from the user,

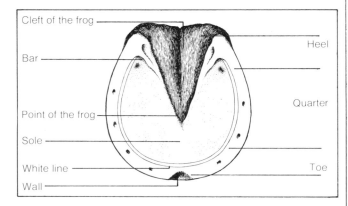

Above: A diagram showing the sectors of a horse's hoof.

Below: The underside of a horse's unshod hoof, showing clearly the white line, frog and sole.

otherwise a slip may result in personal injury, or, if the horse suddenly jumps, serious damage may be done to the sole or frog of the foot.

It is important to clean the sulcus or groove on both sides of the frog. Small stones, grit and other foreign bodies often become wedged in the groove and may cause problems. Thrush often develops in the grooves around the frog because of wet, muddy conditions and lack of cleaning. Damage may be done to the more sensitive areas in the sulcus by digging too deeply with the tip of the hoof pick.

After heavy debris is removed, a hoof knife can be used to remove any loose horn on the sole, as it can be the seat of infection. Loose or ragged pieces of frog should be trimmed off with the knife. As a safety precaution, the knife should always be used, going away from the user. Finally, after the hoof knife is used, give the sole and wall of the hoof a vigorous brushing to ensure that the cleaning is thorough and complete.

When the hoof is being cleaned, take the opportunity to inspect the sole for any bruising, corns, puncture wounds and thrush, and the wall for any cracks and brittleness. This is also an appropriate time to check the shoes to make sure the nails are secure, the clenches are not protruding and the shoe is sitting snugly on the wall of the hoof.

Dressing

In order to remain supple and resilient, the hoof should be dressed every day with a hoof oil (neatsfoot oil), otherwise it tends to become brittle and to crack. Brittleness of the hoof is caused by evaporation of moisture from the hoof wall. The natural, shiny coating on the hoof wall is called *stratum tectorium* and it helps to prevent evaporation. With excessive rasping of the hoof wall, this *stratum tectorium* is removed and consequently evaporation with drying out of the hoof is more evident.

In dressing the hoof with oil, use a 4 cm (1½ in) paint brush and first apply the oil liberally to the sole, making sure that it penetrates the grooves on either side of the frog and between the heels, then finish off by painting the wall right up to the coronary band.

Above: A horse's hoof being picked out correctly starting at the top and using downward strokes.

Above: A horse's hoof being painted with hoof oil. It should be applied regularly to cover the whole of the wall of the hoof.

Above: Hoof oil being applied to the underside of the horse's hoof to help keep it supple and resilient.

EXERCISE

All horses have a right to good general health. Quite a number of factors contribute to the horse's healthy state; a significant one is exercise.

The wild horse on the open range exercises naturally by means of grazing, mob movement and avoiding predators. Similarly, but in a more restricted sense, working horses, which were fairly common up to the early 1950s, exercised through daily work, grazing and being turned out in a large paddock. It is the horse stabled for long periods or confined to a pocket handkerchief yard that needs a daily exercise programme for its continuing good health.

Paddock exercise can be adequate if the paddock is at least the minimum size of 0.5 hectares (1 ¼ acres) per horse and if the horse is not lazy but walks to investigate things of interest in the paddock, grazes on the pasture, trots to the water trough and indulges in an occasional canter and buck. Such paddock exercise is adequate for the horse that is resting, turned out or retired, but it is by no means adequate for the weekend, pleasure riding horse or for the horse actively engaged in competition. In their cases, it is just supplementary exercise that gives them an opportunity to stretch their legs and to be mentally refreshed.

If the confined horse is used for pleasure riding one or two afternoons a week or is ridden at a weekend show or gymkhana now and then, it does need regular exercise on the other days of the week in order to be healthy and fit for what is required of it. In a simple form, the regular daily exercise would consist of a 10-minute walk at the beginning as a warm-up, followed by an hour of trotting and cantering and concluded by a 10-minute walk to cool down. The exercise may be given by means of lungeing or riding.

If the horse is being prepared for a strongly competitive event such as racing, polo, jumping or endurance riding, it needs exercise not only to keep it healthy, but additional exercise to develop its maximum fitness so that it can give its very best in the competitive event.

Fitness

Fitness means more than just being healthy. It is the level of a horse's development at a particular time in relation to a performance or an event in which it has to compete. Maximum fitness would allow the horse to compete or to perform to the best of its ability.

The fitness needed by a horse will vary according to the activity it has to carry out. For example, a jumper in a horse show requires a different kind of fitness than the stayer in a 3 km (2 mile) race.

Fitness is an individual characteristic. Some horses acquire it more quickly than others, some hold it for longer and others reach a state of maximum fitness greater than the maximum reached by other horses following the same programme. The fitness level achieved is not only a result of the training programme but is also a result of something in the inherent nature of the horse and the interaction of training and inherent nature.

Fitness has three components: physical, mental and skill. These three aspects interact, in that an improvement in one usually results in an improvement in the others. However, in a training programme, an active attempt should be made to improve each. According to the kind of event for which the horse is being prepared, and according to the inherent nature of the horse, the emphasis given to each aspect will vary. Certainly for a jumper, the skill of jumping would be emphasised. For a stayer or sprinter in racing, greater emphasis would be

Above: In this picture, horses are seen in 'follow the leader' formation exercising themselves in a paddock.

placed on racing, although the skill of leaving the starting barrier would be considered important.

The physical aspect of fitness is concerned with developing the horse's endurance, strength, power, agility, flexibility and balance. In terms of systems of the body, it is mainly concerned with the cardio-vascular, muscular, skeletal, articular, respiratory and nervous systems. Actual participation in competition contributes to their development but they should also be developed separately and together in a conditioning programme that is preparing the horse for competition.

The components of physical fitness and the various systems of the body are developed through many kinds of exercises or activities such as lungeing, racing over different distances at different speeds, cantering or galloping carrying different weight loads and using sand dunes and other forms of terrain for exercising.

Mental fitness might simply be described as the horse having the right temperament, the will to try or willingness to give of its best. Suffice to say that some have it, some do not. Mental fitness is not only important when competing but it is also vital when the horse is training if it is to get maximum benefit from its training programme.

The horse's inherent nature may be one of the major contributing causes to a low level of mental fitness, but other factors are also very significant. Such factors are personal relationships with humans and other animals, boring training routines of sheer hard work and no play, lack of variety in training and no satisfaction experienced from a word of praise, a gentle touch or a titbit.

Skill fitness is often referred to as the horse's level of neuromuscular co-ordination. More simply, it is the horse's ability to execute the skill that is required in a

Above: Young horses gallop around much more than most older horses when free, as shown by this yearling.

Below: Hacking out is a useful means of building up fitness. Horses enjoy this exercise especially with company.

particular event. The skill in itself may be broken down into a sequence of finer skills. For example, the skill of jumping may be broken down into the approach, the takeoff, the flight, the landing and the recovery. The levels of physical and mental fitness not only contribute to the level of the skill fitness at one performance but they also play a considerable role in helping a horse to keep performing at its highest level of skill.

The fitness programme is designed by the trainer. Usually there is a common core of fitness needs for all horses, as well as individual programmes for horses with individual needs. The veterinary surgeon plays an important role in any fitness programme.

It is best if the major part of the fitness programme is carried out in the environment in which the horse has to compete. For example, the racehorse should train for the most part on a racecourse, private or public; the endurance horse should work in the hills and on the flat, on terrain similar to the conditions it will meet in competition; the jumper should work over fences.

The fitness programme can be divided into three phases: pre-conditioning, conditioning and performance.

The pre-conditioning phase covers a period when a horse is first admitted to a stable or when it returns to the stable after a visit to the paddock. It is a time of settling in, of evaluating the horse's fitness needs, of formulating a tentative training programme and of checking aspects of the horse's physical condition to make sure that it is ready to undertake the next phase of the programme. While resting, whether in a paddock or stable, horses are apt to be infected with parasites. After resting, treatment for parasites should be carried out. A month later the manure should be examined for worm eggs. Worms and worming are discussed on pages **78-80**. Checks for worms should be carried out every 6 weeks.

The teeth should be checked for abnormal growth, irregular wear and injuries caused to surrounding tissue. Teeth problems such as sharp edges causing lacerations to the inside of the cheeks can cause the horse to go off its feed. Teeth should be examined regularly about every 6 weeks. For further information on teeth, see pages **81–83.**

There should be a check on the horse's vaccination programme. Young horses should have been vaccinated for tetanus and strangles; older horses should have a booster. During a rest, horses' feet usually change. Many lose their shape, alter in size and become asymmetrical. Corrective trimming and shoeing can remedy the problems and will prevent injuries occurring during training and competition, not only to the feet but also to the fetlocks and knees. See pages **84–87.**

The aim of any physical fitness programme is to produce maximum fitness in a horse by the time the event for which it is being prepared is to take place.

A good conditioning programme is noted for two main factors, notably variability, ie, a variety of exercises and activities, and progression, ie, the programme imposes on the horse a workload that becomes progressively more demanding. Progression can be incorporated into a programme by proceeding from simple to more difficult exercises, increasing the weight load carried in an exercise and shortening the time for a constant amount of work to be done. It can also be done by keeping the time constant and gradually increasing the workload within that time, lengthening the distance for the exercises and making the terrain increasingly difficult but not dangerous for the horse undertaking the exercise.

The trainer must assess the horse's performance from day to day and from week to week. This assessment should be as objective as possible; time and distance are useful measures. The assessment should be recorded so that the horse's development and the conditioning programme can both be evaluated at regular intervals.

A suitable area and time must be allocated for exercise, equipment must be set up and records kept. Exercises could be arranged in an easy, hard, easy, hard sequence or from very light, leading up to a heavy load, and tapering off to a reduced load, about 5 to 10 per cent below the normal load for the event; the tapering should take place a week before participation in the event for which the horse is being prepared. Finally, one needs to prepare for the unexpected, such as knowing what to do if the sand track is unavailable for training on a particular morning.

All horses, no matter what they are being trained for, should be exercised each day, and programmes should change, according to horses' response to them.

Immediately a horse has performed very well, let it know by comment, touch or offering a titbit. This encourages it to perform just as well next time.

The exercises prescribed in any conditioning programme are done early in the morning. In the afternoon, the horse should again be exercised comparatively lightly, by being given a 20-minute walk with a 10-minute pick where possible. The horse may be led or ridden. If neither of these is possible, a walking machine can be used.

Exercises for developing maximum fitness in the conditioning phase may be given in several forms, such as lungeing, riding and swimming.

Lungeing is a good form of exercise that can be given in a comparatively small space but it should only be used as a complement to other forms of exercise. It can be used to develop discipline, to teach the horse to respond to aids such as the whip and voice, and to exercise the horse at the walk, trot and canter.

The horse is worked in one direction, then in the opposite one, making it lead with alternate forelegs. In this approach, all the muscles of the limbs and body are used; muscle tone and flexibility are developed.

If a horse is fresh or above itself and tends to buck wildly when an attempt is made to ride it, lungeing for half an hour can settle it down to the point where the rider can manage it.

Walking is an excellent exercise to begin the conditioning phase of the programme. Walk the horse for about 4 km (2½ miles) each day for the first 2 weeks and intersperse the walking with trotting.

In any daily programme of exercise, always walk the horse for 10 minutes at the beginning to warm it up, and for 10 minutes at the conclusion to cool it down.

For the regular 20-minute walk that the horse has

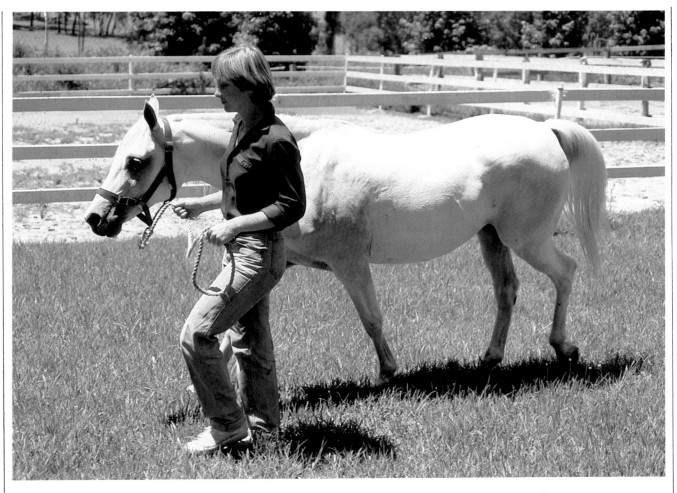

Above: The horse in this picture is being taken for a walk on a lead rein.

Below left: A horse walking machine used in yards with many horses.

Below: Lungeing is a very effective means of exercising the horse. It is used in the training of young horses, helping to make them obedient. It is also used to exercise older horses without riders.

each afternoon according to its fitness programme, it may be led, ridden or put on a walking machine. The walking machine may be labour and space-saving, and suitable in wet weather, but it is the least satisfactory because it lacks the personal relationship between handler and horse.

Following the 2 weeks of walking, the horse is trotted and cantered for varying distances for 3 weeks. A racing thoroughbred, for example, might trot 800 m (800 yd) and canter 1,500 m each day.

After 3 weeks, trotting and cantering are continued, but galloping is added. To quote the racing thoroughbred as an example, it is galloped at three-quarter pace every second day for 800 m, progressing to the point of galloping flat out for the last 200, 400 or 600 m. Similarly, the workload should be varied and progressively increased by changing such constants as weight, time, terrain and distance. The trainer of course is constantly checking the horse for signs of stress (too much workload) or of being underdone (too little workload).

Swimming is an excellent form of exercise, serving as a change of routine to alleviate boredom, to help maintain fitness that has been developed, to provide hydrotherapy for horses with leg injuries and as an alternative to the morning exercise when conditions are not suitable for it.

Above: When swimming the attendant can control the horse's head with a pole.

Below: A swimming pool designed for horses with a sloping ramp as an exit.

Above: The veterinary surgeon is taking a blood sample from a horse. An analysis of the blood will help in assessing what treatment, if any, is needed to bring the horse to his peak fitness.

Swimming has very little effect on the horse's cardio-vascular or respiratory system and furthermore is not a total substitute for canter work. Horses can swim in the ocean, in a river or in specially designed pools.

When first introducing the horse to the water, allow it to stand knee deep for a while. It should always wear a head collar, a rearing bit and a strong, long lead so that it is always under control.

The horse can be held from the back of a small rowing boat when swimming and taken into water deep enough for its feet to be just off the bottom. The first time, the boat moves in a small semi-circle, back to shallow water, where the horse can stand. Most horses are natural swimmers but a few panic. When you are happy with the horse's confidence in the water, gradually increase the actual swimming time or the distance at each visit.

Once the horse has reached its peak of maximum fitness it is ready for the performance phase. Because it will give of its best, it will perform repeatedly in rigorous competition for a reasonable time and without loss of form, and the risk that it will be injured in competition is minimal.

Taking part in a competitive event is in itself a form of exercise, but if the events in which the horse is competing are a week or more apart, additional light exercise is also necessary. The more variety that can be given to this light exercise the better, as it will help to maintain the horse's mental fitness, which is most important at this stage.

With the aid of blood tests and serum enzyme and electrolyte tests, the veterinary surgeon can suggest treatment without side effects to maintain the peak fitness of a horse for a longer period than would otherwise be the case. Again, it is through such tests that the veterinary surgeon can suggest that the horse be rested or turned out for a spell, before the trainer comes to such a decision based on the horse's lack of appetite and loss of weight.

It is not sufficient to say that you are improving a horse's fitness when you exercise it. It is possible that it may be getting too much exercise, and consequently it is under stress, a condition that leads to fatigue and breakdown; again, it may be getting the wrong kind of exercise and show no improvement in fitness at all.

The maximum fitness for each horse is never the same. Whilst each horse has common components of fitness that have to be developed, such as strength, agility, etc, each horse, too, has to develop these components to different levels in order to achieve maximum fitness for its particular task.

The trainer, as an observer, can evaluate a horse's fitness with some reliability and validity. He can interpret the horse's ability to cope with the training programme by the interpretation of certain signs. For example, he can evaluate the volume of feed, especially grain, that the horse is consuming. A horse will often go off its feed when it is getting too much work. He can also evaluate the condition of the horse's coat and general muscle development. Sometimes with too much work a horse's muscle tone deteriorates and it loses weight.

Another factor is the horse's approach to work. The horse should be keen and bright and appear to enjoy the exercise. Some horses, when given too much work, turn sour, resent the exercise and perform poorly. The performance of the horse can be measured against the clock or some other objective measuring device.

By doing a blood count, a serum enzyme and electrolyte evaluation, a heart and/or pulse rate and a respiratory rate check, the veterinary surgeon can be of great assistance in assessing a horse's fitness.

When a horse exercises or performs competitively, its body tissues have a greater demand for blood, which carries oxygen and other nutrients and sources of energy to the tissues, especially the muscles, and takes away the waste products, including the lactic acid, which are produced during exercise in a greater quantity than normal. If the blood content is low, this means that the oxygen fails to reach the muscle tissue in the volume that it should and the waste products are not taken away from the muscles as quickly as they should be. Consequently, the horse with a low blood count has less chance of performing well.

Serum enzyme levels have a direct bearing on muscle function. After strenuous exercise, the muscles release certain enzymes into the blood. The type and amount of these enzymes are good indicators of the degree of muscle damage or breakdown. If the level of enzymes in the blood is high, it indicates that the horse is not coping with the exercise, its muscles are being damaged and the type and/or quantity of exercise should be changed. On the other hand, a low level could indicate that the horse can tolerate more exercise, other factors being equal.

Serum electrolyte levels if high, low, or not in the correct proportion to each other, can have an adverse effect on the horse's response to its training programme and on its performance. Electrolytes are administered orally, by stomach tube, or intravenously when low, and of course are withheld when the levels are high. Drugs can be administered to help horses retain fluid and electrolytes when the levels in the blood serum are low, and other kinds of drugs when administered help horses to excrete fluids and electrolytes when the levels detected are high.

Horses are notably free sweaters and the loss of fluid with electrolytes is accentuated when they are worked hard and often. Loss of fluid and electrolytes sets up dehydration, which in turn causes a horse's performance to go off.

The extent of the rise of pulse, heart rate and respiratory rate during exercise and the rate of return to normal after exercise are important. In simple terms, the fitter the horse, the smaller the rise and the quicker the return to normal.

PERIODIC CARE

WORMS AND WORMING

All horses have worms although the young and the old are most susceptible. Many stables, yards, paddocks and the general environment of the horse are contaminated with worms and worm eggs and will continue to be so while the horses pass manure. The worms and immature migrating larvae can cause damage ranging from temporary anaemia to death from a ruptured bowel.

Signs of Worms

These are fairly obvious and include weight loss, a dull harsh coat, poor appetite, tail rubbing, reduced performance and poor stamina, diarrhoea, colic and other abdominal pains, coughing in young foals and bot fly eggs on the coat.

Many healthy-looking horses have worms, but no mature worms will appear in the manure if the worm burden is not heavy. One cannot say with absolute

Below: A foal showing the typical signs of worms: a dull, harsh coat, evidence of weight loss and a distended abdomen.

certainty that a horse has worms on signs or symtoms alone; numerous other diseases such as poor nutrition and irregular teeth can give rise to similar symptoms.

Treatment

If owners suspect worms, they have three courses of action open to them. They may seek their veterinary surgeon's advice and a diagnosis based on the signs and symptoms evident in the horse. Secondly, they may have the horse's faeces (manure) tested in the veterinary surgeon's laboratory to find out if the horse's condition is due to worms, if worms are present, what type they are and how heavily infected the horse is. Only one ball of fresh manure is required for the microscopic examination in the laboratory. The third possibility is for the owner to drench the horse with a preparation and see if it improves; this is less acceptable because it may not be conclusive and takes much longer and, during this time, the condition of the horse may deteriorate.

Worm Eggs

The female worm lays eggs in the intestines of the horse and they are passed into the environment in the horse's

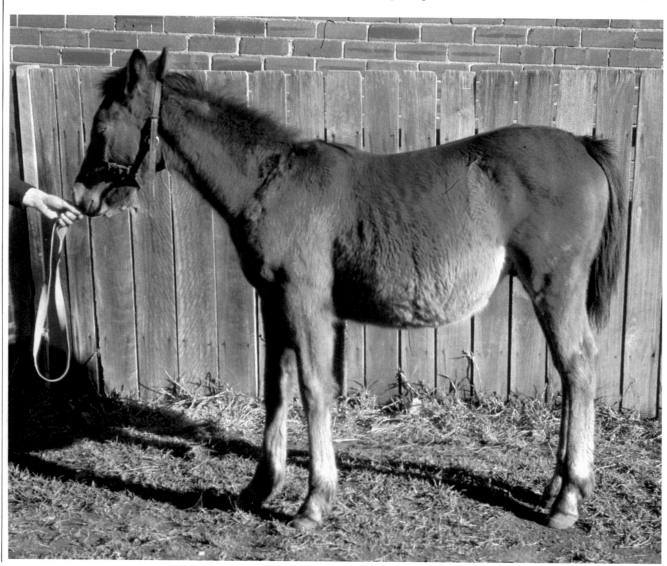

manure. All worms have a distinct type of egg, so the worm present in the intestine can be identified by the egg found in the manure. The number of eggs in the manure indicates the number of worms in the intestine.

Methods of Worming

A stomach tube is an effective tool, but it should only be used by your veterinary surgeon or by trained personnel. It is the most efficient and direct method of drenching a horse.

Pellets and granules are very convenient and easy to use; they can simply be added to the feed. However, there is no guarantee that every horse will eat them.

Worm pastes are convenient but not easy to administer, especially if the horse is head shy.

The fact that the horse has been given a worming preparation by any one of these methods does not automatically mean that it is worm-free. Firstly, some worms have developed a resistance to certain worming preparations; secondly, the worming preparations are only effective against the adult worms in the intestine. The migrating immature larvae in other areas of the body at the time of worming are *not* affected.

To guard against these two problems, have a manure sample tested by a veterinary surgeon 6 weeks after the horse has been wormed. However, as pinworm eggs are not usually found in the manure, their absence does not guarantee that the horse is not suffering from pinworm.

Worming Programme

Pregnant mares should be wormed every 6 weeks with a final worming 4 weeks before foaling. Do not use organo phosphate compounds in the last 3 months of pregnancy.

Worm the mare and foal when the foal is 6 weeks old and continue every 6 weeks until it has been weaned. The foal can be infected with intestinal threadworm via the milk of the mare during the first few weeks after foaling.

Worm all non-pregnant mares, weanlings, yearlings, teasers and stallions every 12 weeks.

Laboratory and microscopic examinations should be done on manure samples twice a year.

It is a good idea to worm all horses on the stud at the same time; all horses in the same paddock should also be wormed together. Outside mares coming onto a stud should be wormed on arrival and kept in a separate paddock for 3 days.

Early spring and late autumn is the ideal time to worm for bots.

Ponies and horses in paddocks should be wormed 4 times a year and a manure test should be done twice a year.

Racehorses, hunters and event horses should be wormed as soon as they come into the stable from the paddocks. If worms are evident in the droppings after treatment, repeat the treatment in 4 weeks; otherwise worm the horse every 6 weeks while in work and just prior to going out to grass. A manure test should be done to see if the worms are developing a resistance to the treatment.

Management for Prevention

Prevention is much better than treatment because, even though you can get rid of the worms, you may not always be able to repair the damage they have done.

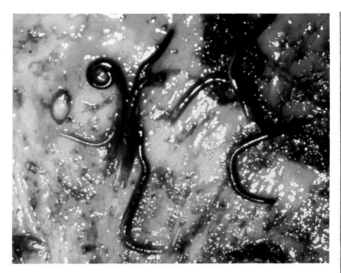

Above: Strongyle which are more commonly known as red worm and are the most frequent causes of worm problems.

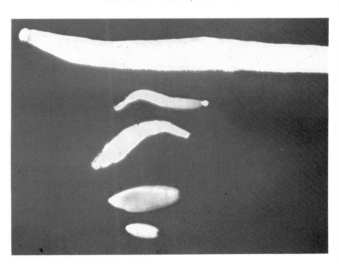

Above: Tapeworm which are much longer than red worm, and cause problems less frequently.

Above: Pinworm which are usually the longest of the types of worm found in horses.

COMMON TYPES OF WORM

Worm	Length	Colour	Shape
Large strongyle (red worm)	up to 5 cm (2 in)	Reddish	Thin with tapered ends
Small strongyle (red worm)	up to 2.5 cm (1 in)	Reddish	Thin with tapered ends
Roundworm (milkworm)	up to 40 cm (12¼ in)	White	Spaghetti-like
Bots	1 cm (¼ in)	Brown to red	Grub-like
Pinworm	up to 10 cm (8 in)	White	Whip-like
Tapeworm	4 to 8 cm (1½–3 in)	Off-white	Flat

In paddocks and yards, do not feed horses off the ground. Provide them with feed bins, water troughs and hay racks.

Give horses water troughs rather than letting them drink from dams as the worm eggs and larvae thrive in the moist, muddy areas around the dam edges. Fence off swampy areas or provide good drainage to dry them out. Don't let water troughs overflow as damp areas around water troughs are danger zones. Harrow the paddocks, especially areas where horses tend to gather around feed and water troughs.

Pick up and dispose of the manure in yards. Slash areas where long grass and weeds tend to grow so that the manure is exposed to the sun that kills the worm eggs. Rest the paddocks for 3 months from horses and rotate them with cattle. Reduce the number of horses per paddock. Overcrowding results in heavy contamination with worm eggs. The horses pick up more worm eggs and larvae because they graze closer to the ground.

In the stable, pick up manure and soiled bedding during the day and change the bedding regularly. Put hay in nets, not on the floor, clean feed bins every day and use automatic watering devices if possible, otherwise clean out the water bucket every day.

Concrete floors are best because they are easier to clean, they can be hosed out effectively and can be thoroughly disinfected.

Control fly activity around the stables with baits and flyscreen doors.

The horse should be thoroughly and regularly groomed to remove unseen eggs from the coat. Wash the horse regularly, especially around the base of the tail, where pinworms deposit their eggs. Remove bot fly eggs from the coat by clipping, the use of a bot knife or by washing.

Above: A horse is less likely to pick up worms if he is fed off the ground in the yard or paddock. This horse is being fed from a bin which hooks onto the fence.

VACCINATION

Vaccination with tetanus toxoid is extremely important for all horses. Active immunity takes 14 days to develop; the horse must therefore be vaccinated before exposure to infection. The initial course usually consists of 2 doses given about 4 weeks apart.

The injection of tetanus toxoid often produces a swelling in the muscle at the site of the injection which disappears in about 4 days. It is not true that if you vaccinate your horse, its performance will be adversely affected for the rest of its life.

Foals should be vaccinated at 3 to 4 months old. Mares should be vaccinated in the last month of pregnancy so that temporary immunity will be passed onto the foal. Outside mares on arrival at a stud should have a booster vaccination. All horses should have a yearly booster because of the frequency of cuts, nail pricks, castration

Above: Bot fly eggs are often found on the legs of horses that are turned out to grass during the summer as in this case.

wounds, foaling lacerations and general trauma.

If a horse has suffered a wound in which tetanus infection is likely, a veterinary surgeon can administer an antitoxin that will give immediate protection and afford temporary immunity for about 2 weeks.

Not only should all horses be vaccinated but all people, especially those dealing with horses, should consult their doctor regarding tetanus vaccination. *See* Strangles page **125** *and* Tetanus page **132**.

In the UK, it is compulsory for race-horses, show horses and horses involved in other fields of competition to be vaccinated with Equine Influenza. Two doses are given 6 weeks apart, then boosters not more than 1 year apart.

TEETH CARE

The horse uses the incisor (front) teeth to pick, tear or cut grasses and pastures when grazing. The molar (back) teeth are used for grinding or masticating the food in preparation for digestion.

Man uses the horse's incisors to tell its age accurately up to 8 years, after which the degree of accuracy decreases.

The knowledge of how to tell a horse's age is most useful when buying a horse with a doubtful or unknown origin or history.

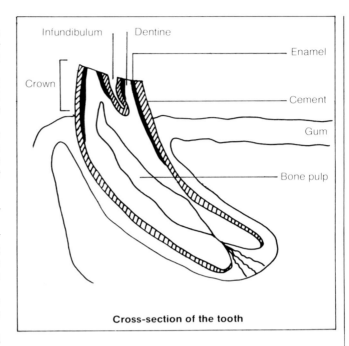

Cross-section of the tooth

Above: The diagram shows the various parts of a horse's tooth seen in cross section.

TEMPORARY, DECIDUOUS OR MILK TEETH

Teeth	Time of Eruption
1st incisor (central)	Birth or 1st week
2nd incisor (lateral)	4 to 6 weeks
3rd incisor (corner)	6 to 9 months
1st premolar 2nd premolar 3rd premolar	Birth or 1st 2 weeks

PERMANENT TEETH

Teeth	Time of Eruption
1st incisor (central)	2½ years
2nd incisor (lateral)	3½ years
3rd incisor (corner)	4½ years
Tusk (Canine)	4 to 5 years (usually male)
1st premolar	5 to 6 months
2nd premolar	2½ years
3rd premolar	3 years
4th premolar	4 years
1st molar	1 year
2nd molar	2 years
3rd molar	4 years

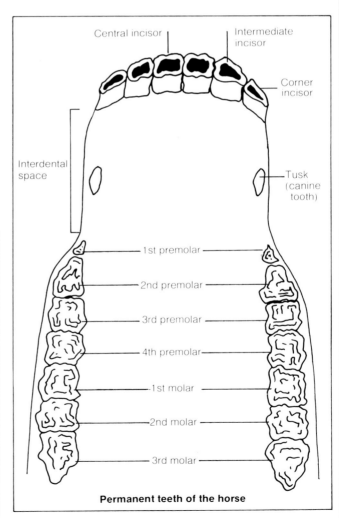

Permanent teeth of the horse

Above: The diagram shows the position of the eruptions of the various permanent teeth.

Above: This picture shows the variety of instruments needed to take care of horse's teeth. Special skills are required to perform this task; therefore, it should not be attempted by untrained personnel, but done by a veterinary surgeon or special horse dentist.

Time of Eruption of Teeth

The horse has two sets of teeth in a lifetime, namely the temporary or deciduous set (milk teeth) and the permanent set. The teeth erupt through the gum in pairs; when one incisor appears on one side of the jaw, the corresponding incisor appears on the other side. The times of eruption for the various teeth are set out in the **accompanying table.**

Abnormalities of Tooth Eruption
Supernumerary Teeth

Sometimes the permanent incisors erupt behind the temporary incisors. The temporary teeth remain firmly embedded in the gum, leaving the horse with one or two extra teeth or sometimes with a complete second row. Food collects between the teeth, causing inflammation and infection. The veterinary surgeon will distinguish the temporary teeth from the permanent ones and extract the temporary teeth by using forceps.

Dental Caps

The head or crown of the permanent molar becomes locked into the roots of the temporary molar as the permanent molar erupts through the gum. The remains of the temporary molar attached to the head of the permanent molar is known as a dental cap.

Symptoms can be identical to those produced by sharp edges of the molars.

Treatment is either by removing the caps with tooth forceps or by levering off the cap by inserting the tip of a screwdriver between the cap and the permanent tooth.

Undershot Jaw

This is commonly known as parrot mouth. It is fairly common and may be inherited. The upper and lower incisors do not meet because the lower jaw is too short.

If the lower incisors tend to push up into the hard palate, they should be filed and checked every 3 months.

Wolf Teeth (First Premolar)

When a horse is being ridden or driven, pressure on the bit with the rein sometimes pulls its gums onto the sharp edge of the wolf teeth, causing pain.

It is advisable in these cases to remove the wolf teeth, as they may cause the horse to pull, hang to one side or toss its head.

Teeth Care

This mainly involves the molars which are associated with the grinding of food. The action of chewing is an up-and-down movement as well as a side-to-side one.

When this type of action, coupled with the fact that the upper jaw is wider than the lower jaw, the outside edges of the upper molars are ground to a razor-sharp edge, as are the inside edges of the lower molars.

The sharp edges on the upper molars lacerate the cheeks and on the lower molars lacerate the tongue causing glossitis ie, inflammation of the tongue.

You can tell that this is happening if you observe the following symptoms: refusal of food, slow eating, excessive salivation and blood coming from the mouth. Quidding the food, ie, dropping food that has been partially chewed from the mouth, is another sign, as is lack of response to the bit, throwing the head, pulling, or hanging to one side. Other symptoms are loss of condition and swelling of the cheeks, which are painful to pressure.

Ask the veterinary surgeon to do a detailed mouth examination. This can be done without a gag, although a gag removes the risk of being bitten and allows one plenty of time to feel and to look at the teeth as well as to check the tongue and the inside of the cheeks.

The sharp edges of the teeth are removed by rasping or floating the teeth with a long-handled rasp. Teeth should be inspected every 4 months.

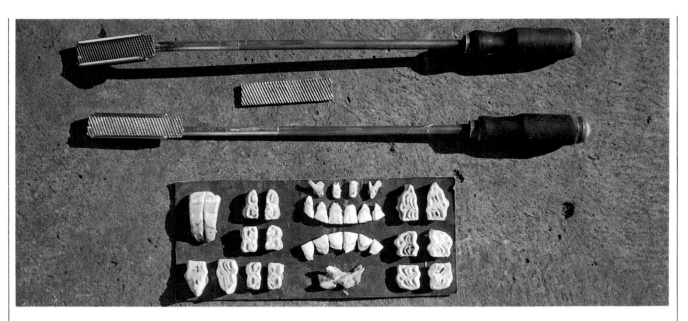

Above: This picture shows a set of horse's teeth laid out. The longer teeth in the centre are the incisors, and the flatter ones are the various types of molars. The instruments laid out above are rasps and a float used for filing the teeth.

Below: The horse is wearing a gag. This serves to keep the horse's mouth open to enable the teeth to be rasped. A long-handled rasp is being used by the expert to remove the sharp edges of the horse's lower molars.

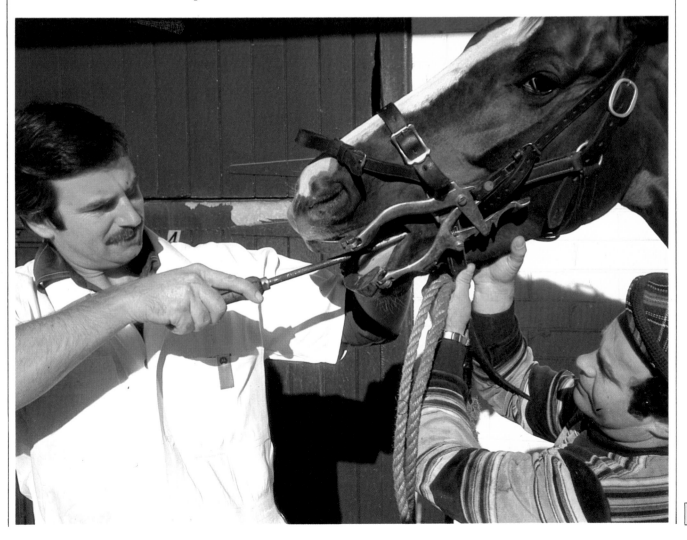

SHOEING

Shoeing is not a simple task. It is a skill that can be acquired only through a detailed knowledge of the anatomy of the hoof, combined with the practical experience of preparing, fitting and nailing the shoe to the hoof. In the UK, it is unlawful for anyone to shoe a horse unless he is listed in the Register of Farriers, to ensure that horses do not suffer through shoeing by unskilled persons. What is unlawful in respect of shoeing varies from nation to nation, and even state to state. It is advisable, therefore, to check *locally* on lawful practices.

Horses are shod to protect feet from wearing away, to prevent feet from cracking, to increase the grip, to correct conformation faults, to correct problems such as cross firing and brushing and to improve the horse's gait. The choice of a master farrier or blacksmith is of great importance to ensure proper hoof care and shoeing.

The following information is given to help the owner understand the range of activities and complexities involved in shoeing a horse.

The Loose Shoe

A loose shoe can be nailed back on. The basic gear needed for doing so consists of a leather apron to protect the farrier's legs from being cut by protruding nails, and a driving hammer for driving the nails and finishing the clenches. The claw of the hammer is used for twisting off the ends of the nails. A pair of pincers may be used for cutting the hoof wall and, with jaws closed, can be used as a clench block to form the clenches.

Prior to tightening a loose shoe, it must be in the correct position. If the clench has lifted and the nail is not holding the shoe tightly onto the hoof wall, the closed jaws of the pincers are placed against the partially clenched end of the nail and the head of the nail struck with the hammer. The clenched end will then need to be bent over further into the wall of the hoof, so that the clench does not protrude. This is partly a safety precaution, partly a technique for making the shoe more secure.

If a nail has broken and supposedly fallen out, care must be taken that the old nail or part of the nail is not still in the hole. The new nail is put in the old hole with the flat side of the nail on the outside. As the nail with the bevel on the inside is driven by the hammer, it is directed to the outside and emerges from the wall. When the nail is secure and the head is still not in the crease of the shoe, the end is bent over and twisted off with the claw of the hammer. The clench is formed by holding the closed jaws of the pincers against the broken end of the nail and striking the nail head with the hammer, seating the head in the crease. To cap it off, a small groove is filed under the clench and the clench seated into the groove with the hammer.

Removing a Shoe

The shoe must not be pulled off because the clenches will make it impossible, or it will break away parts of the hoof wall. This may cause lameness in the horse or make it very difficult to put on another shoe due to the lack of a solid wall in which to drive a nail.

The correct approach is to cut the clenches on the hoof wall with a clench cutter (buffer) or to rasp them off. If the rasping is done roughly, there is a danger that the horse's natural protective coating on the hoof wall will be damaged.

The hoof is then picked up and placed between the thighs just above the knees. In this position it can be firmly gripped by the legs and more leverage can be

Above: The farrier is seen here taking off a shoe by levering it off with pincers.

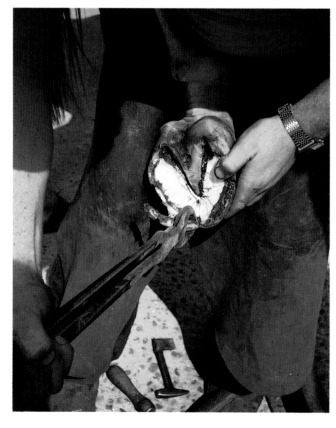

Above: After the shoe has been removed the hoof wall is trimmed with hoof nippers.

placed on the shoe without rotating the hoof. In addition, both hands are free to lever off the shoe with the pincers. Starting at one heel of the shoe, the jaws of the pincer are placed between shoe and hoof and the pincer rocked from side to side until the heel is loose. Then the other heel is given the same treatment.

The same procedure is then repeated near each nail until the shoe has been freed from the hoof. The nail holes are then checked to see that no nail remnants remain in them.

The farrier should remove horses' shoes about every 6 weeks from the feet and reset new shoes. Horses that are working unshod should have their feet trimmed every 4 to 6 weeks.

To Shoe the Normal Foot

The debris in the sole, frog and grooves is cleaned out with a hoof pick. Dead and ragged pieces of the frog are cut away with a hoof knife. Any loose or flaking sole is removed with the hoof knife. The wall is trimmed with the hoof nippers, starting at the heels and working towards the toe. A rasp is used to smooth and level the ground surface of the wall and to establish the correct angle between the face of the wall and the sole at the toe.

Hot shoeing gives a better guide to the level of the ground surface of the wall and the fit. Cold shoes must be hammered into shape, and it must be that the shoe is shaped to fit the foot, not vice versa.

The point of the frog is used as a guide to centre the shoe. The point of the nail is placed at the outside edge of the white line. The flat edge of the nail is on the outside and the bevel on the inside so the nail will emerge about 2 cm ($\frac{3}{4}$ in) above the ground surface. The protruding point of the nail is bent over with the claw of the hammer and wrung off by twisting the hammer. This partly forms the clench and prevents injury to the farrier if the horse pulls the leg away quickly.

If the nail head is too small and fits down into the crease of the shoe, it will come loose in a few days. A nail is needed with a head that protrudes from the crease by about 2 mm ($\frac{1}{16}$ in). Three nails on each side are adequate unless the horse is used for such sports as polo, in which case 4 nails on each side are necessary.

When all the nails are in, the nail heads are seated in the crease and the clenches formed. To form the clench, the closed jaws of the pincers are held against the broken end of the nail and the head is struck with the hammer, driving it into the crease. In forming the clench, the shoe is automatically tightened onto the wall.

A groove is filed below the clench and the clench then seated in the groove with the hammer. The foot is lightly rasped below the clenches.

CORRECTIVE TRIMMING

Trimming a hoof to correct a fault of conformation or gait should be done carefully. The problem should not be corrected by severely trimming the foot at the first attempt, but done little by little. The only tools necessary are a rasp and a pair of hoof nippers.

Knock knees in young foals can be successfully treated in most cases by confining them to the stable and trimming the hoof. The outside edge of the hoof should be kept trimmed by rasping it repeatedly until the leg is straightened.

Bow legs in the foal may be corrected by trimming the inside edge of the hoof with a rasp at weekly intervals.

Above: A farrier, or blacksmith as he can also be called, at work rasping the foot of a horse. This blacksmith is wearing a special pair of over trousers to give him added protection. Holding the hoof between the legs means that trousers are subjected to a great deal of wear. The blacksmith has the shoe and pincers on the floor ready for use.

In many cases of contracted heels, the heels are too high and do not allow the frog to touch the ground. The heels should be trimmed with hoof nippers and rasp until the frog just comes in contact with the ground when the horse is bearing weight on that foot. With constant trimming, the frog pressure will promote heel expansion.

Long toes and low heels are undesirable features because this combination puts a lot of stress up the back of the leg, involving the sesamoid bones, the flexor tendons and the suspensory ligament. The toe should be shortened with the hoof nippers and then rasped. Nothing should be taken off the heels, so that in time the heels will grow and become raised.

If the horse is going to remain unshod, the hoof wall is cut back when trimming the wall with the hoof nippers so that it extends beyond the sole by about $\frac{1}{2}$ cm ($\frac{3}{16}$ in). If the horse is going to be shod, trim the wall back level with the sole at the toe and as low as necessary at the quarters and heels to establish the proper foot angle and contact of frog with ground. A smooth finish is secured by rasping but not by taking too much off the hoof wall because, in doing so, too much of the wall's protective coating (*stratum tectorium*), may also be removed.

Above: This is a bar shoe. It is used to help contracted heels when the frog won't touch the ground, as it promotes the expansion of the hoof and brings that important pressure to bear on the frog.

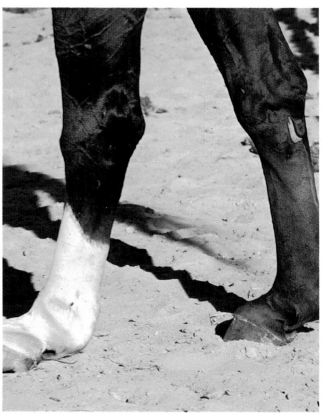

Above: This horse has very weak pasterns and is 'Getting down Behind' on his fetlocks. With this condition, he is likely to graze the skin on the back of his fetlocks when he is cantering or galloping.

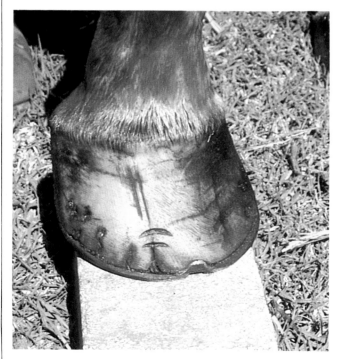

Above: This horse has cracks on his hoof and where one has split, the wall clips have been inserted to prevent it getting any higher and wider.

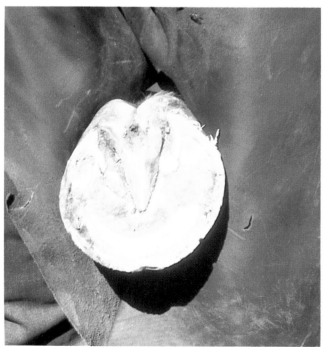

Above: This horse has a corn in his heel. A small amount of the sole has been pared away to drain the collection of blood and promote healing.

CORRECTIVE SHOEING

Before any attempt is made to correct defects in a horse's action by corrective shoeing, the horse should be carefully examined in regard to conformation, stance, relationship of pastern to hoof, type of feet, position of frog in relation to the ground, abnormal wear and action. The following are some common faults and their treatment.

Contracted Heels

If the frog cannot be made to touch the ground by trimming the heels, a bar shoe can be used to bring pressure to bear on the frog.

Cross Firing

Cross firing occurs when the toe or inside wall of the hindfoot strikes the inside quarter of the opposite forefoot. It is a very common fault in pacers. The toes of the forefeet should be rasped square and a square-toed shoe fitted. This causes the forefeet to break in a straight line and stops interference. The hindfeet should be shod with a three-quarter shoe.

Over Reaching

The hindfoot steps on the heel of the forefoot on the same side. Often the toe of the hindfoot steps on the heel of the shoe on the forefoot, pulling it off. Conformation faults, improper shoeing and poor co-ordination associated with fatigue are some of the causes.

The front leg can be made to move faster than the hindleg by shortening the toe of the hoof and by rolling the toe of the shoe and raising the heel. The crease of the shoe is removed to reduce friction. The action of the hind feet can be slowed down by lengthening the toe and lowering the heel of the hoof.

Getting Down Behind

The alternative phrase often used is 'getting down on the bumpers'. Both phrases describe those horses that, when cantering or galloping, graze the skin covering the back of the fetlock of the hindlegs. Horses with long, sloping pasterns are prone to this problem.

The toe of the foot is cut back as short as possible, leaving the heel intact. The horse can be shod with a variety of shoes, depending on the severity of the problem. A shoe with an extended heel, with a raised heel or a bar shoe should suffice.

Brushing

This is the term used when the inside edge of the foot in motion touches the inside of the fetlock of the opposite leg. It may occur with the forelegs or the hindlegs. It can be caused by poor conformation, such as turning out or turning in from the fetlock, or by poor co-ordination induced by fatigue. The recognised treatment is for the toe of the offending foot to be trimmed square and the hoof shod with a square-toed shoe, with the inside branch of the shoe rolled and set slightly in from the border of the inside (medial) wall.

Horses that continue to give trouble after corrective shoeing and trimming often respond to the treatment of allowing the feet to grow then being worked on a hard, smooth, level surface to allow the feet to be worn naturally. This helps the feet to find their own natural level; when this is achieved, the horse may be shod.

CRACKS, CORNS AND BRUISING
Cracks

Cracks in the hoof wall can vary markedly from short and shallow to long and deep. The crack can start at the ground surface of the hoof wall or at the coronary band.

Treatment can vary according to the position, length and depth of the crack. Basically, if the crack starts at the ground surface, treatment is designed to prevent its expansion by putting shoe clips on either side, as well as by rasping the weight-bearing edge of the hoof wall so that no pressure is borne by the wall in the area of the crack.

A groove should be burnt or filed at right angles to the upper end of the crack to stop its progress.

If the depth of the crack involves the sensitive tissues, the horse will probably be lame. If so, it needs to be treated by a veterinary surgeon, who will administer antibiotics and a tetanus injection and apply tincture of iodine locally to the crack.

Prevention includes trimming and reshoeing every 6 weeks, minimal rasping of the hoof wall, daily hoof dressing and the use of boots to prevent damage to the coronary band.

Corns

A corn is a collection of blood under the sole in the region of the heel.

Corns are commonly caused by the heel of the shoe turning inwards; this puts pressure on the sole.

Normal treatment is to correct the shoe if necessary and to drain the blood by carefully paring off the minimum amount of sole surface. A veterinary surgeon should be called to treat the horse, both with a tetanus injection and antibiotics, if infection is present or the opened corn is at risk of becoming infected. Apply tincture of iodine to the opening and cover with an adhesive bandage to prevent further contamination.

Bruising

Bruising of the sole is caused by sharp stones or walking on hard, rough, uneven ground that damages the toe or quarter areas of the sole.

If the bruising is severe, the horse will show signs of lameness and react to pressure on the sole.

If the sole is cleaned with a hoof knife, the bruising will be evident by the presence of blood under the surface.

In the case of mild bruising, rest and time will allow the blood to disperse; in severe bruising, the sole over the bruised area can be cut away with a clean hoof knife to provide drainage. Apply tincture of iodine to the opening, as well as a drawing agent (magnesium sulphate), and cover the bruised area with a bandage to prevent contamination. A veterinary surgeon should be called to administer a tetanus injection. If the bruise is infected or there is danger of infection, antibiotics should also be administered.

STABLING

Stable Structure

The ideal position for a stable is an elevated site, protected from the prevailing winds, facing the morning and early afternoon sun and adjacent to an area suitable for a grazing paddock. The site should be well drained.

A stable 3.6 m (11 ft) long by 3.6 m (11 ft) wide by 3 m (9 ft) high will accommodate most types of horse. The stable should be dry, well-drained and well-ventilated, but free from draughts.

The stable floor should be hard, non-slip, non-porous and durable. It should not absorb urine or water, nor should it be subject to rising damp from the ground. The ideal flooring surface is concrete or non-porous brick. As well as being non-absorbent, these surfaces lend themselves to cleaning and disinfecting. There should be a slope on the floor, leading to a drain outside the stable so that waste water flows away easily.

The stable walls should be solidly constructed to withstand the strain of being leaned on, pushed against, run into, kicked and chewed. Brick is best, although hard wood serves the purpose adequately. Some excellent prefabricated stalls are assembled on a prepared, concrete slab.

The roof should be of sufficient height to allow good ventilation and to give the horse plenty of head room. Insulation of the roof is necessary to keep the heat out in summer and the warmth in during the winter months.

The doorway should be a minimum of 1.3 m (4 ft) wide and 2.4 m (7 ft 4 in) high to allow sufficient room for the horse to go through without brushing or hitting the door jamb. The stable door should open to the outside; both top and bottom halves of the door are best made with solid material and both halves should have a bolt at the top and bottom so that secure fastening is possible for each. The door should open outwards to a full 180 degrees so that neither handler nor horse will be caught by a half-open door.

The top half of the stable door is usually left open to allow the horse to look out, thus relieving its boredom and allowing the ventilation of the stable to be improved.

If the bottom half of the stable door is secured, both bolts should be fastened. If only the top bolt is fastened, the horse may be able to undo it and get away. If the bottom bolt is not fastened, the horse may get its foot caught in the gap at the bottom between the edge of the door and the door jamb.

If possible, a window should be built into a stable wall in order to aid ventilation and to allow the horse to look out in another direction to that of the stable door to relieve its boredom. The window should be about shoulder height, glazed with reinforced glass or protected by a metal grid. The window can be hinged at the bottom so it opens inwards from the top to allow air to enter above the horse.

Water can be supplied to the stable by automatic water feeders which, though costly to install, are great labour-saving devices, but they do need frequent checking and cleaning. Alternatively, large hinged rings about 4 ft (1.3 m) up the wall can be fitted to hold a water bucket, or a metal container can be placed in the corner of the stable.

A good artificial lighting system should be installed. A power point should be close by, but out of reach of the horse.

Feed and Tack Rooms

The feed room should be dry so that feed does not get damp and go mouldy. It, or at least the bins in which the feed is stored, should also be vermin-proof.

The tack room must be dry, as leather can become

Below: A horse free in a well equipped stable. Precautions have been taken for his safety with grills on the window and a fitted manger, although it would have been even safer to box the latter in.

mouldy. Some form of heating is advisable. The tack should be under lock and key as saddles, bridles and other gear are costly items.

Manure Pit

The manure pit should be a solid brick structure with a concrete floor and a lid that seals off manure from flies. It is best placed away from the stables with easy truck access for removal. Alternatively, a manure heap can be used when the manure is stacked neatly in a pile far enough away from the stables for any flies not to be a nuisance.

Bedding

Straw makes a soft, comfortable bed which is not readily compacted. It comes in bales, is easy to handle, readily available, absorbs urine and the soiled, unwanted bedding can be given to mushroom growers and gardeners for fertiliser. The only disadvantage is that some horses will eat the straw, too much of which can cause impaction colic. As they tend to eat both oat and barley straw more than wheat, the latter is the most popular type of straw for horses.

Wood shavings or sawdust are commonly used. They make a comfortable bed, but are more easily compacted. They tend to collect in the sole of the hoof, especially when mixed with urine and manure. However, horses do not eat shavings.

Shredded paper is used for horses with allergies and

Below: Most horses get bored if kept all the time in a stable and can easily develop bad habits. Try and allow them to run free in a paddock and it is easiest if it is adjacent to the stables.

coughs as it is dust free and is not eaten.

Peat moss makes a good bed but is expensive.

Paddock or Yard Adjacent to Stable

Ideally the yard or paddock has direct access to the stable so that the horse can move easily from one to the other. The land should be well drained and slope away from the stable. The area given to the paddock will vary according to the land available.

A paddock of approximately half a hectare (1 ¼ acres) in area would be ideal for each horse. Such a size would not only provide opportunities for the horse to pick grass and exercise, but would also help to prevent vice problems associated with the boredom of stable life. The feed bill would not be so great, the stable bedding would last longer and stable maintenance costs would be reduced.

Trees in the paddock could serve the dual purpose of providing shade in summer and acting as a windbreak in winter. They would need to be protected with tree guards or with wire netting wrapped around the trunk, or the horses would ringbark them very quickly.

Finally, the paddock should have a water supply, preferably automatic non-overflowing, and be surrounded by a fence about 1.8 m (6 ft)high and solidly built. The kind of material used in building a fence ranges from wooden post and rail, board, wire (but *not* barbed wire), various plastics to pipe. They all have their advantages and disadvantages and will appeal to one person or another according to the emphasis placed on such factors as cost, maintenance, durability, strength and safety.

If a half-hectare (1 ¼ acre) paddock is not possible and only small yard, say about 8 m (24 ft) square, is available, it should be surfaced with ash and rolled to prevent it becoming a messy bog in wet weather.

Horses that are kept in stables with access to a yard or paddock usually have fewer vices and respiratory problems, a better appetite and longer-lasting bedding than other horses.

FIRST AID

The horse's ability to react suddenly and to run quickly were its greatest means of protection from predators or danger in earlier days. Even now, when a horse senses danger or is frightened, it will often react in a wild, violent, blind panic, having no regard for ropes, fences, or any other objects in its path. Consequently, it often suffers a variety of self-inflicted wounds and damages its body. While exercising, especially at the gallop, a horse can cause a great damage to itself, particularly to its limbs.

Much hurt could be prevented by correct handling, stabling and shoeing. These areas are covered in other sections of this book and you are advised to read them in conjunction with this section on first aid.

FIRST AID KIT

- Scissors
- Roll of gauze bandage 5 cm (2 in wide)
- Roll of Elastoplast 8 cm (3 in) wide
- Roll of cotton wool
- Antiseptic wash (eg, Hibitane)
- Crepe cotton bandages 8 cm (3 in) wide
- Antibiotic powder
- Antibiotic pressure spray
- Clean bucket
- Thermometer
- Tincture of iodine

Bleeding

The first step in treating any wound is to control haemorrhage (bleeding). If the blood is slowly oozing from the wound, apply direct pressure to the site by means of a piece of clean gauze or sheeting held between the fingers. Don't dab or wipe the wound; this tends to promote further bleeding. Hold the pressure on the wound for 10 seconds, then remove the hand holding the gauze or sheeting and evaluate the depth and breadth of the wound. If the bleeding recommences, apply further pressure.

If the blood is not oozing but flowing freely, take a wad of gauze or a suitable absorbent material and apply heavy pressure to the wound with a clean hand. Over the wad of gauze, wrap firmly but not too tightly 8 cm (3 in) wide Elastoplast and leave it in place for about 30 minutes. Then remove the bandage and evaluate the wound. Do not use cotton wool because small, fine fibres tend to collect in the wound, act as a foreign body and slow down the healing process.

In cases of arterial bleeding, the blood is normally bright red and spurts out with a pulsating action. Apply very heavy pressure with gauze in hand directly over the site of the bleeding. Then wrap 8cm (3 in) wide Elastoplast tightly around the gauze. Not only does the bandage apply pressure, but it also immobilises the edges of the wound, thereby helping to stop bleeding; movement of the horse stimulates blood flow and indirectly quickens bleeding. Consequently, if a horse is bleeding, keep it calm and quiet, preferably tied up in a stable. Leave the bandage in place and call a veterinary surgeon for further advice.

When a horse is bleeding from an inaccessible area such as inside the nostrils, restrict its movement then externally apply cold to the area in the form of slowly running water from the hose or ice packed in a towel.

To sum up: don't stand and watch a horse bleed to death. Immediately apply direct pressure and stop the horse from moving about. Tourniquets are not recommended. They are often difficult to apply and, if applied incorrectly, can accentuate rather than retard blood loss.

Wounds

There are several types of wound. Most wounds seen in the horse are contaminated. Because of a horse's susceptibility to infection, a veterinary surgeon should be consulted with regard to tetanus injection and treatment with antibiotics.

This horse has a severe cut on his off hind. The firmly applied Elastoplast bandage controls haemorrhage.

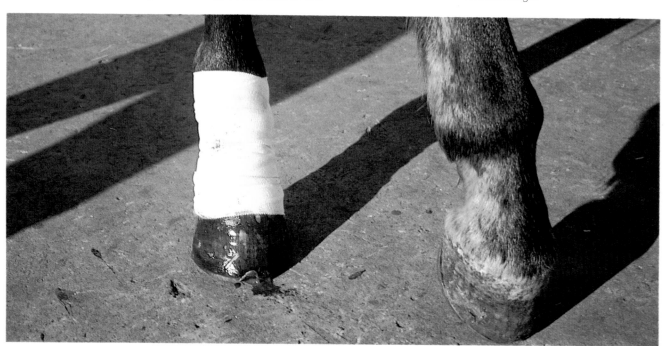

Abrasions

The hair and surface layer of the skin are removed by friction from contact with a brick wall, rope, hard ground, gates, and other similar objects. Abrasions are normally painful to touch, haemorrhage a little, and are often contaminated with grit and dirt.

The dirt and foreign material can be removed by directing running water from the hose with firm pressure directly onto the wound. Be careful about the pressure; if it is too severe, it may tend to drive foreign material further into the tissues.

As an alternative, the wound may be cleaned with peroxide, which has a germicidal effect as well as a foaming action that helps to flush out debris. Once the wound is clean, pat it dry with clean gauze and dust it with antibiotic powder or spray it with one of the aerosol packs containing antibiotics and triple dye. Leave the abrasion open unless it is oozing freely, in which case cover it with a gauze bandage.

If the abrasion covers a large area, do not exercise the horse until it is obviously healing.

Contusions

These wounds are characterised by bruising and swelling of the skin and underlying tissues. However, they are not necessarily associated with a break in the skin but may be caused by kicks, falls or collisions.

If there is no abrasion or break in the skin, the swelling is best dealt with by the application of alternate hot and cold foments. To make a hot foment, put hot water into a bucket containing 2 tablespoons of salt. The temperature of the water should be so hot that you can just put your hand into the water and leave it there. Remember that if the water is too hot, it will scald the horse's skin. If it is too cold, it will not serve its purpose

Below: This is a typical abrasion on the pastern which might have been caused by catching the foot under a gate or fence.

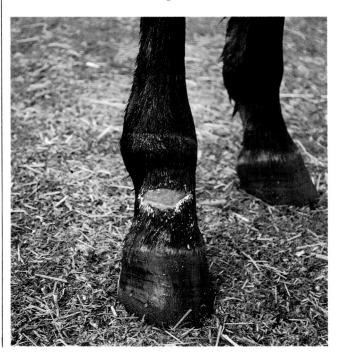

of increasing the blood circulation to the area, for the blood aids in the repair of damaged tissue and carries away debris and damaged cells.

Drop a large wad of cotton wool into the bucket containing the hot water, then hold it on the contused area until it cools off. Repeat this procedure for 10 minutes, morning and night, and be sure that water is kept at the same temperature during the 10-minute procedure.

To apply a cold foment, hose the wounded area with a fair amount of water pressure. The cold water constricts the blood vessels, reducing the oozing of fluid into the contused area. The pressure has a massaging effect, stimulating circulation and flow of fluid away from the site.

Be aware that, if there is a break in the skin, the contused area is an excellent environment for the development of bacteria. Antibiotics are therefore essential, no matter how small the break in the skin.

Puncture Wounds

These occur frequently, mainly because of the nature of the horse in relation to the environment. Puncturing of the sole by horseshoe nails left lying around, or penetration of the skin by a splinter or piece of wire when the horse rubs against a fence, are common. Puncture wounds may or may not be accompanied by haemorrhage, but they are generally painful.

To treat puncture wounds, clean the site of the puncture thoroughly with an iodine-based scrub, or Hibiclens, removing any dirt, debris or dead tissue. Try to make the opening to the puncture as large as possible to allow for proper drainage, and always carefully check the wound to see that no foreign body remains embedded. Any remnant of foreign body left in the wound will delay the healing process. Finally, paint the opening and as far into the puncture as possible with tincture of iodine.

After the wound has been cleansed and sterilised, it should be kept open as long as possible while drainage is taking place. The horse should be given hot foments to relieve pain and to aid healing. The administration of antibiotics and anti-tetanus vaccine are necessary precautions in the treatment of puncture wounds. Many puncture wounds go unnoticed. If infection or dirty foreign bodies are lying in or underneath the skin, an abscess will probably form. In cases of this nature, contact your veterinary suregon, who will provide necessary drainage, antibiotics and anti-tetanus vaccine.

Lacerations

These are probably the most common types of wound, and a frequent cause is barbed wire. The wound edges are often irregular, jagged and gaping. Sometimes whole sections of skin and underlying tissue are torn away. Lacerations are not usually acutely painful and the haemorrhage is variable according to the type of blood vessels that have been severed.

However, treatment can be complicated. Call a veterinary surgeon who will tell you whether or not the wound needs to be stitched. If it cannot be stitched, clean it thoroughly by hosing or by the application of peroxide. Remove any hair, dead tissue or foreign bodies and apply antibiotic powder, zinc cream, or a mild astringent to the exposed flesh. Beware of strong antiseptics that not only fail to destroy bacteria but will irritate the wound, destroying the important cells necessary for wound healing. They do more harm than good.

Above: The fleshy tissue is higher than the skin and is known as proud flesh.

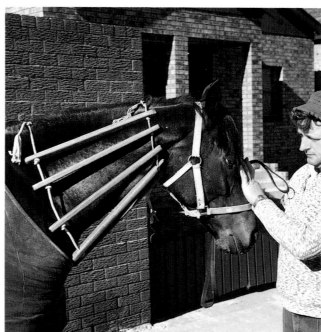

Above: This horse is wearing a cradle to stop him biting bandages or nuzzling a blister.

If one of the horse's legs has been lacerated, cover the wound with gauze held in position by a firmly applied Elastoplast bandage. If the pressure of the bandage is too tight, the blood supply to the area will be impaired, slowing down wound-healing. A firm pressure bandage controls swelling, helps to immobilise wound edges and stops the production of proud flesh. If the leg does not swell, leave the bandage on for 2 days.

When the bandage is removed, it will be soggy and discoloured with discharge from the wound. The odour will probably be offensive and this is normal, provided the horse is on a good antibiotic cover. Hose the wound, clean away any discharge, debris or dead tissue and dress as before.

Continue the process just described until the fleshy tissue has filled in the cavity to skin level. Then leave off the bandages, allowing the air and sunshine to dry the surface of the wound.

If the fleshy tissue (granulation tissue) becomes raised above the level of the skin it is called proud flesh. The skin cannot grow up and over the proud flesh, so the latter must be cut back. The best method of doing this is to apply a copper sulphate solution to the proud flesh, keeping it well away from the sensitive skin at the wound edges. Little by little, day by day, cut the proud flesh back to the level of the skin, then stop. The skin should then gradually close over the wound. If the proud flesh is excessive, a veterinary surgeon will have to cut it back surgically.

Do not exercise the horse. Confine it to a stable or yard until the skin has completely covered the wound.

Incised Wounds

Characteristics of incised wounds are that the edges are clean cut, fairly well-opposed and there is minimum tissue damage. Call your veterinary surgeon to suture the wound. It should be stitched within 8 hours of the accident and the stitches removed 10–12 days later.

BLISTERING

A blister is a counter-irritant usually made from red mercuric oxide or tincture of iodine. It is applied to the skin for the purpose of creating intense local inflammation in an already chronically inflamed area such as a splint, sore shin, osselet, bony enlargement or sprained ligament or tendon.

The blistering process causes an increase in the blood supply to the blistered area, which becomes swollen and hot. After the effects of the blister subside, it is often noticed that the original area of inflammation or swelling has subsided as well.

The area to be blistered should be clipped so that the blister can be applied directly to the skin. Vaseline should be applied liberally around the blistered area, especially below, as a preventative measure to stop the blister burning additional areas of skin.

The severity of a burn caused by the blister is determined by the length of time the blister is rubbed into the skin. The usual time taken is from 5–10 minutes.

It is necessary to ensure that the horse cannot touch the blister with its mouth, nostrils or (particularly) its eyes. If it does, it will suffer further burns in the contact area. Apply vaseline around the eyes, lips and nostrils. If the blistered area is on a leg, it can be covered with a bandage. Normally tying up the horse with two side reins prevents it from contacting the blistered area.

Six hours after blistering, wash off the blister with warm water and a mild soap. Then thoroughly hose the area and smear vaseline over it. Untie the horse.

On the day following the blistering, the area will be swollen and hot. After 4–7 days, the surface layers of the skin will begin to flake and peel off. The area should be kept clean and an antiseptic ointment should be applied to keep the surface soft and free from infection.

Gradually over a period of 3–4 weeks, the swelling and heat should subside and the area should return to normal.

Above: By kneeling on a horse's extended neck, he can be prevented, without hurting him, from trying to stand up. By doing so, the horse will be prevented from floundering and causing himself further injury.

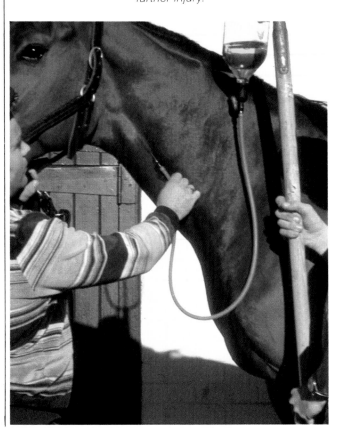

SHOCK

Shock is a term used to describe a state of collapse following many forms of serious stress such as car accidents, massive haemorrhage, heavy falls, overwhelming infection (septicaemia), twisted bowel (colic) and dehydration. The symptoms can vary, depending on the cause and include depression, prostration, rapid breathing and pallor of the gums and of the conjunctiva (membranes around the eye).

Contact the veterinary surgeon immediately, but while waiting for his arrival, take the following steps.

1 Keep the horse warm but not too warm ie, maintain the normal body temperature. Warmth can be overdone to the point of accentuating the shock if the horse becomes too hot.

2 Control any bleeding (see page **90**).

3 Ask any people in the area to be quiet or to move away, as a noisy group of spectators can aggravate shock.

4 Keep the horse calm and quiet by tying it up or putting it in a stable. If it is lying outstretched and is spasmodically struggling to get up but is unable to do so, rather than letting it flounder with the risk of further injury, put a head collar and lead on it and prevent it from getting up by kneeling on the extended neck and head with your full weight.

5 If the horse has an obvious fracture of the lower limb, apply a splint to prevent any further damage at the site of the fracture while waiting for the veterinary surgeon. A splint can be readily made by wrapping a pillow or a roll of cotton wool around the leg, with the fracture in the centre of the cotton wool or pillow. Bind the pillow or cotton wool to the leg with crepe bandages applied as tightly as possible. To add extra rigidity, a broom handle should be incorporated in the bandage, with a final few layers of 8 cm (3 in) wide Elastoplast applied as before and as tightly as possible. The splint not only immobilises the fracture but also helps to relieve a certain amount of pain.

BANDAGING

See page **53**.

Apply a bandage with an even, firm pressure. Check to see that the leg does not swell and, if it does, this is a sign that the bandage has been applied too tightly. Remove and re-apply it.

Do not fall into the trap of applying a plaster bandage too tightly. Unroll a manageable part of the bandage, then wrap that part around the leg, unroll another part, wrap it around the leg, and so on. If you unroll as you wrap on, the bandage will invariably be too tight.

Uneven pressure applied over a tendon can produce a bow in it. Many horsemen use cotton wool under bandages, but this material can form hard balls that act as pressure points. A layer of sponge rubber under a bandage will ensure an even distribution of pressure.

When bandaging, the main points to keep in mind are: apply an even pressure and do not bandage too tightly. When taking the bandage off, assume the same position as when applying it. As you unwrap it, roll the bandage up, making sure the tapes are folded into the first part of the roll. If it is not dirty, the bandage is then ready for immediate use.

Left: This horse is being administered with a transfusion by a veterinary surgeon as a treatment for his state of shock.

ADMINISTRATION OF MEDICATION

Above: Tablets, capsules and boluses may be placed in the mouth by hand.

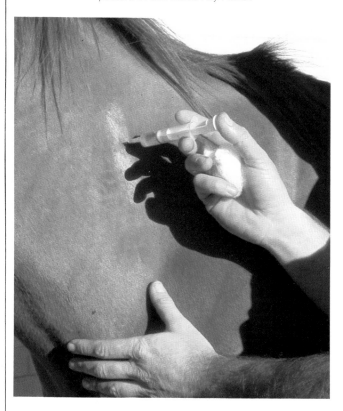

Above: this horse is being given an intra-muscular injection by a veterinary surgeon.

There is nothing more frustrating and worrying than the refusal of medication by a horse. If the medication is not administered correctly, the horse's condition will not improve and may worsen, and in most cases the medicine is wasted.

If an owner finds it impossible to give medication to his horse, a veterinary surgeon can administer it in an uncomplicated manner if the horse's condition is serious. If long-distance travel is involved, the horse can be hospitalised to ensure regular medication.

Whether the medicine is given orally, by stomach tube, by injection or via the rectum depends upon the type of medicine, palatability, speed of onset and duration of its action, the condition and temperament of the horse, and the temperament of the owner.

Oral Administration of Drugs

Pelleted Preparations in the Feed

These are numerous vitamin, mineral supplements, worm preparations and others that have additives such as flavouring to make them palatable so that they can be mixed in as part of the normal feed. They are pelleted to prevent wastage.

Powders and Liquids in the Feed

Provided these are palatable, they can be thoroughly mixed with the feed so that the horse cannot selectively avoid the powder or liquid and eat the rest of the food. Powders tend to collect in the bottom of the feed bin in inaccessible corners and when the horse is eating he tends to blow his nostrils into the feed, causing some of the powder to be blown out of the feed bin. If powder and liquid preparations are not palatable, they can be mixed with molasses or honey then mixed with the feed or placed on a large wooden spoon and wiped over the horse's tongue.

Powders, Liquids in Drinking Water

Many electrolyte mixtures in powdered form can be given in the drinking water. Leave the horse in his yard or stable for a number of hours without water. Add the powder to a bucket about a quarter full of water and offer it to the horse.

After it has finished, top the bucket up with fresh water.

Liquids and Pastes by Syringe

Many worming pastes come in a syringe. Put a head collar on the horse with a lead attached. Make sure the mouth is empty before introducing the syringe. Standing on the left side of the horse's head facing the horse, put the syringe in the corner of the mouth so that the nozzle rests on the back of the tongue.

After pressing the plunger of the syringe, hold the horse's head up to ensure that the full dose is swallowed, but not too high, otherwise the horse may have difficulty in swallowing.

If there is liquid in the syringe, don't squirt it rapidly onto the back of the tongue, as some may go into the windpipe and cause inhalation pneumonia. Just gently dribble it onto the tongue, allowing sufficient time for the horse to swallow.

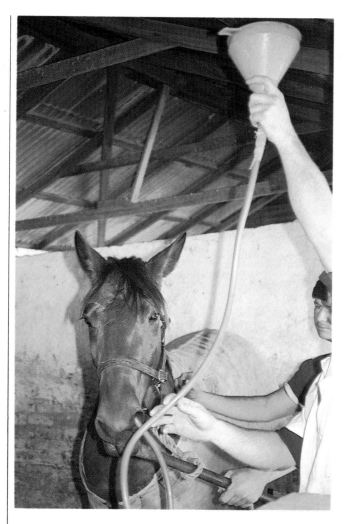

Above: A stomach tube being used on a horse. Most horses are not disturbed by this method.

Tablets, Capsules and Boluses Placed in the Mouth

These can be given by hand or with a balling gun. A gag may be used, but it is not necessary. If one is used, it can be applied in the same way as a bridle. The gag has the advantage of opening the mouth wide so that a tablet can be placed in the very back of the mouth without the fingers, hand or arm being bitten or abraded.

To administer medication by hand without a gag, stand on the left (near side) of the horse's head, facing the horse. Put your left hand into the right side of the horse's mouth, grasp a good handful of the tongue and pull it out between the lips on the right side of the mouth. As well as keeping the mouth open, this will stop the horse from biting your hand because it will bite its own tongue first.

With the right hand, place the tablet, capsule or bolus as far back on the tongue as possible, then quickly release the tongue that you are holding in the left hand. This action carries the tablet into the back of the throat. Lubrication of the tablet prior to introduction helps it to slide down more smoothly. Hold the head in a slightly elevated position.

Using the balling gun, grasp the tongue as previously described and introduce the gun between the incisor (front) teeth, discharging the bolus or capsule on the base of the tongue. If it is discharged too far to the back

of the mouth, damage can be done to the throat.

Do not put irritant materials in gelatine capsules, as they sometimes become caught in the throat or oesophagus (food pipe), dissolve and release the irritant material with the risk of causing severe local damage. I recall one occasion on which a capsule containing a physic burned a hole through the oesophagus to the skin, necessitating euthanasia of the horse.

Drenching with Bottle in Mouth

To carry out this procedure, the horse's head is elevated sufficiently to allow the liquid to flow to the back of the throat rather than the mouth. If the head cannot be held high enough by hand, attach a rope to the noseband of the head collar. Raise the head by pulling on the rope thrown over a rafter.

A plastic bottle with a long neck is introduced into the mouth where there is a gap between the teeth. Slowly trickle the solution into the horse's mouth, allowing plenty of time to swallow. There is always the danger of fluid getting into the windpipe, causing secondary pneumonia, so remember to drench slowly with the bottle.

Nasal Administration of Drugs

The stomach tube is an efficient, safe, professional method of giving liquid medication. In the author's opinion, the use of this technique should be left to the veterinary surgeon or trained personnel because in inexperienced hands many horses have died from the stomach tube inadvertently being passed into the lungs, resulting in fatal inhalation pneumonia.

Administration of Drugs by Injection

This is the route most often used by veterinary surgeons. It is quick, efficient and convenient. Injections can be given under the skin (subcutaneous), into the muscle (intramuscular), into a vein (intravenous) or into a joint space (intra-articular). The type of drug and the disease determine how and where it will be given. This technique for the administration of drugs should be employed only by veterinary surgeons or trained personnel.

Administration of Drugs Via Rectum

Extreme care should be taken when giving an enema to a foal. Use a soft tube and make sure it is well lubricated. Do not insert the tube more than 6 cm (2½ in) into the rectum, and insert it gently. Allow the fluid to flow by gravity. This is much safer than forcing it in under pressure because of the risk of rupturing the rectal wall.

Administering a Bran Mash

Sick horses are prone to constipation. A bran mash can be used to encourage a sick or convalescent horse to eat, as well as being used as an effective means of treating and preventing constipation.

To make a bran mash, place 1 kg (2 lb) of bran, 30 g (1 oz) of salt and 300 ml (10 fl oz) of molasses into a clean bucket. Add 2 litres (3½ pints) of hot water and stir thoroughly. Allow the mixture to stand for 10 minutes before offering it to the horse.

DISEASES AND PROBLEMS A-Z

GENERAL SIGNS OF ILLNESS

Horses are creatures of habit, and any variation of or departure from their normal habits should be viewed with suspicion. By following a routine checklist each day, you may become aware of a problem in its very early stages. This will enable you to rectify the situation or to contact a veterinary surgeon before it becomes too serious. The checklist should include the following items.

Appetite

Each morning and evening you should check the feed bin to see how much the horse has eaten. If the horse has eaten very little or nothing at all, check the palatability of the feed and whether or not there has been any change in quality or type.

Some horses can be fussy about their food. If there is no logical explanation for loss of appetite, this is one of the first signs of illness.

Droppings

Check the droppings in the stable, yard or paddock, morning and night. Usually there are 10–15 droppings per day. The presence of very few droppings could be a sign of constipation; none could be a sign of an intestinal obstruction.

Very hard, small dry balls of manure indicate dehydration and/or constipation. Fluid, watery droppings indicate diarrhoea.

If worms, odour, mucus, blood and undigested food are observed in the manure, they are signs of varying health problems.

Coat

Depending on the time of the year and housing conditions, the quality of the coat can vary markedly. A dry, harsh coat, excessive sweating or tight skin when pinched can be signs of illness.

Urine

Normal urine can vary markedly in colour from clear and colourless to cloudy and yellow, and from water-like to thick in consistency. If you suspect that there is something wrong with the urine, collect a sample in a clean screwtop jar and put in the refrigerator until the veterinary surgeon arrives.

If no urine has been passed within about 24 hours and the horse appears to be straining frequently, it could be indicative of an obstruction (stone in the bladder). If excessive urine is passed, it is often referred to as 'flooding the box' and a sign of it is very damp bedding. This is also abnormal.

Reddish-brown or blood-tinged urine is abnormal.

Eyes, Nose and Mouth

Discharge from any of these orifices, if excessive in volume and/or yellow in colour, is abnormal. The mucous membrane lining the eyes, nose and mouth is normally a glistening pink colour. If it is white, yellow, bluish or brick-red in colour, it too is abnormal.

Legs

The lower limbs should be hard and cool with good definition around the joints and tendons. If the legs are puffy, swollen and/or hot, further investigation by the verterinary surgeon is indicated.

Temperature

A normal thermometer can be used to take the temperature of a horse by inserting two-thirds of its length through the anus into the rectum, with the bowl of the thermometer resting on the wall of the rectum. Make sure you shake the mercury down in the thermometer before inserting it into the rectum. Leave the thermometer in the position for approximately one minute but keep hold of it so it does not get sucked into the rectum. If the horse's temperature is outside the range of 37.7°–38.6°C, call a veterinary surgeon.

Position

If the horse is lying down for lengthy periods of time, getting up and down, looking at its flanks or pawing the ground continuously, these can be signs of abdominal pain. Even if you don't observe the horse showing these signs, you can often infer their presence if the bedding is piled in a heap or strewn everywhere, or if the horse's body is covered in bedding.

Respiration

The normal respiration rate is 10–15 breaths per minute. Rapid, shallow, heavy or noisy respiration is abnormal and requires veterinary attention.

Above: Check the number of droppings when you pick them up from the paddock or stable.

SPECIFIC DISEASES & PROBLEMS

Abortion
• *See* Breeding, page **143**

Abrasions
• *See* First Aid, page **91**

Abscess

An abscess is a collection of pus, generally circumscribed in a sac enclosed within the tissues of the body.

Causes
Abscesses that can be seen or felt under the skin are caused, in most cases, by a foreign body penetrating the skin and underlying tissue. When rubbing its neck against the fence, a horse may cause a splinter of wood to penetrate its skin; when grazing it may pick up a grass seed in its cheek; when walking in the yard or paddock, a nail may puncture its foot. However, abscesses appearing under the jaw are not usually caused by penetration of a foreign body but by an internal infection such as strangles (see page **125**).

Horses sometimes develop internal abscesses on the liver, lungs and elsewhere. These are associated with a generalised bacterial infection.

Signs
In the early stages while the abscess is forming, the swelling is diffuse, hot, painful and hard. As the abscess matures, it becomes more localised, softer, less painful and forms a point. At this stage, when pressed by the

Below: This horse has a large, hard, painful abscess on the rump.

finger, it will often show a pit or identation. Depending upon the size and position of the abscess, the horse may be lethargic, off its food, or have a temperature.

Treatment
In the early stages, if a puncture site is obvious, thoroughly cleanse the area with an iodine-based scrub, removing any dirt, debris, or dead tissue. Check the wound to see that no foreign body remains embedded in it.

Apply a hot foment to the area (see page **91**) and then smear a drawing agent over the swollen area. Call the veterinary surgeon, who will administer antibiotics and anti-tetanus vaccine.

The treatment may cause the forming abscess to subside and the tissue to return to normal. If the abscess points, the veterinary surgeon will lance it to drain it. The wound should be kept open as long as possible while drainage is taking place.

If there is a large pocket after the pus has been drained out, it should be irrigated twice daily by squirting a syringe full of peroxide into the cavity. Drainage can be aided by gently pressing from the outer extremities of the abscess towards the opening.

This treatment should be continued until the opening has almost closed over.

Anaemia
• *See* Blood Disorders, page **98**

Aneurysm
• *See* Verminous Aneurysm, page **133**

Anthrax

This is a very acute disease caused by the bacteria *Bacillus anthracis*. The disease occurs all over the world, affecting all animals, including humans.

Cause
The bacteria in suitable conditions can survive in soil for 40 years. Infection can enter the body by ingestion, inhalation or through a break in the skin.

Signs
These can vary according to the route of infection. Generally there is a high temperature, severe depression, diarrhoea and abdominal pain, followed by swelling under the jaw, chest, abdomen and in the lower limbs. Death follows in 2–4 days.

Treatment
Contact a veterinary surgeon immediately. Isolate the horse from all other animals while waiting. If the horse dies, do not attempt a post mortem but seek advice from the appropriate authorities regarding disposal of the body and disinfection.

Arthritis

Arthritis is inflammation of a joint (which is made up of bones, cartilage, ligaments and joint capsule). The joint capsule produces fluid that lubricates the joint.

Causes
Inflammation of the joint is caused by trauma that may be due to a kick, cut, fall or penetrating foreign body. It may also result from infection entering the joint through a wound or localising in the joint from a general

infection (see Joint Ill page **153**). Poor conformation placing abnormal stress on a joint or joints may cause arthritis, and so may nutritional deficiencies (eg, calcium).

Signs

Acute arthritis involves all the signs of inflammation. The joint is warm and painful to the touch and swollen. One or all components of the joint may be involved. The joint capsule and ligaments may be stretched or torn, the cartilage bruised or scored and the bones fractured. Acute arthritis may subside, leaving a normal joint, or it may lead to chronic arthritis.

Chronic arthritis is associated with a joint that has been swollen for a long time. The swollen joint is firm or hard, often not warm to the touch, and less painful. Although in many cases movement of the joint is restricted, over a period of time it becomes permanently damaged.

Treatment

This varies according to the cause. A veterinary surgeon is best able to diagnose arthritis and pinpoint the cause.

While waiting for the veterinary surgeon, apply a pressure bandage to the affected joint. Immobilise the horse by putting it in a stable or tying it up. Cold hose the joint and pack it with ice if there are no obvious signs of infection. An antiphlogestine poultice will help reduce the swelling.

Chronic arthritis varies in its response to liniments, blisters (see page **92**), pin firing, anti-inflammatory agents and radiation therapy.

Atresia Ani
• *See* The Foal, page **151**

AZOTURIA (TYING-UP)

Years ago this condition was called Monday morning disease because draught horses, pit horses, and other working horses in good, well-muscled condition exhibited symptoms on Monday mornings after they had rested over the weekend and had been fed a high-grain diet.

The condition is characterised by stiffness, pain and muscle tremor involving the muscles of the hindquarters, except in severe cases where the muscles of the forequarters may be involved as well. Tying-up is a less severe form of azoturia.

Causes

Horses worked at irregular intervals and fed high-grain diets are most susceptible to azoturia.

Ingested grain is converted to glycogen, which is stored in muscles and elsewhere. If the horse is rested for periods of 1–2 days whilst on a high-grain diet, large quantities of glycogen are stored in the muscles. Glycogen is used by the muscles as a source of energy when work is being done; the waste product from the chemical change that takes place is lactic acid. If the glycogen is suddenly broken down to release energy when the horse exercises hard, a large volume of lactic acid is produced. If this lactic acid cannot be expelled from the muscle tissue, it damages the muscle fibres, causing the condition known as tying-up. If large areas of muscle fibres are damaged or even destroyed, azoturia results. The danger lies in the sudden demand for a lot of energy; hence too much exercise too soon after time off work is very bad.

Some horses that are not on grain diets tie-up because they are hypersensitive to lactic acid or because their particular metabolism does not cope with it efficiently.

Signs

These can vary widely. In mild cases, during or after exercise, the horse steps short in th hindlimbs, giving the appearance of stiffness. In severe cases, the horse will show stiffness, pain, sweating and muscle tremor. The stiffness, involving both the hindlimbs and frontlimbs, may progress to the point at which the horse cannot move and may lie down. The affected muscles are very hard to the touch, indicating cramp, and the urine may vary in colour from dark brown to reddish black, according to the severity of the condition.

Treatment

Call the veterinary surgeon who can confirm the condition, not only by its history and clinical signs, but also by taking a blood count and by doing certain serum enzyme tests.

Stop exercising the horse when you notice that it is tying-up. In some cases, to continue with any form of movement, even walking, can precipitate an attack of azoturia. If it appears no better, call the veterinary surgeon. Walking aids in the circulation of blood to the muscles with consequent removal of lactic acid, thus helping to prevent severe cramping.

Keep the horse warm by seeing that it is well rugged. Tempt it with fluids containing electrolytes which, if drunk in any quantity, will help to flush out the kidneys.

With the aid of information gained from a blood count, the veterinary surgeon can administer a muscle relaxant, diuretics, tranquillisers and anti-inflammatory agents if required, as well as specially prepared fluids and electrolytes by stomach tube or intravenous methods. An injection of vitamin E and selenium can be used therapeutically and as a preventative measure.

All grain should be eliminated from the diet and the horse should be offered a bran mash as a mild laxative. Horses susceptible to frequent typing-up should have a low-level grain diet. Normally the grain level in the diet should be in proportion to the amount of work done. For example, if in any one week a horse works for 6 days followed by a day off, reduce the quantity of grain in the feed for that day. Recovery can take place within hours, though in severe cases it may take weeks.

Exercise the horse every day and consult a veterinary surgeon about the regular use of a particular vitamin supplement (ie, vitamin E and selenium) as a preventative measure.

Back Injuries
• *See* Spondylitis, page **131**

Bleeders
• *See* Blood Disorders, page **99**

BLOOD DISORDERS

Anaemia

Anaemia is not a disease; it is a symptom of something else. It is a decrease of the haemoglobin and red blood cells whereby the levels are below normal, thus reducing the oxygen-carrying capacity of the blood.

A stressed horse readily shows signs of anaemia. On the other hand, the unstressed horse with anaemia may not show any signs at all.

Causes

Anaemia can be caused by acute haemorrhage, which is indicated by internal bleeding from a ruptured blood vessel, or external bleeding from a cut or puncture

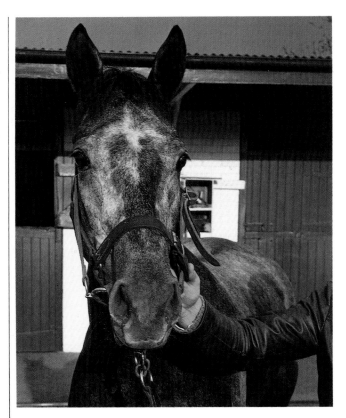

This horse is known as a bleeder. It is a condition commonly found in racehorses. He displays the obvious signs: blood is trickling from both his nostrils after exercising.

wound. Chronic haemorrhage is indicated by blood loss associated with blood-sucking parasites, or blood loss associated with biting lice.

Anaemia can also be caused by the destruction of red blood cells; this may result from infection. Piroplasmosis is a disease caused by a blood parasite called babesia, which destroys the red blood cells and is transmitted by ticks.

Also equine infectious anaemia is a virus infection that causes severe anaemia.

Phenothiazine, which is used as a worm drench, when given in a dose above the recommended level causes the breakdown of red blood cells. Another cause of the destruction of red blood cells is isoimmune haemolytic jaundice (see page **151**).

Anaemias caused by the depression of red blood cell production are associated with chronic infections and nutritional deficiencies such as lack of iron, copper, pyridoxene and folic acid.

Signs
Symptoms of anaemia are lethargy, loss of appetite, restlessness, loss of condition and a rough coat.

The colour of the tissue around the eye (conjunctiva) reflects the status of the red blood cells in the horse. The normal colour is pink; white indicates severe anaemia. However, in many cases the colour of the conjuctiva does not fall into either category. In these cases, a full blood count is essential. The purpose of a blood count is threefold; recognition of the not-so-obviously anaemic horse, indication of the degree of anaemia and diagnosis of the cause, which will determine the type of treatment to be given.

Treatment
No treatment should be initiated until the cause has been diagnosed.

Bleeders

Bleeding is a condition common to racehorses, not the equine-equivalent of human haemophiliacs.

A bleeder is potentially dangerous to itself, to its rider and to other horses and riders in the field. During races there have been cases of horses bleeding severely, collapsing and bringing down others in the field. Some owners and trainers have argued that the bleeding is caused by the nose hitting the ground when the horse has collapsed. This argument has been refuted on film showing blood streaming from the horse's nostrils before its collapse and fall.

Causes
Bleeding can be due to a defect in the blood clotting mechanism, high blood pressure or fragile capillaries in the nose or lungs.

Signs
The most obvious sign is that the horse will bleed from one or both nostrils after a race, track work or sometimes swimming. Usually, it is more serious if the bleeding is from both nostrils as it may well mean that the haemorrhage is further back and therefore more dangerous. Bleeding from one nostril only usually means it is confined to that nasal passage and therefore less likely to affect the lungs. The bleeding may begin during the exercise, immediately after, or sometimes hours after the exercise has finished. The blood may lie inside the nostrils, drip to the ground, or flow very freely. Some horses bleed in the lungs. The only signs of this may be laboured breathing, distress and coughing.

Treatment
Contact a veterinary surgeon, as this problem can be fatal. He can evaluate a defect in the clotting mechanism by taking a blood sample and doing specific tests for clotting. Using an instrument called a rhinolaryngoscope, he can examine the nasal passages, throat and upper windpipe to see if a ruptured vessel in any of those areas is causing the haemorrhage. Various drugs can be used to harden fragile capillaries, reduce blood pressure and rectify the deficiency in the clotting mechanism. Rest is essential for any capillary rupture to heal properly. Feeding the horse at ground level, thus making it put its head down to eat, may help to strengthen the capillaries in the nostrils.

Blood Poisoning (Septicaemia)
• *See* The Foal, page **152**

Bog Spavin
• *See* Leg Injuries and Problems, page **114**

Bone Spavin
• *See* Leg Injuries and Problems, page **114**

Bots
• *See* Worming, page **80**

Botulism
• *See* Forage Poisoning, page **107**

Bowed Tendon
• *See* Leg Injuries and Problems, page **115**

Broken Knees
• *See* Leg Injuries and Problems, page **116**

Broken Wind
• *See* Respiratory Problems, page **124**

Bruising
• *See* Shoeing, page **87**

Brushing
• *See* Corrective Shoeing, page **87**

Capped Elbow
• *See* Leg Injuries and Problems, page **116**

Capped Hock
• *See* Leg Injuries and Problems, page **116**

Carpitis
• *See* Leg Injuries and Problems, page **117**

Cataract
• *See* Eye Problems, page **104**

CHOKE

Choke occurs when the oesophagus becomes obstructed
by food or a foreign body.

Causes
Horses that bolt their feed and those with teeth abnormalities are more susceptible when fed dry grains.
Boluses administered orally may lodge in the oesophagus. Foreign bodies such as wire, nails and pieces of
wood are often responsible for choke.

Signs
The horse is obviously distressed, refuses to eat, extends
its head and neck, salivates, coughs, grunts and paws
the ground. Food and saliva may be regurgitated through
the nostrils. A lump may be seen and felt on the left side
of the neck. The agitation will finally give way to
depression.

Treatment
Call the veterinary surgeon and, while waiting, try to
determine the cause of the obstruction. Solid objects are
more serious than a blockage caused by grain, hay or
grass. Do not allow the horse to drink as the water may
be inhaled into the lungs, causing pneumonia.
    If a lump can be felt in the neck, gently but firmly try
to massage it upwards or downwards, depending on its
position.
    Greedy horses that bolt their feed can be forced to eat
more slowly if large stones are placed in the feed bin and
if hay is put into a hay net.
    Check the horse's teeth every 6 weeks for abnormali-
ties. Those prone to choke on dry grains can be fed boiled
feeds.

Colds
• *See* Viral Respiratory Diseases, page **126**

COLIC

Those diseases of the horse that cause abdominal pain
are generally referred to as equine colic. There are
numerous types of colic, ranging from mild pain and
quick recovery to severe pain and eventual death. It is

*Above: A capped hock which is a swelling on
the point of the hock.*

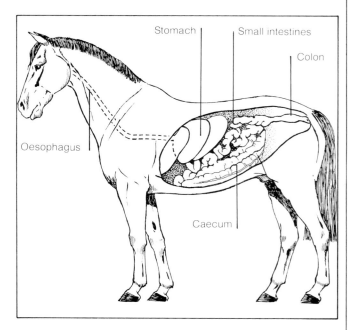

*Above: This diagram illustrates the digestive
system of the horse.*

*Right: A horse with colic often keeps lying down
and getting up again as a sign of the severity
of the abdominal pain.*

much easier to prevent colic than to cure it, though the cure rate has markedly improved. It is interesting that many cases the author has seen come from the same people, time and time again. This points to a management problem.

Causes

The causes of colic are many. One group of causes stems directly from poor management, the other from causes unrelated to management and over which man has little control.

It is necessary to look at the state of the horse's teeth. The horse has a grinding action with the teeth, which leads to the development of very sharp edges on the inside of the lower molars and the outside of the upper molars. If they are neglected, the teeth develop razor-sharp edges that severely lacerate the inside of the cheeks and gums. The horse finds it difficult to grind the food; poorly digested food will upset intestinal motility and could lead to colic.

Excessive low-grade roughage makes digestion difficult for the intestine. Large boluses form, which lead to impaction.

Debility, exhaustion and excitement can lead to changes in intestinal motility, and therefore cause colic. Slowing of the intestinal movements leads to build-up of food, impaction and obstruction. Hypermotility, or speeding-up of gut movements, can also lead to painful spasmodic colic.

Lush green feed gives rise to excess gas production due to fermentation processes in the gut. This causes flatulent colic.

Engorgement with grain can cause gastric dilation resulting, in some cases, in rupture of the stomach or acute founder (laminitis).

The immature larvae of the red worm, *strongyllus vulgaris*, migrate into the muscular walls of arteries, causing a fibrous swelling known as an aneurysm which can block the artery, subsequently cutting off the blood supply and bringing about necrosis (death) of the portion of the bowel supplied by that artery. Routine and correct worming procedure cannot be over-emphasised in the prevention of colic.

Signs

Symptoms vary markedly with the severity of the pain as well as the length of time that the horse has been suffering from colic.

Generally speaking, the signs range from the horse

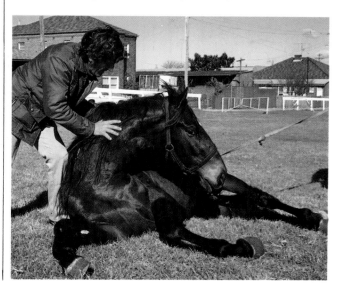

being restless to pawing the ground, looking at its flanks, standing with all four legs extended, sweating, looking depressed, lying down, rolling, kicking and showing little or no interest in food and water. The horse's faeces can vary from none at all to reduced amounts of small hard pellets or to fluid, diarrhoea-like droppings.

Treatment

If the horse is exhibiting more than one of the symptoms described, contact a veterinary surgeon immediately. It is important for you to observe all the horse's habits so that you can give the veterinary surgeon an accurate history.

He will then carry out a clinical examination, including pulse rate, temperature, respiration rate and stethoscope examination of the heart and intestine. It will also be necessary for him to carry out a rectal examination, paracentesis (puncturing the abdominal cavity) and a blood count.

Following examination, a diagnosis can be made as to whether the case is a medical one (needing drug treatment) or a surgical one. Time is of the utmost importance if surgical cases are to be successful. Many people think that a horse with a twisted bowel is doomed to death. This is *not* so if the veterinary surgeon is contacted early.

Conjunctivitis
• *See* Eye Problems and Injuries, page **104**

Constipation
• *See* The Foal, page **152**

Contagious Equine Metritis (CEM)
• *See* Metritis, page **136**

Contracted Heels
• *See* Corrective Shoeing, page **87**

Corneal Injuries
• *See* Eye Problems and Injuries, page **105**

Corns
• *See* Shoeing, page **87**

Coughing
• *See* Respiratory Problems, page **124**

Cracked Heel
• *See* Foot and Hoof Injuries, page **108**

Cracks
• *See* Corrective Shoeing, page **87**

Cross Firing
• *See* Corrective Shoeing, page **87**

Cryptorchidism
• *See* Rig, page **127**

CYSTITIS

Inflammation of the bladder is not a common problem in horses. Mares are affected more frequently than colts or geldings.

Causes
These include damage to the bladder or urethra (opening

of the bladder) during foaling, infection of the uterus or vagina, spreading to the bladder or stones in the bladder.

Signs

Frequent straining to urinate with little or no urine being passed on each occasion. The urine may vary in colour from clear to dark red, indicative of blood being passed. The skin around the vulva and between the legs of mares may be scalded, due to the continual dribbling of urine.

Treatment

Contact a veterinary surgeon but, while waiting, collect a urine sample from the horse in a clean glass receptacle with a screwtop lid. A urine sample is helpful, sometimes essential, in making a correct diagnosis. Do not use a honey jar; this may artificially affect the urine sugar level. If the veterinary surgeon is delayed, store the sample in the refrigerator.

If the skin has been scalded by urine, wash the area with warm soapy water, dry thoroughly and apply zinc cream or vaseline. Clean, fresh water should be available to the horse at all times.

The veterinary surgeon will select and administer an appropriate antibiotic for infections of the bladder.

DEHYDRATION

Horses sweat freely, are often exposed to the environment for lengthy periods of time in a paddock, and some are regularly and vigorously exercised in preparing for and taking part in such activities as weekend competitions, racing and endurance riding. They are, therefore, more susceptible than most animals to dehydration, ie, they lose more than normal amounts of fluids and electrolytes that cannot adequately be replenished by normal diet.

Electrolytes are made up of a delicate balance of salts, including sodium, potassium, chloride, bicarbonate, phosphate and magnesium. Body fluids and cells contain electrolyte ions in varying proportions. For example, body fluids have concentrated sodium and chloride ions, whereas the fluid inside cells contains concentrated potassium ions.

When a cell functions, eg, when a muscle cell contracts, potassium and other ions from inside the cell pass through the cell wall to the body fluid. Sodium and chloride ions pass from the body fluid to the inside of the muscle cell. Muscle fatigue sets in, ie, the muscle becomes incapable of further contraction, when ions in the body fluid equal those within the muscle cell. When muscles are resting, the reverse action takes place.

Cramping and tying-up result if excessive loss of electrolytes in the sweat is not replaced because there are insufficient electrolytes in correct balance in the horse's diet.

Daily feeding of an electrolyte mixture will ensure that the electrolytes are replaced as they are lost, thus preventing dehydration. However, there is a limit to the quantity of electrolytes a horse will accept in its feed. Horses in training or performance horses that require greater amounts of electrolytes can be given them by stomach tube.

Causes

There is a continual loss of electrolytes and fluid through faeces, sweat and urine. This continual loss is accelerated by the following factors: exercise, heat, travelling, diarrhoea, loss of appetite, lack of access to water and free sweating.

Signs

Dehydration may be identified by a dry, starry coat, sunken eyes, lethargy, loss of appetite, hard, dry balls of manure, fatigue, cramping, tying-up, lack of will to win, poor performance and poor recovery from exercise. When the skin is pinched, lack of return or slow return to normal can indicate dehydration.

Treatment

A balanced electrolyte mixture can be administered orally by means of the feed or drinking water, by nasal stomach tube (the electrolytes being dissolved in water) or intravenously, the electrolytes being contained in a specially prepared sterile solution.

Blood tests can be done to evaluate which electrolyte is deficient and a solution concentrated in that electrolyte can then be administered. Drugs that act on the kidney can be injected into the horse, causing retention of certain ions in the body.

DIARRHOEA

Diarrhoea in mature horses is uncommon. When it does occur, it attracts attention and causes some alarm because often the cause is not determined and the symptoms do not respond to the treatment. Many cases of diarrhoea can be prevented by proper management, including feeding, worming, teeth care and cleanliness.

Causes

These include bad teeth, broken teeth or teeth with sharp edges, all of which give rise to incomplete mastication. Other causes are worms and poor nutrition. The quantity and quality of the food may be the cause, eg, large amounts of succulent, lucerne hay (quantity) and mouldy hay (quality) fed to the horse at irregular intervals. Infection that may be bacterial, viral, or protozoal can cause diarrhoea, as can excitement such as is experienced at the races or horse shows. Nervousness or excitement upsets intestinal movement.

Signs

Diarrhoea is recognised when the faeces passed are cowlike, porridgelike or just a discoloured water fluid. A horse with severe diarrhoea can squirt discoloured fluid a metre (3 ft) or more from the anus, splattering the walls of the stable. When there is evidence of diarrhoea on the ground and a group of horses are in the paddock, the sick horse will, in most cases, have diarrhoea matted in the tail and around the hindquarters. The colour of the faeces may vary from pale to yellow to black with streaks of blood and mucus.

The horse's appetite can fluctuate from normal to non-existent. Most horses with diarrhoea exhibit signs of discomfort when defecating (passing a motion) such as switching the tail, looking at the flank and tucking up the abdomen.

Horses with severe diarrhoea can exhibit signs of colic. If the diarrhoea continues for 2 or 3 days, they lose weight and become weak, depressed and dehydrated.

Treatment

Some horses do not respond to any treatment. In these cases, the only thing to do is to turn them out into a paddock for a lengthy spell. This was the successful treatment for Tulloch, one of Australia's outstanding racing thoroughbreds, a horse that suffered from chronic diarrhoea. (Chronic diarrhoea is often called Tulloch's disease.)

Call a veterinary surgeon, who will not only treat the

symptoms but will examine the horse and take a sample of its faeces to ascertain the cause so that the correct treatment can be given. Treatment varies according to cause. For example, treatment for diarrhoea caused by worms is markedly different from that caused by salmonella.

While you wait for the veterinary surgeon, you can help the horse by isolating it, reducing its total volume of feed by half or by not feeding it at all. Remove from its diet powdered milk, bran or succulent lucerne hay, and replace these supplements with ordinary, dust-free hay.

Allow the horse frequent small amounts of water containing electrolytes. Check the teeth and note the date when the horse was last wormed.

Assess the quality of the feed that the horse has been eating. For instance, check for mouldy hay. Reduce the horse's exercise, if it is in hard work, to a 10–minute walk morning and night. If the hard work is in the form of chasing a young filly in the next paddock up and down the fence, remove either the colt or the filly to another paddock out of sight.

• *See also* The Foal, page **152**.

DUNG EATING

Eating manure, bedding and dirt is both an unhealthy and an unpleasant habit that horses sometimes acquire.

Causes
These include poor nutrition, involving vitamin and mineral deficiencies, boredom as a result of being confined to a small stable or yard, insufficient food and lack of access to natural pasture for grazing and the presence of sweet additives in the feed, such as honey, glucose, molasses and powdered milk, which give the dung a sweetish taste.

Signs
You should be suspicious, if, when mucking out the stable or yard, you find no dung in the bedding. (Of course, keep in mind that the horse may be constipated.)

Treatment
Provide a well-balanced vitamin and mineral supplement and adequate quantities of good quality feed, and remove any sweet additives from the diet. To relieve the boredom of a stable or small yard, give the horse access to a paddock with good quality natural pasture.

If a paddock is not available, provide the horse with a hay net filled with good quality hay and freshly cut grass. Pick up and remove the dung 4 times a day. Regular worm treatment is essential.

EAR MITES

The presence of ear mites is not common. However, sometimes the signs are not obvious to the unpractised eye and the problem goes undetected for a long time.

Causes
The presence in the ears of tiny mites.

Signs
One or both ears tend to droop. The horse is often very sensitive to the touch of the hand on the ears or to the touch of the bridle as it is being put on or taken off over the ears. The horse may hold its head to one side, shake it and rub the ears on doorways, walls and fences. Wax may be discharged from the ear.

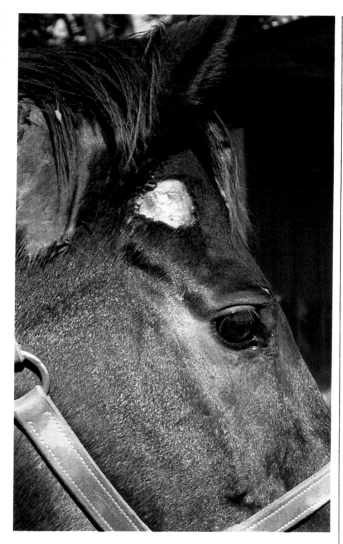

Above: Irritation by mites has made this horse rub the skin away.

Treatment
Contact a veterinary surgeon, who will examine wax from the ear canal under the microscope. Mites in the wax give a positive diagnosis. The veterinary surgeon will then prescribe the correct ear drops.

A twitch and/or tranquilliser may have to be used so that the ears can be thoroughly cleaned of all wax and the prescribed drops applied.

ENCEPHALITIS AND MENINGITIS

Encephalitis is inflammation of the brain and meningitis is inflammation of the membranes covering the surface of the brain.

Causes
These are viruses, bacteria, trauma, tumours, certain migrating parasite larvae and various poisons.

Signs
Include excitement and overreaction to normal external stimuli, followed by depression, staggering, knuckling over, walking in circles, lying down, general muscle tremor, rigidity, paddling movements of the legs, and coma.

Treatment

Call a veterinary surgeon immediately. While waiting, if possible place the horse in an area where it will cause minimal damage to itself. Provide fluids and protection from the environment (warmth or shade.) Reduce external stimuli to a minimum by keeping the noise level down and handling the horse as little as possible. Provide a bran mash to help prevent constipation.

Equine Infectious Anaemia
• *See* Anaemia, page **99**

EYE PROBLEMS AND INJURIES

Cataract

The lens is the area of the eye surrounded by the pupil. Cataract is crystalisation of the lens. The bluish cloudy appearance that the lens of the horse's eye develops with advancing age is not to be confused with a cataract.

Causes

Congenital causes, trauma, infection and chronic inflammation of the eyeball are all known causes of cataracts.

Signs

In immature cataracts, the lens is partly or wholly cloudy but allows some light to pass through it. Some sight is present. A mature cataract is dense and silvery-white and fills the entire pupil, which is usually dilated. Light cannot penetrate the opaque lens, resulting in total blindness in that eye. A cataract can form in one or both eyes.

If the horse is totally blind in both eyes, it will walk into walls and other objects, often subjecting itself to severe abrasions. A horse that is totally blind in one eye will often walk into objects on that side. When approached on its blind side, the horse will often jump with fright when touched.

A horse partially blind in one or both eyes may shy or balk at objects unnecessarily. Again, it may have difficulty in negotiating objects when the light is subdued, as it is at dusk.

Treatment

Once a cataract starts to form, treatment cannot prevent its further development. When it has reached maturity it can be removed surgically and the horse's sight is restored.

Conjunctivitis

The conjunctiva is the membrane lining the inside of the eyelids around the eye, seen when you pull the upper or lower eyelid away from the eyeball. Conjunctivitis is inflammation of the conjunctiva.

Causes

These are: the entry of foreign bodies such as chaff, dust or grit, and mud into the eye; infection, both bacterial and viral; eye injury.

Signs

The conjunctival membrane is very red and swollen and produces a discharge, varying from copious amounts of clear, watery fluid that runs down the cheek to thick, yellow-green pus that lies in the corner of the eyelids, sometimes matting them together.

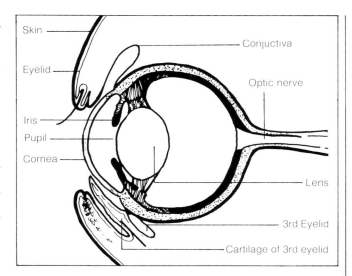

Above: A diagram of the various sections of the eye of the horse.

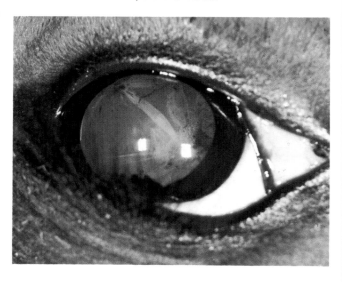

Above: This horse has a cataract. You can see the lens is cloudy.

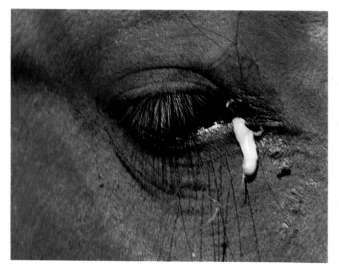

Above: A yellow-green pus discharge is a sign of conjunctivitis.

One or both eyes may be involved. If both eyes are involved, the cause is often a viral infection or allergy.

Treatment
Call a veterinary surgeon, as other complications are often associated with conunctivitis. One such complication is ulceration of the surface of the eyeball which, if incorrectly treated, may lead to a permanently damaged eye or blindness.

While waiting for the veterinary surgeon to arrive, bathe the eye for 10 minutes 4 times a day, with water that is not too hot for your hand. While bathing the eye, wipe away the discharge adhering to the eyelids. If possible, keep the horse in a dust-free environment, out of the wind and out of direct sunlight. If a foreign body is present in the conjunctiva, remove it, provided that this can be done readily. If not, leave the eye alone; you may increase the irritation of the conjunctiva and may even damage the eyeball itself.

There are numerous different types of eye ointments, all of which have a specific purpose. Eye ointments should not be used indiscriminately for conjunctivitis because some can make certain conditions worse.

Above: A corneal injury causing tears and the eye has become opaque.

Corneal Injuries

As the cornea or surface of the eye is exposed, it is more subject to injury than other parts of the eye. In many cases, injury is followed by ulceration. Blindness or poor vision in one or both eyes can make a horse dangerous to ride.

Causes
Dirt or mud may be thrown up from the hooves of a horse in front into the eyes of a horse following behind. When horses are packed up tightly in a race, one may be accidentally hit in the eye with a whip.

A horse being ridden around and between trees and bushes can be poked in the eye by a twig. When a horse is feeding, a piece of chaff can be blown into the eye. Infection can also damage the cornea.

Signs
An obvious sign is the sight of tears streaming down the cheek, and the eyelid or eyelids being partially or completely closed.

The appearance of the cornea or surface of the affected eye can vary from a dull, hazy appearance in a small area to the whole corneal surface of the eye being opaque and bluish-white in colour. A small pit, varying in depth, may be seen if the cornea is ulcerated. Often it can only be seen by a veterinary surgeon using special techniques for examining the eye. Scar formation following corneal ulceration is common. Its effect on vision depends on the size, position and thickness of the scar.

Treatment
Call your veterinary surgeon. Early veterinary treatment will help to minimise scar formation and maintain proper vision.

While waiting, bathe the eye in hot water and clean it as well as you can, using a clean wad of cotton wool soaked in water of such temperature that your hand can just tolerate the heat. Be careful to see that you do not cause any further damage to the eye while bathing it.

If a foreign body is present and can be readily removed, do so. Otherwise call the veterinary surgeon.

Remove the horse to a shaded area or darken the stable; corneal injury is very sensitive to direct sunlight. Wind, dust and flies will aggravate the problem.

Above: This horse's damaged eye has extensive scar formation.

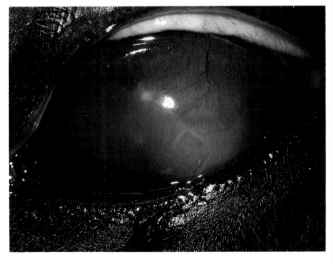

Above: This horse is suffering from an eye problem which is due to a corneal ulcer.

Entropion

Entropion is turning in of the eyelid that causes the eyelashes to rub on the surface of the eyeball (cornea), thus irritating it.

Causes
Some foals are born with this condition, often with both eyes affected. The lower eyelid is the one more commonly involved. Chronic conjunctivitis and lacerations of the eyelids can cause entropion in adult horses.

Signs
One sign is weeping of the affected eye, as evidenced by a continual wet patch below it. Partial closure of the eyelid of the affected eye or rubbing the eye to alleviate the constant irritation may be observed.

Treatment
Contact your veterinary surgeon. This condition can be successfully cured by surgery. In young foals, the affected lid may be corrected by turning out the lid 6 or more times a day and applying an eye ointment.

Fistulous Withers

Fistulas or long, pipelike, narrow-mouthed ulcers may appear on the withers as non-infected, localised swellings or as an extensive weeping infection, starting at the withers and running under the skin, sometimes along two thirds of the shoulder blade. To prevent the formation of fistulas, check that the saddle fits the withers properly. Correct saddling procedure should be followed as a matter of routine.

Causes
Infection; the bacteria found in the discharge are the same as those that cause abortion in cattle and poll evil in horses.

Trauma; in most cases, injury to the withers by the saddle precedes infection. In a few cases, however, there is no observable evidence that trauma or infection is the cause.

Signs
The disease may erupt suddenly with all the signs of acute inflammation such as swelling, heat and pain, or it may develop slowly and insidiously without any obvious signs of inflammation, the first real sign being discharge at the point of eruption.

Fistulas may develop on one side of the withers or on both and, in acute cases, the horse is stiff in its movements of the forelimbs. When the swelling erupts, the fluid is straw-coloured, and in a few days this changes to a whitish-yellow discharge of pus. The site of the eruption may dry up, heal and scar, but later another eruption will occur in a different spot on the withers.

Treatment
If a small, localised swelling develops on or near the withers, do not use a saddle on the horse until the swelling has disappeared completely and the skin has regained its toughness and elasticity. If the horse is in training, its fitness programme can be continued by lungeing, leading off a pony and swimming.

Bathe the swelling 4 times a day for 10 minutes each time, using water just hot enough for the hand to tolerate it. After bathing the swelling, apply a drawing agent such as antiphlogistine.

Above: Fly veils are a simple and inexpensive way of protecting the eyes of a horse from flies. This fly veil has dangling threads which prevent the flies from being able to collect in the corners of the eyes.

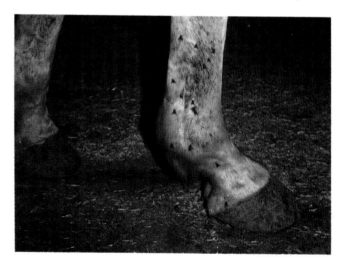

Above: This horse's leg is being attacked by flies. Stable flies are larger than house flies and have a nasty bite. They are attracted to the legs making the horse stamp its feet.

Call your veterinary surgeon, who will advise you and administer the appropriate antibiotics. He will take a swab from the discharge to identify the bacteria and to determine what antibiotic is the most effective. A lengthy course at a high level of the antibiotic is administered, as the condition is apt to recur.

If the infected area is extensive, involving sinuses running under the skin, surgical drainage as well as administration of the antibiotics is necessary.

Place water and feed containers at an appropriate height when the horse is suffering from fistulas, as some horses refuse to bend down because of the pain.

FLY IRRITATION

Causes
The flies that commonly cause irritation are the house fly and the horse fly, both of which are prolific breeders in soiled bedding and manure.

Signs
The house fly seems to be attracted to the corners of the horse's eyes, causing conjunctivitis and weeping, which in turn attracts more flies.

The horse fly is larger than the house fly and has a savage bite. It can attack the horse on any part of its body, but seems to be most attracted to the legs. When attacked by this fly, the horse becomes restless, stamps its feet, switches its tail and bites the skin on which it is being bitten by the fly if it can reach it. Raised lumps, up to 1 cm in diameter, often appear at the site of the fly bite.

Treatment
This is similar to the treatment for conjunctivitis (page **104**). The use of fly veils and fly-repellent ointment applied around the eyes are also helpful. If possible, put the horse in a stable with fly screens on windows and doors. Rug it with a fly sheet.

Fly spray and pest strips in the stable assist in reducing the fly population; spraying the horse with pyrethrum is effective for several hours. Frequent removal of soiled bedding and manure to a flyproof manure storage pit is also a preventative measure in the control of flies.

FORAGE POISONING (BOTULISM)

Botulism is the technical term for forage poisoning. It does not occur very often, as its cause (feeding on mouldy hay or chaff and on grain contaminated by vermin) is widely known and avoided.

Cause
Botulism is brought about by the ingestion of food or water contaminated by bacteria (*Clostridium botulinum*) that multiply and produce their toxin or poison.

The botulism organism is found in soil, silage and carrion. Warm, moist and poorly ventilated conditions are suitable for the growth and multiplication of the organism. The same conditions are also suitable for the growth of moulds, so that there is often an association between botulism and mouldy feed. It is therefore common sense not to use mouldy, damaged, decomposed hay, chaff or grain as feed. Feed contaminated by carrion or vermin should also be avoided.

Signs
These are difficulty in grasping food with the lips and teeth, drooling saliva, inability to drink, paralysis of the tongue, slow mastication, inability to swallow, wobbliness in the hind and forequarters and knuckling over and stumbling that precede going down.

Signs of botulism develop 5 days or more after the ingestion of the toxin. When a large amount of toxin has been ingested, the horse may be unco-ordinated for a short period and then collapse, with constant paddling movements of the limbs. Death usually follows quickly, but may be delayed up to 48 hours.

Treatment
The mortality rate from botulism is high so contact a veterinary surgeon immediately. While waiting, treat the horse for shock (see page **93**).

Vaccines are available but they are seldom used because of the infrequency of the disease in horses.

FOOT AND HOOF INJURIES
Founder (Laminitis)

The terms 'founder' and 'laminitis' are synonymous, both being used to describe inflammation of the sensitive laminae that cover the pedal bone inside the hoof. The condition can be acute or chronic and is usually confined to the front feet, although all four feet may be involved.

Causes
These include ingestion of an excessive amount of grain, particularly wheat and barley, drinking large amounts of water while still hot after exercise, ingestion of excessive amounts of lush pasture and intermittent, severe exercise on hard surfaces. Other causes are the retention of the placenta after foaling and diarrhoea and other gut disorders. Some causes are unknown.

Signs
Signs of acute founder are readily observed. The horse is reluctant to move and tends to lie down or to change its weight continually from one foot to another. If only the front feet are involved, the horse will stand with its hindlegs well up under the body and its forelegs well forward, so that as much weight as possible is taken off the front feet. If forced to move, it will shuffle along, putting the heels to the ground first.

The affected feet are hot because of the inflammation and increased arterial blood supply. The throbbing of the arteries running down either side of the pastern can be felt with slight pressure of the fingers.

The horse refuses to eat, sweats and trembles. These symptoms reflect the pain that the horse is suffering. In severe cases, its hoof or hooves may fall off.

With chronic founder, the horse is intermittently lame, putting first the heels of the affected feet to the ground. The feet are often warm, the sole is dropped and is convex instead of being concave, and ring-like impressions are present on the hoof wall. Seedy toe (see page **109**) and excessive flaking of the sole are usually present in chronic founder.

Treatment
If your horse has acute founder, contact a veterinary surgeon. While waiting for him to examine and treat the horse, you can help by removing the cause if possible. For example, if the horse has been eating an excessive amount of grain, change it to a grain-free diet.

You may cool the horse's feet in a variety of ways: by hosing them, by packing them in ice or by standing the horse in a dam, in a stream or in a wet muddy area which, if not available naturally, can be man-made.

It is a good idea to move the horse about for short periods at frequent intervals in order to stimulate circulation in the feet.

Feed the horse with a warm bran mash as a gentle laxative (see page **95**).

Some horses recover completely from acute founder, depending on its cause, its severity and the speed with which the horse is treated. If rotation of the third phalanx (pedal bone) has taken place, the chance of recovery is not good.

The treatment for chronic founder is long-term, covering the use of anti-inflammatory agents prescribed by the veterinary surgeon. It also involves corrective trimming and shoeing, whereby the heels are trimmed and rasped as much as possible with minimal or no rasping of the ground surface of the wall at the toe. A wide bar shoe is placed on the foot to protect it and to prevent further dropping of the sole, caused by downward rotation of the pedal bone.

In some cases, corrective trimming and shoeing over a long period of time can slowly but surely restore the foot to its original state.

Mud Fever

This is a dermatitis or inflammation of the skin at the back of the pastern and between the heels. It is found more frequently in the hindlimbs than the forelimbs.

Causes
Standing or exercising in wet or muddy conditions predisposes the skin to infection. The skin at the back of the pastern may be abraded by exercising on sandy surfaces or by rope burns.

If the area is constantly wet and washed with soap, it may become irritated.

Signs
The affected areas are sore to the touch. In the early stages, the skin is inflamed, after which it becomes raw and bleeds. Hair may be lost and deep cracks with thickened skin on either side may develop. In severe cases, swelling of the pastern and fetlock accompany lameness.

Treatment
Keep the horse's legs as dry as possible by reducing hosing to a minimum, by putting the horse in a well-drained, dry yard and by working it on dry surfaces.

Wipe any grit from the backs of the pasterns and from between the heels after exercise. Grit can have a very abrasive action, especially when embedded in cracks in the skin.

If the condition is old, dry and hard, apply zinc cream to soften the skin and minimise cracking. If the skin is moist and oozing, apply gentian violet to dry it out.

Leave the skin open to the air, as bandages often keep the surface moist as well as collecting grit that acts like sandpaper. If the pasterns are swollen and oozing, call a veterinary surgeon for professional advice and treatment.

Nail Pricks

Causes
When the shoeing nail is placed incorrectly on the inside of the white line or, when being driven, it crosses the white line and penetrates the sensitive tissues of the foot, the horse is referred to as having been 'pricked'.

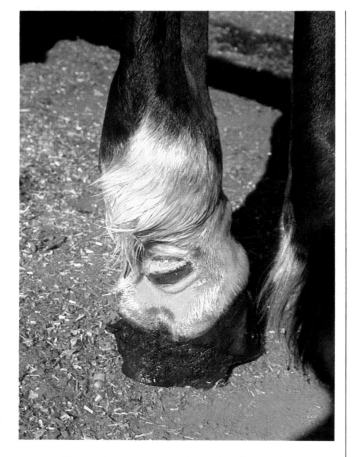

Above: A severe case of cracked heels with inflamed and broken skin.

Signs
The most obvious is mild lameness shortly after shoeing, and this generally worsens each day, so that 3–7 days after being shod, the horse is acutely lame, just touching the ground with the toe of the foot.

The hoof wall is warm to the touch and often the pastern is swollen. Severe pain is exhibited by the horse pulling the foot away when it is squeezed with hoof testers or pincers or tapped with a hammer. The pain is worse when pressure is applied over the offending nail.

Removing the shoe is often a painful procedure. Carefully examine each nail and nail hole in the hoof for moisture, blood or pus. Arteries on either side of the pastern supplying the hoof pulsate more rapidly and strongly than normally.

Treatment
Leave the shoe off. Clean around the nail hole with tincture of iodine, removing debris and dirt. With a clean hoof knife, enlarge the hole to allow for proper drainage. Soaking the hoof in hot water for 10 minutes 3 times a day aids in healing and relieving pain. The water, with a teaspoon of an iodine-based solution added, should be so hot that your hand can just tolerate it. The level of the water should not go above the coronary band of the hoof because it tends to swell and soften.

Fill the hole with a drawing agent such as magnesium sulphate paste, or paint the hole with tincture of iodine and cover the sole with Elastoplast.

The administration of antibiotics and tetanus anti-toxin by the veterinary of surgeon are necessary precautions in the treatment of puncture wounds.

Navicular Disease

The navicular bone is a boat-shaped bone lying in close proximity to the pedal bone within the hoof. It lies under the centre of the frog. Horses with navicular disease put weight on the toe to protect the frog and heel from concussion. In some cases, over a long period of time, lack of frog pressure leads to contracted heels.

Navicular disease encompasses changes in the navicular bone, navicular sac or bursa and the flexor tendon that wraps around the navicular bone and attaches to the pedal bone. The disease is almost exclusively a front limb lameness.

Causes
Inherited conformation such as short upright pasterns increases the concussion and stress on the navicular bone, bursa and deep flexor tendon. Concussion associated with hard work on hard surfaces may cause navicular disease and improper trimming and shoeing may increase the stresses placed on the navicular bone.

Signs
In the early stages, the horse sometimes exhibits slight lameness that seems to fluctuate from one front foot to the other. As the disease progresses, the horse steps short in both front legs, assuming a proppy, stilted gait, particularly at the trot. The horse will often resent trotting and try to break into a canter. When turning, rather than crossing its front legs, it will tend to shuffle around in order to lessen pressure on the navicular bone.

Treatment
Because of the difficulty of accurate diagnosis and the complexity of treatment, consult a veterinary surgeon if you suspect that your horse has this disease.

Depending on the severity of the disease, treatment can involve corrective shoeing (raised heel and rolled toe shoes), which can give good results in horses used for pleasure riding and poor results in performance horses; anti-inflammatory and anti-coagulant agents, and also more recently, a vaso-dilator drug to improve the blood supply to the leg; desensitisation of the affected part of the foot by cutting certain nerves supplying the area concerned. Whatever the treatment, the range of success varies.

Pedal Osteitis

This condition is inflammation of the pedal bone. Associated with it is demineralisation of the pedal bone and formation of a roughness on its outer edge.

Causes
These include an inherited conformation that increases the amount of concussion on the pedal bone, concussion associated with hard work on hard surfaces and poor hoof care.

Signs
This is a problem of the front feet. In the early stages, lameness is sometimes present; at other times it is absent. Sometimes one cannot tell if the disease is present in the right front leg or the left front leg. As the inflammation progresses, lameness is obvious in all gaits, and is characterised by a short step — the horse fails to stretch right out. A veterinary surgeon is essential to make a correct diagnosis with the aid of clinical examination, nerve block and X-ray.

Treatment
Consult your veterinary surgeon. Treatment and its success vary according to the severity and distribution of inflammation in the pedal bone. The treatment may involve rest, corrective shoeing, anti-inflammatory agents, a calcium supplement in diet or neurectomy (ie, denerving).

Quittor

Quittor is a chronic, purulent inflammation of the lateral cartilage in the hoof, characterised by discharge at the coronary band.

Cause
Injury near or on the coronary band covering damage to the cartilage and soft tissues in the area of the heel can cause quittor.

Other causes are a foreign body penetrating through the sole in the region of the heel, and over-reaching.

Signs
These are redness, swelling, heat and pain in the region of the heel and the associated coronary band. Discharge from small openings or cracks above the coronary band which dry up and erupt again are also signs, and so is fluctuating lameness associated with build-up of discharge.

Treatment
Contact a veterinary surgeon who will administer the appropriate antibiotics and tetanus injections. This treatment may not prove effective and complete surgical removal of the diseased cartilage may be necessary. Even this treatment may not effect a cure.

Seedy Toe

This hoof condition is characterised by separation of the wall from the sole at the toe, leaving a socket or cavity running under the wall.

Causes
These are chronic founder, poor hoof trimming and

Above: A severe case of seedy toe with the hollow cavity visible under the wall.

shoeing and a foreign body such as a small stone wedging between the wall and sole at the toe.

Signs

If the hoof wall over the seedy toe is tapped, it emits a hollow sound.

When the shoe is removed and the sole is pared back at the toe, a hollow cavity is visible, often filled with black, foul-smelling, greasy, decaying hoof.

Treatment

With a hoof knife, cut away the dead, black horn lining the cavity until you reach good healthy horn. Paint the inside of the cavity daily for 7 days with a solution containing 10 per cent formalin. Most cases that recur do so because the dead horn has not been completely cut out.

If the seedy toe is of a deep nature, call a veterinary surgeon, as antibiotics and a tetanus injection may be indicated.

Thrush

Thrush is an infection located in the grooves on either side of the frog. In more severe cases, the frog itself is involved.

Causes

Predisposing causes that provide a breeding ground for the infection are poor hoof care, particularly lack of attention to daily cleaning and hoof trimming at the time of shoeing; damp, dirty stable conditions, where the horse stands in bedding soaked with urine and manure; poorly drained yards, with the horse standing for lengthy periods in mud or in other damp and dirty places.

Signs

A foul-smelling, black tarry discharge can be seen in the grooves on either side of the frog. The horse may be lame if the sensitive tissues in the depths of the grooves are involved.

Treatment

Trim away any excess or infected frog and clean out the discharge from the grooves. If the sensitive tissues are involved, the horse will flinch or pull the foot away when you dig deeply into the grooves.

Paint the sole, including the depths of the grooves, with a solution of 10 per cent formalin. Be careful not to bring the skin into contact with formalin, as severe burning may result. Repeat the treatment daily until the condition has cleared up completely.

Contact a veterinary surgeon, as antibiotics and tetanus injections may be indicated.

Cleanliness is the keynote to the prevention of thrush. It is, therefore, very important to clean thoroughly both hoof and stable every day.

When trimming and shoeing the horse, it is essential to maintain frog contact with the ground. If this is not possible, a bar shoe should be fitted to exert pressure on the frog.

FORGING

Forging is similar to over-reaching. The toe of the hindfoot strikes the sole of the forefoot on the same side when the horse is in motion.

• *See* Corrective Shoeing, page **87**

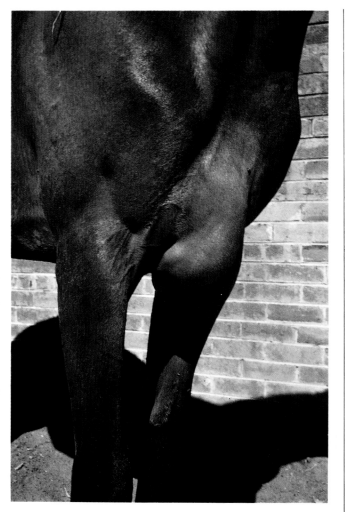

Above: A haematoma which is a large blood-filled swelling. In this case, it has formed on the horse's chest.

Founder
• *See* Foot and Hoof Injuries, page **107**

Fractures
• *See* Leg Injuries and Problems, page **117**

Galls
• *See* Leg Injuries and Problems, page **122** *and* Saddle Sore, page **129**

Getting Down Behind
• *See* Corrective Shoeing, page **87**

GLANDERS

Glanders has been eliminated in most well-developed countries, although it is still prevalent as a contagious disease in some of the less-developed parts of the world. Man is susceptible to the disease and in some cases it has proven fatal.

Cause

The bacteria *Actinobacillus mallei* is the causative agent. It can survive in water for up to 4 weeks. It is readily destroyed by dessication from the sun and by certain disinfectants such as iodine. Infection is mainly by ingestion but it may be by inhalation or by abrasion of the skin.

Signs

Horses that develop a chronic form of the disease show weight loss, nasal discharge, coughing, pneumonia, ulcerations of the nasal cavity and of the skin, often erupting on the inside of the hock. The nodules under the skin are up to 2 cm (¾ in) in diameter and discharge a honey-like pus.

Treatment

Isolate the horse or horses and contact a veterinary surgeon or appropriate authority immediately.

Glossitis

• *See* Teeth Care, page **82**

GUTTURAL POUCHES

The Eustachian tube extends for about 10 cm (4 in) from the middle ear to the throat. A section of it is distended to form a sac known as the guttural pouch. These pouches are only found in horses and other solipeds; their precise function is obscure.

Signs

The pouches can become infected or distended with air causing swelling below the ear where the head meets the neck, causing discomfort and difficulty in breathing.

Treatment

Surgery is the recommended treatment.

HAEMATOMA

This is a circumscribed swelling of variable size and position, located under the skin and containing blood.

Causes

The condition is caused by a horse running into a fence, crashing into a doorway, falling over, being kicked by another horse, or by any blow that damages the skin and underlying tissues severely enough to rupture local blood vessels. The blood leaks into the surrounding tissues, forming a haematoma.

Signs

Often the swelling is not sore to the touch. It can vary in size according to the size of the vessel ruptured and the size of the rupture itself. It is not uncommon to see a haematoma the size of a football. The swelling in the early stages is soft to the touch. If you tap it, it feels as though you are tapping a fluid-filled cavity.

Treatment

In the early formation of a haematoma, ice packs and cold hosing help stop the bleeding and reduce the swelling. If a blood-filled cavity has formed, continue applying cold foments and call a veterinary surgeon. He will usually leave the haematoma for 4–5 days before draining it. This allows the ruptured vessel to seal itself off, and also allows the bleeding to stop before the cavity is opened.

If a haematoma of any size is not opened and drained, the blood may be converted over several months into a hard fibrous swelling that will remain as a permanent blemish.

HEART PROBLEMS

The heart is a four-chambered, muscular pump, made up of special muscle fibres. The heart pumping action is controlled by electrical impulses released from a small node situated in the heart muscle, but this automatic control is overridden by other factors when a horse is excited or disturbed.

The function of the heart is simply to circulate blood to the numerous tissues and organs throughout the body. Basically, blood goes from the heart to the lungs where the red blood cells are replenished with oxygen and their waste products are removed. The oxygenated blood then goes to the tissues and organs, where it exchanges its oxygen for carbon dioxide and other waste products. It is then said to be deoxygenated blood, and is then transported back to the heart and again pumped to the lungs, where the waste products are removed and the blood is reoxygenated.

Causes

The horse may be born with a heart defect. Viruses and bacteria may also damage the heart muscle and valves. An unfit horse put into hard training too quickly or a fit horse subjected to prolonged periods of stress may also suffer a heart problem.

Signs

Symptoms of heart trouble include poor performance during preparation or training, as well as fatigue and poor exercise tolerance. The horse has laboured, rapid breathing and rapid heart rate following moderate exercise. Another sign is that respiration and heart rate take a long time to return to normal after exercise. These signs are not specific for heart disease, but you should be suspicious if your horse exhibits them.

Heart murmur, detected with a stethoscope, is associated with incomplete closure of the heart valves. When the heart muscle contracts on a supposedly closed chamber, some blood leaks through the partially closed valves, thereby reducing the cardiac output, the oxygenation of the tissues, the exercise tolerance and the performance of the horse.

Myocarditis or inflammation of the heart muscle is detected by a veterinary surgeon using an electrocardiogram, enabling him to evaluate abnormalities in the heart and to assess the heart size. It is not an uncommon condition and is seen in performance horses such as the polo, endurance, event and racehorse. In some cases, horses show signs of a good first-up performance when resuming after a rest or spell. Then the performances become progressively worse as the horse competes more and more. In other cases a horse racing over a distance of 1,200 m (6 furlongs) may be in a winning position at the 1,000 m (5 furlongs) mark and racing keenly, but in the last 200 m (furlong) it fades from a winning position to finish at the tail of the field.

Treatment

If a horse is born with a heart murmur or acquires a murmur from damage to a heart valve, no treatment is available. Most of these horses lead a normal life, but some do not. The author knows of a number of racehorses with heart murmurs that race and win.

If a horse has myocarditis, consult a veterinary surgeon who will prescribe the appropriate treatment. In training a racehorse subject to myocarditis, it is advisable to get the horse fit and at its peak a few weeks before the event, then taper the workload and keep the horse as fresh as possible with light exercise prior to the race. Space the races so that the horse has plenty of time to recover, as well as using them to help maintain the horse's fitness. If the horse requires a gallop before the race, make sure it is at least 4 days away from the event, allowing the horse and its heart muscle sufficient time to recover.

Horses with myocarditis often race better if they are nursed along during the race until 100 m (half furlong) or so from the finishing post and are then called on to make their final sprint to the line, assuming that they are within catching distance of the leaders.

They sometimes respond well to treatment and altered training methods, while other horses with myocarditis become progressively worse with more exercise and racing.

HEATSTROKE

All horses subject to strenuous exercise or exposed to very hot, humid conditions are susceptible to heatstroke. They generally recover in a few hours, though those that convulse and have a very high temperature are not likely to do so.

Causes
Strenuous exercise alone over a lengthy period of time such as during an endurance ride can cause heatstroke, as can exposure to heat wave conditions, especially without adequate shelter. Another cause is confinement in a poorly ventilated, hot stable or in a horsebox during transit. Unfit horses exercised on hot days can also develop heatstroke.

Signs
These include weakness, stumbling, refusal to move or eat, dry skin (sweating ceases), convulsions, collapse, coma, high temperature (41°C or more) and marked dilation of the blood vessels in the skin.

Treatment
Immediately place the horse in the shade and if possible in a breeze. If an electric fan is available, use it to cool the horse.

Hose the horse all over from head to foot with cold water, and provide large quantities of drinking water. Stop exercising the horse for a number of days, then gradually increase the amount of work.

Hernia
• *See* The Foal, page **151**

Infertility
• *See* Breeding, page **139**

Joint Ill
• *See* The Foal, page **153**

Kidney Disease
• *See* Spondylitis, page **131**

LAMENESS

Lameness can render the horse useless or can cause it to perform below its normal level of efficiency.

Lameness can be the result of soreness in a limb that the horse will then favour, or the result of reduced flexibility in a joint, whereby the horse's ability to stretch out is restricted.

Like humans, horses vary in their way of moving. One

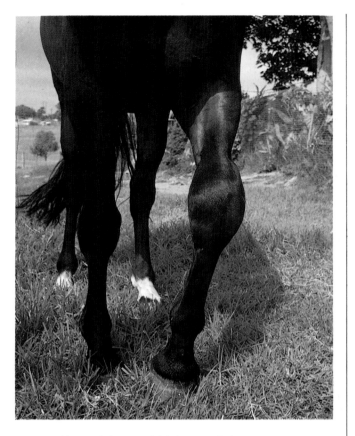

Above: A horse which is acutely lame cannot put its feet squarely on the ground.

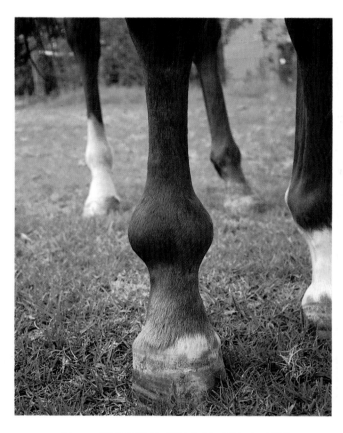

Above: This fetlock joint is severely swollen. Compare with the other legs.

breed of horse moves in a different fashion to another and within the same breed, horses move differently. The lameness of most horses is obvious, but in some cases the observer must have a certain expertise in order to make a correct judgment.

Lameness may be not only a veterinary problem; it can also involve economic and emotional problems. For instance, imagine the economic concern over a racehorse bought for £150,000 going lame just before a race in which it is the favourite, and, if successful, it will be sold for £500,000; or again imagine the upset in a family when, on the eve of a pony club camp, their child's pony is found to be very lame.

In the majority of cases, lameness is located in the forelimbs because they bear 60–65 per cent of the horse's weight as well as providing some force to assist the hindlimbs in propelling the horse forward. In most cases, too, lameness may be concentrated in the section of the leg between the foot and the knee. It is quite rare for hip and shoulder problems to cause lameness.

Causes

These are injury, infection, poor nutrition (calcium imbalance), inherited defects. Lameness can also be caused by disorders of the nervous system and disorders of the circulatory system.

Signs

These vary markedly. Lamenesss is acute when the horse cannot put its foot to the ground and sub-acute when it uses the leg but has a distinct limp. Lameness can be described as chronic if the horse is vaguely lame, if its lameness is intermittent and if it has been going on for a long time. Sometimes the horse is lame when it first walks out of the stable, but then the lameness disappears, or the lameness may only come on after work. Signs associated with lameness may also include inflammation, heat, swelling and pain on palpation, though there may also be no obvious signs in some cases. The location and causes of some lameness are readily detected; eg, there may be a nail puncture in the sole of the foot.

You can check for lameness. Always check the horse in the stable first, looking at it as it stands squarely and motionless. Check to see if it is bearing its full weight on all four legs, if it has any swellings and if there are any signs of injury such as cuts, bruises and grazes.

Ask a handler to lead the horse out of the stable so that you can examine it in motion on a hard, even surface, preferably concrete or asphalt. The handler should look straight ahead, not at the horse, so that the horse is led freely and without any interference to its straight-forward movement and head action.

Ask the handler to walk the horse away from you in a straight line for 25 m (30 yd), then turn it sharply to the left (near side) and walk it back straight towards you. Step aside to allow it to pass and to observe it from the side. Continue to watch the horse walking for 25 m then ask the handler to turn it sharply to the right (off side) and bring it back, past you.

The same procedures are repeated at the trot, then in a circle, first one way and then the other, with you standing in the centre.

Keep an eye on the horse's head because when the horse steps on the lame leg, the head goes up to help take some of the weight off it. Correspondingly, the head goes down when the good leg takes the weight. Consequently, this phenomenon is often called 'head nod associated with lameness'.

If the horse is lame in the two front or two black legs, it will have a stilted, proppy action. The length of stride may be shorter in the lame leg. This action is called 'stepping short'.

If observing a horse at the walk or trot, and if the lameness is obscure and difficult to isolate, it can often be made more apparent if a rider is placed on the horse's back. If the observer listens carefully to the sound made by the horse's hooves on a hard surface such as concrete or asphalt, an irregularity in the rhythm may indicate lameness.

Lameness can sometimes be detected by palpation. Start at the foot, feeling with your hand to detect heat, then tap gently with a hammer in various spots to detect pain. If the lameness involves the foot, remove the shoe, check the nails and nail holes and clean the foot thoroughly, looking for puncture wounds, bruising, corns and cracks. Feel the leg, particularly the joints, for swelling and heat. Then press, squeeze and bend, testing for pain and flexibility.

Treatment

If the lameness is not obvious and cannot be simply rectified, call a veterinary surgeon, as he has a detailed knowledge of the anatomy and physiology of the horse, he is experienced and has probably treated other cases similar to the one in question and he has the knowledge and equipment necessary for X-ray, hoof testing and nerve blocks.

You can help by preparing a well-organised history of the horse, covering such matters as when it was last shod, when it was last ridden, and how hard, when it became lame – before, during, or immediately after exercise, or the next day – and what kind of surface it was ridden on.

The veterinary surgeon should be called when the horse is lame, not after a week's rest when the horse is sound.

Don't call him if the horse has been treated with anti-inflammatory drugs, as these mask the lameness and make the task of diagnosis more difficult. If you are uncertain about which leg is lame, don't pretend that you know and tell the vet that it is the right foreleg. This will mean that he might waste time checking the right foreleg, when all the time the lameness may be in the near side hindleg.

Laminitis (Founder)
- *See* Foot and Hoof Injuries, page **107**

LAMPAS

Lampas is a swelling of the mucous membrane covering the hard palate behind the upper incisor teeth.

Cause

It may be associated with feeding or eruption of the permanent incisor teeth.

Signs

If the swollen membrane of the hard palate extends below the level of the tables of the incisor teeth, it may cause discomfort to the horse when feeding and consequently it may go off its feed.

Treatment

No special treatment is required. The problem will rectify itself within a few days. Any tooth irregularities in the horse should be corrected.

Leg Deformities
- *See* The Foal, page **152**

LEG INJURIES AND PROBLEMS

Bog Spavin

This is a soft, fluid-filled swelling located on the upper, inner side of the hock. It is associated with inflammation of the joint capsule. In many cases, the swelling is an unsightly blemish having little or no effect on the usefulness of the horse.

Causes
These are faulty conformation such as a straight, upright hock, which produces abnormal strain on the joint capsule, and stretching and tearing the joint capsule of the hock, as a result of a sudden, sharp movement commonly met in such activities as polo and jumping.

Signs
A soft swelling on the upper and inner side of the hock. More often than not, no heat, pain, or lameness is associated with the swelling.

Treatment
In the early phases, cold hosing, rest, immobilisation by stabling and application of a pressure bandage may be recommended. In chronic cases, treatment by a veterinary surgeon can vary from blistering to draining the fluid and injecting an anti-inflammatory agent into the joint capsule.

Bone Spavin

Bone spavin is a bony swelling on the lower, inner side of the hock, caused by arthritis of the bones in the area. Some horses with an obvious bone spavin show little or no signs of lameness; others may be very lame but with no signs of swelling. Horses with bone spavin may still be useful, but fluctuating lameness may recur at varying intervals.

Causes
In many cases, bone spavin is due to poor conformation, such as sickle and cow hocks. Despite what many people think, the condition is not hereditary. What is inherited is the poor conformation that predisposes the horse to bone spavin. The condition can also be caused by stress and strain being placed on the hock because of participation in such activities as polo, show jumping and racing, especially by young horses.

Signs
These include a hard, bony enlargement that can be felt and seen in the lower and inner side of the hock. Lameness is evident when the horse is cold but often disappears as it warms up with exercise, although in some cases the lameness may worsen. The lameness is characterised by reduced flexion of the hock and a shortening of the stride in the affected leg.

Treatment
Diagnosis initially is made from an increased severity of lameness after the hock flexion test, more commonly known as the spavin test, which is an integral part of a routine vetting for purchase by a veterinary surgeon.

The veterinary surgeon may advise any one of a number of treatments or a combination of them, if necessary. These treatments include rest in a paddock for a minimum of 6 weeks and corrective trimming and

Above: A bog spavin which is a soft swelling on the upper inner side of the hock.

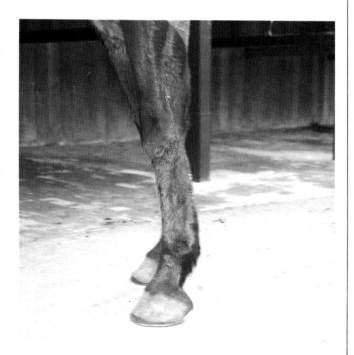

Above: A bowed tendon. The swelling due to strain makes the leg appear bow shaped.

shoeing. In the latter treatment, the toe of the foot should be rasped square and a shoe with a raised heel and a rolled square toe should be fitted. This causes the leg to move in a straight line rather than deviating outwards, thus alleviating strain on the inside of the hock.

Other treatments are radiation, anti-inflammatory agents, pin firing and surgery to sever a section of the tendon that runs over the spavin.

Bowed Tendon

Tendon is the tough, sinewy tissue that attaches muscle to bone. A tendon is made up of numerous fibrils and is surrounded by a tendinous sheath. The tendons involved in the condition known as bowded tendons are the superficial and deep flexor tendons, located in all four legs behind the cannon bone, running from knee to fetlock. The more commonly involved ones are in the front legs.

Bowed tendon is very common in racehorses, often causing premature retirement. The bow is actually caused by swelling fibrils, oozing inflammatory fluid and by capillary haemorrhage. The size of the bow varies according to the number of fibrils stretched or torn and the position of the injury. One can get some idea of the stress placed on the flexor tendons when one considers the force of the impact when the horse with a body weight of about 500 kg (1,100 lb) lands on one leg as it is galloping, say, at 60 km per hour (almost 40 mph).

Recovery from bowed tendon is more likely with modern advanced treatment. However, unless the tendon is returned to its original state, any weakness in the form of a damaged bowed tendon is likely to show under extreme stress, such as in racing.

Causes
There are many predisposing factors, including conformation (long sloping patterns), shoeing (long toe and low heel), fast gaits, forced training (unco-ordinated leg movement due to fatigue), and excessive demand (the horse at full gallop or trot is asked to give that 'little bit extra'). In addition, external damage may cause bowed tendon. It is usually brought about by a blow from another foot.

Signs
In the early stages, the symptoms are swelling, heat and pain on pressure. Depending on the number of fibrils torn in the tendon, the horse may be severely lame or it may just step short with the injured leg when made to walk. The acute signs may last for weeks, but in many cases, with time, the swelling will reduce and localise, leaving a hard, fibrous bow in the tendon.

Treatment
Contact a veterinary surgeon. While awaiting his arrival, apply cold to the swollen tendon in the form of running water from a hose for 30 minutes. The running water also has a gentle massaging effect on the tendon. Alternatively, pack ice in a towel and hold it over the swelling, or bandage it with cotton wool soaked in iced water. Following the cold treatment, wrap a cotton crepe bandage firmly and evenly around the leg from just below the knee to the fetlock joint. Leave the bandage in place unless the leg swells further and causes excessive pressure. If it does, remove the bandage and reapply.

Immobilise the horse by putting it in the stable with a deep bed of straw or other suitable bedding. If the tendon is grossly swollen, immobilise the horse further by tying

Above: A broken knee which is the term used for broken flesh not broken bones.

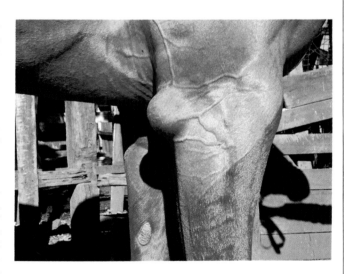
Above: A capped elbow which is a soft, fluid swelling on the point of the elbow.

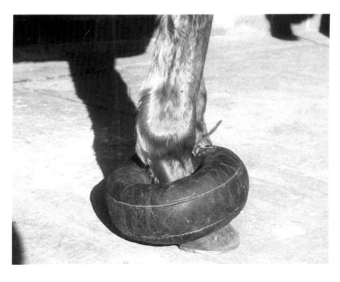
Above: This special leather roll stops the foot from hitting and damaging the elbow.

it up. Rest is most important. Do not exercise the horse, even if the swelling is only minor, until veterinary opinion has been sought.

If a farrier is available in the early phase of tendon sprain, have the horse shod with a shoe having a raised heel in order to reduce the tension on the tendons.

Most recent research advocates rest as being the most successful form of treatment. Such veterinary practices as tendon splitting and carbon filament implant can actually increase the damage to the tendon structures, and are no longer recommended.

Broken Knees

This term refers to a break in the skin over the front of the knees. This break can be anything from a slight graze to a deep wound involving the joint space. These wounds take a long time to heal, often leaving a thickened scar with telltale white hairs.

Causes
The most common cause is a fall. The horse stumbles, loses its footing and falls to its knees. Cantering on bitumen, on concrete roads, up steep, rocky inclines, or over uneven ground or fallen timber, increases the risk of a fall.

Other causes are a kick from another horse or a piece of wood that, when trodden on, flies up from the ground and hits the horse on the knee.

Signs
The hair may be removed, with the skin bruised and oozing a few beads of blood. At the other end of the scale, a large area (about 5 cm square/¾ in square) of skin and hair, including the connective tissue underneath may be gouged away, often to the point of exposing the bone, leaving raw, bleeding flesh grossly contaminated with dirt.

If the joint space is opened, a light, honey-coloured fluid may be seen seeping from the hole. Wounds involving the joint space are serious, as irreparable damage may be done, rendering the horse chronically lame.

Treatment
Regular treatment for broken knees is most important. The treatment steps are very clear: control haemorrhage, and use a hose to clean the wound of debris. Spray it with a topical antibiotic and cover the wound with a sterile gauze bandage to prevent further contamination and to control bleeding and swelling.

Call a veterinary surgeon for advice and treatment. Keep the horse confined to stable and relatively immobile, as movement slows down the healing process. Daily cold water hosing promotes healing and reduces swelling; if the wound is infected, hot bathing should precede cold hosing. Finally, pat the wound dry and apply a wound ointment (zinc cream) or antibiotic powder.

Capped Elbow

This is a swelling on the point of the elbow. In the early stages it is soft and fluid-filled, later becoming hard as the fluid is organised into fibrous tissue. A specially padded leather roll strapped around the pastern while the horse is in the stable will protect the elbow when the horse lies down. If the horse is hitting the elbow when in motion, corrective trimming and shoeing are indicated.

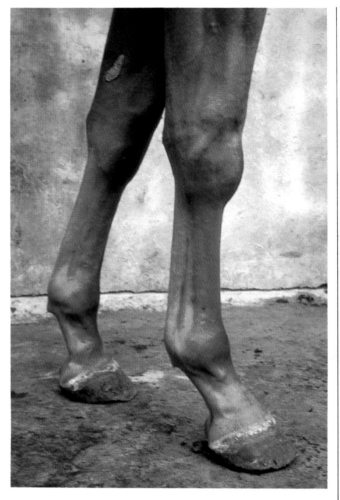

Above: A big knee – a general swelling of the knee from a blow.

Cause
When the horse is lying down with its front legs curled under, one of its front shoes may hit or press on the point of the elbow. The shoe on the foot of the affected limb of a horse with very flexible joints and a flamboyant action may also hit the point of the elbow while in motion.

Signs
A round, soft, fluid-filled swelling up to 10 cm (4 in) in diameter can be seen on the point of the elbow. In most cases the swelling is not sore to the touch and lameness, if present, is only slight and of a temporary nature.

Treatment
In the early stages, cold compresses (ice wrapped in a towel), cold hosing and reduction of exercise to walking may be sufficient to reduce the swelling. If it persists for 3 or 4 days or becomes larger, call a veterinary surgeon, who will drain the fluid and inject a drug into the lump to prevent it refilling.

Capped Hock

This is a swelling on the point of the hock. It is soft and fluid-filled, later becoming hard as the fluid is organised into fibrous tissue. To prevent capped hock, remove the horse from the stable to a yard or paddock if it is a kicker.

Causes

Horses in confined spaces such as stables, horseboxes or trailers are susceptible to capped hocks. Kicking, rubbing or striking the point of the hock against a hard object is the most common cause.

Signs

In the early stages, a round, soft, fluid-filled swelling up to 10 cm (4 in) in diameter can be seen on the point of the hock. The swelling is not sore to the touch and lameness, if present, is only slight and temporary. Old swellings are filled with fibrous tissue and are hard to the touch.

Treatment

In the early stages, cold compresses (ice wrapped in a towel), cold hosing and reduction of exercise to walking may be sufficient to reduce the swelling. If the swelling persists for 3 or 4 days or becomes larger, call a veterinary surgeon, who will drain the fluid and inject an anti-inflammatory agent into the lump to prevent it refilling with fluid.

Carpitis

This is inflammation of the knee joint.

Causes

Concussion associated with such activities as racing, polo, jumping, hunting and eventing causes carpitis; so does trauma caused by a kick from another horse, or a horse pawing at a stable door hitting the front of its knee. Forced training of immature horses and poor conformation are other causes.

Signs

The horse is lame (see Lameness, page 112). The knee generally may be swollen or the swelling may be in a localised circumscribed area of the knee. Recent swellings are soft, whereas old swellings may be very hard. The horse will show signs of pain when the knee is bent. Flexibility of the knee is restricted.

Treatment

The swelling, if soft, is due to excess production of joint fluid from the joint capsule. If hard, the swelling may be due to fibrous tissue, arthritic spurs (new bone growth) or a fracture of one of the small bones in the knee.

Call a veterinary surgeon to X-ray the knee to determine the exact cause of the swelling. Treatment may involve any one or more of the following: draining the joint, rest, injecting an anti-inflammatory agent into the joint, pressure bandage, blistering, pin firing, surgery and/or radiation therapy.

If the horse is not lame and the knee has a soft swelling, the owner should rest it for 14 days, cold hose the knee 20 minutes twice a day and apply a pressure bandage.

If the swelling is still evident or the horse is sore at the end of 2 weeks, seek the opinion of a veterinary surgeon.

Fractures

Until very recently, if a horse broke its leg, it was destroyed. With today's advancement of surgical, medical and engineering techniques, this is not the case. Most fractures encountered in the horse involve the bones of the limbs. Fractures can vary from a small chip fracture of the knee the size of a thumbnail to a completely shattered humerus or femur. To understand the causes of fractures, one needs to know something of the dynamics of locomotion.

Causes

Fractures in many cases are due to repeated concussion or to failure of synchronisation between a joint and the muscles that operate it. The forelimbs are more susceptible to concussion than the hind ones as the latter are protected by the constant flexion of the joints of the limb, particularly the stifle and hock. The forelimb from the elbow down is completely locked into a rigid rod when the horse is standing squarely on all four feet and a horse in motion bears far greater weight on the forelimbs than on the hindlimbs. The forelimbs are therefore subject to more fractures and injuries from concussion and trauma than the rear limbs since, not only do they bear the weight of the body in movement, but also aid the hindlimbs in propelling it forward.

Signs

These vary according to the size of bone fractured and the position and type of fracture. One or more of the following signs may be evident: lameness, swelling, pain, haemorrhage, anxiety, sweating, trembling, the limb hanging limply or bone protruding.

Treatment

If the horse has an obvious fracture of the lower limb, apply a splint to prevent any further damage at the site of the fracture while waiting for the veterinary surgeon. A splint can be readily made by wrapping a pillow or a roll of cotton wool around the leg with the fracture in the centre of the cotton wool or pillow. Bind the pillow or cotton wool to the leg with crepe bandages applied as tightly as possible. To add extra rigidity, a broom handle is incorporated in the bandage, with a final few layers of 8 cm (3 in) Elastoplast applied as tightly as possible. The splint not only immobilises the fracture, but also helps to relieve a certain amount of pain.

Numerous factors influence the prognosis for the

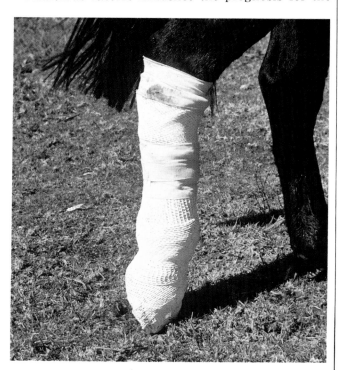

Above: A fractured leg which has been protected by a fibreglass cast.

healing of fractures. Immature horses are more likely to recover from fractures than adults. Lighter, smaller horses have a better chance of fracture healing than do the larger breeds. A quiet, docile temperament is also important. Fractures of bones that bear weight directly have a poorer prognosis than fractures of those bones that do not. Fractures of the lower limb have more chance of healing than those above the knee and hock.

Repair is brought about by what is called close reduction or open reduction. Closed reduction is the technique used to immobilise a fracture utilising material such as splints, fibreglass and plaster casts. Open reduction involves surgery, when an incision is made and the ends of the fractured bone are immobilised by the use of pins, plates, screws and wire. The metal used for these is of an inert nature so that the surrounding tissues do not reject the device. Radiographs are taken to determine what method of reduction is to be used and what type of immobilisation is to be employed.

Immobilisation of fractures in the horse poses the problem of finding materials strong and rigid enough to combat the weight and strength of the horse, as well as allowing it to remain mobile. Today, with the improvement in production of plaster and fibreglass, casts can be applied to a horse's leg under general anaesthetic that dry and develop great strength and rigidity.

For certain fractures, such as those of the sesamoid bones, splint bones, and chip fractures in the knee, surgical removal of the fragments is the best treatment.

A recent development is the immersion tank. The horse, with the fractured leg immobilised, is placed in the tank containing saline solution. Its buoyant effect provides support and immobilisation during healing.

Leg Deformities
- *See* The Foal, page **152**

Locking of the Hind Leg

This is due to luxation of the patella, where it either 1) becomes positioned on the top of the medial femoral condyle (medial luxation), or 2) dislocates laterally out of the groove (lateral luxation).

Medial luxation occurs when the patella glides upward during maximal extension and catches on the medial femoral condyle, thus causing the stifle and hock to become locked in an extended position with the fetlock flexed. Medial luxation is rare in the horse.

Lateral luxation of the patella is characterised by flexion of the stifle and hock, and the limb collapses.

Cause
This problem is seen in all breeds and is inherited.

Signs
When the stifle becomes locked, the leg assumes a fully extended position with the hoof bent backwards. When the horse is forced to move with the stiff leg, the front of the hoof drags along the ground.

The limb may remain locked in a position of extension for hours or the kneecap may be released every few steps, allowing the leg to flex (bend) suddenly. Often a snapping sound is heard as the kneecap is released.

Treatment
Contact a veterinary surgeon, but in the meantime, if the horse is backed or frightened, the kneecap will often snap into position, releasing the limb.

Surgery under local anaesthetic offers a complete and permanent cure and the results are immediate.

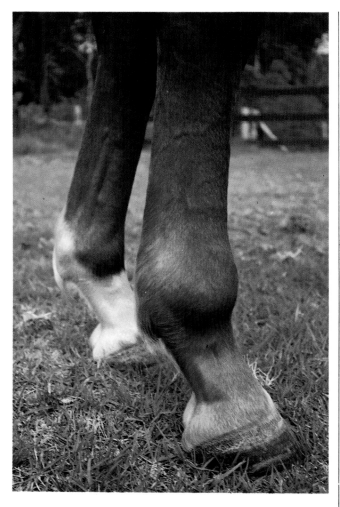

Above: An osselet which is a hard swelling just above the fetlock joint.

Above: A high ringbone can be seen above the hoof on this horse's left leg.

Osselets

This condition is most common in young racehorses, both thoroughbreds and standard breds. It is characterised by a hard swelling, often in both front legs, at the front of and just above or below the fetlock joint.

Causes
These can include subjecting immature horses to a hard training and/or racing programme or the conformation faults of short or long upright pasterns that increase the effect of the concussion on the front of the fetlock joint.

Signs
A swelling, usually hard, appears just above or below the front of the fetlock. Pain on bending the fetlock and lameness are evident. The actuall swelling may only be a thickening of the joint capsule and soft tissue, or it may be due to new bone growth.

Treatment
Rest is essential. Cold hosing and the firm application of bandages soaked in Epsom salts and iced water will help to reduce inflammation and swell. Call a veterinary surgeon, who will prescribe appropriate treatment that may involve X-ray and radiation therapy.

Preventative measures can be taken by corrective trimming of the feet of horses with long or short upright pasterns. Allow the toe to grow longer and lower the heels by trimming and rasping. Allow young horses plenty of time to mature and check the horse's diet to see that there is a correct balance in the calcium-phosphorus ratio.

Patella Locking
• *See* Locking of the Hind Leg (**opposite**)

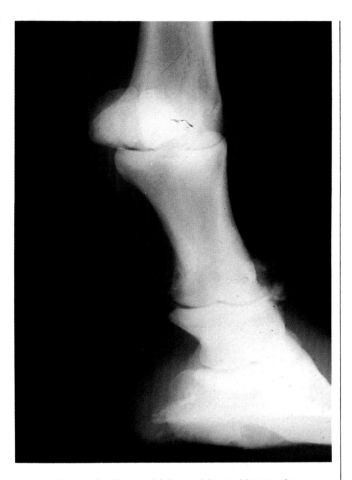

Above: An X-ray which provides evidence of a high ringbone, a swelling by the upper joint.

Ringbone

Ringbone is a bony swelling below the fetlock, usually located near the upper or lower joint of the pastern. The bony swelling near the upper joint is generally obvious to the naked eye and the average horseman thinks of it as the only kind of ringbone. In fact, there are two kinds. That just described is known as high ringbone; the other is known as low ringbone, as it is near the lower joint of the pastern, which is encased by the hoof wall. Unless the bony swelling known as low ringbone is large enough to distend the coronary band, it cannot be seen. If the joint surface is not involved, the horse may lead a useful life, even though the bony swelling may persist.

Causes
The condition is not inherited but the conformation that predisposes the horse to ringbone is inherited. Short or long upright pasterns increase the concussion impact on the bone causing an inflammatory reaction on its surface which stimulates a bony growth or swelling.

Base-wide, base-narrow, toe-in and toe-out conformation predispose one side of the pastern or the other to excessive strain, which in turn causes ligament and joint capsule strain or trearing. This sets up inflammation where the ligaments or capsule are attached to the bone, and this subsequently stimulates new bone growth.

Injury, such as a kick or blow to the pastern, can trigger off a ringbone condition. A diet low in calcium and high in phosphorus can also be a predisposing cause.

Above: The near foreleg has sesamoiditis – a swelling at the back of the fetlock.

Signs

If the ringbone is caused by injury and is seen in the early stages, there will be evidence of heat, swelling, pain on pressure and lameness. Ringbone resulting from poor conformation may develop slowly over a long period of time. Many such cases are not diagnosed until the horse shows signs of lameness. On closer examination, a bony swelling, varing in size, can be seen and felt on the pastern.

Treatment

Seek veterinary advice but, in the meantime, immobilise the affected limb with a firm pressure bandage from the hoof to just below the knee. Stop all exercise and minimise movement by confining the horse to a stable. Cold hosing and antiphlogestine poultices will help to reduce inflammation.

With the aid of an X-ray, the veterinary surgeon will vary the treatment according to the position, size and nature of the ringbone. The treatment ranges from radiation therapy to pin firing, blistering and the giving of anti-inflammatory agents.

Check the affected horse's diet and correct any calcium-phosphorus imbalance.

Sesamoiditis

Sesamoiditis is inflammation of the two sesamoid bones at the back of the fetlock joint. They act as a pulley for the flexor tendons that pass over them and provide attachment for the suspensory ligament.

Causes

The sesamoid bones are subject to a pulling effect from the ligaments attached to them. The constant pulling can aggravate the surface of the bones and set up inflammation. This can be further aggravated by conformational faults such as long, sloping pasterns or by activities such as racing, jumping and hunting.

Signs

Symptoms of sesamoiditis are lameness, swelling at the back of the fetlock and pain on the application of pressure over the sesamoid bones and on bending the fetlock joint. The only sign in some cases may be the horse stepping short. Veterinary expertise with the aid of X-rays is necessary to diagnose the problem.

Treatment

Rest and immobilisation are desirable; a pressure bandage should be applied from just below the knee to the top of the hoof. Paint the back of the fetlock joint with a cooling lotion. Trimming and rasping the hoof to shorten the toe and fitting a shoe with a raised heel tapering down to a rolled toe will help to relieve the strain on the sesamoid bones.

Consult a veterinary surgeon who, with the aid of an X-ray, will vary treatment, which may involve anti-inflammatory agents, 6 months' rest or radiation therapy.

Sore Shins

Sore shins are common among young thoroughbreds. The forelimb is the usual site; occurrence in the hindlimb is comparatively rare. The condition is caused by excessive demands on the horse to exert itself physically. Sore shins (bucked shins or metacarpal periostitis) result from tearing of the periosteum (membrane covering

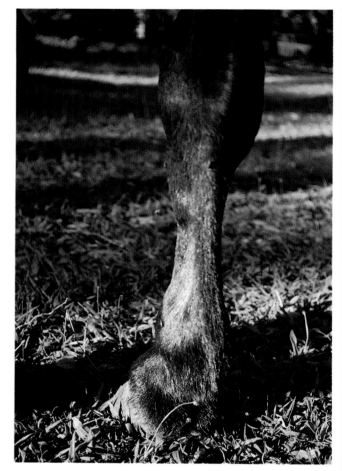

Above: A large splint can be seen on the inside of this foreleg.

bone) along the front of the metacarpal (cannon) bone.

Some trainers think that sore shins are inevitable. This idea is quite false; many cases can be avoided by paying attention to diet, foot trimming, shoeing, track surface and training methods.

Causes

Concussion is probably the most frequent cause of sore shins, particularly in young horses. The common digital extensor tendon running across the front of the cannon bone is very loosely tied down to it by fibrous bands. The periosteal attachment to the bone in young horses is immature and is therefore more readily pulled away from the bone, causing inflammation.

Injuries to the periosteum from direct trauma may also produce sore shins. Sore shins in mature horses or in one leg only is often caused by trauma, such as hitting the cannon bone on a yard rail or feed bin.

Small saucer-like and hairline fractures can be underlying causes of sore shins. These cases generally show severe inflammation, localised to a small area on the front surface of the cannon bone. All severe cases of sore shins should be X-rayed to eliminate the possibility of such fractures.

Signs

The condition is readily diagnosed, since the swelling on the front of the cannon bone is warm to the touch and painful when pressure is exerted. Lameness will increase with exercise and the stride will be characterised by a short anterior phase. If only one limb is involved, the horse will tend to rest it. If both limbs are involved, the horse will shift its weight from one to the other.

Treatment
Rest is essential if complete recovery is to occur. The use of counter-irritants, pin firing, anti-inflammatory drugs, X-ray therapy and cobalt 60 are of real value. The selection of treatment depends on the severity of the case and on the actual cause of the sore shins.

Splints

Splints, a condition mainly of young horses, most often affects the forelimbs. Splints are most commonly found on the medial (inside) aspects of the limb between the 2nd and 3rd metacarpal bones. This disease is associated with hard training, poor conformation, malnutrition or immaturity.

Causes
The concussion that results from working on hard surfaces may cause disturbance to the fibrous interosseus ligament between the 2nd and 3rd or the 3rd and 4th metacarpal bones. This disturbance may cause irritation of the periosteum, which could lead to periostitis and new bone growth, a condition commonly referred to as splints.

Splints also may be produced by trauma, resulting from blows to the outside of the limb or from interference to the inner side. Any trauma induced by slipping, running, jumping or falling may be enough to disturb the interosseus ligament before it becomes ossified.

Faulty conformation may cause splints by placing abnormal stresses on the interosseus ligaments. Deficiencies of calcium, phosphorus, vitamin A or vitamin D in the horse's diet may also predispose it to splints.

More splints occur on the medial (inner) side between the 2nd and 3rd metacarpal bones than on the lateral (outer) side between the 3rd and 4th metacarpal bones, because of the shape of the proximal ends of the bones and the fact that the 2nd metacarpal normally bears more weight.

Signs
Lameness is the most common sign in 2-year-olds undergoing heavy training, but occasionally cases occur among 3- and 4-year-olds.

Heat, pain and swelling over the affected area may occur anywhere along the length of the splint bone and more commonly at its junction with the 3rd metacarpal bone. Splint formation near the knee may cause arthritis to develop in the knee. Excessive bone growth may put pressure on the suspensory ligament and cause chronic lameness.

After the original inflammation subsides, the enlargement usually becomes smaller but firmer as a result of the ossification at the site of the swelling. In the early stages the greatest bulk of the swelling is fibrous tissue and this normally resolves to a much smaller size. The reduction in swelling is usually due to a decrease in the amount of fibrous tissue, not to a decrease in the size of the actual bone formation. Some cases of splints may never cause lameness.

Fracture of the splint bone is commonly confused with splints. Whenever one suspects splint bone fracture, X-rays should be taken by a veterinary surgeon.

Treatment
Treatment varies according to the size, position and nature of the splint. It can range from anti-inflammatory preparations to blistering, pin firing, surgical removal and cobalt treatment. In every case it is important to analyse the horse's diet and blood to determine if deficiencies exist that predispose the horse to the condition.

Prognosis is favourable in all cases except those in which the bony growth is large and encroaches on the suspensory ligament and/or the carpal knee joint.

Stringhalt

Stringhalt is observed when the horse is in motion. One or both hindlimbs are alternately raised with a high stepping, jerky, almost spastic type of movement. The condition can be mistaken for a more common one in which the kneecap becomes fixed, locking the leg (see page **118**).

Causes
This condition is uncommon and the true cause is not known, although diseases of the nervous system are implicated. In Australia, horses grazing on pastures containing the dandelion weed may develop stringhalt.

Signs
When the horse is motionless, there is no evident sign of this disease; when it moves or turns, the hindlimbs are raised alternately with a sudden high action as if the horse were reacting to a sharp pain in the foot.

Treatment
Check the pasture for dandelion weed and move the horse to a different paddock. If there is no improvement, call a veterinary surgeon, who may recommend surgical removal of a section of tendon that crosses that outside of the hock.

Swollen Legs

Swollen legs may affect horses that are in training, not training, on a high-grain diet and confined to a small stable or yard. The swelling may be in one leg or in all four, but it is more commonly seen in both hind legs. Such a condition is often referred to as 'humor'.

Above: A wind gall – a soft round swelling seen above the fetlock joint.

Cause

If infection or trauma of the limb or limbs is not obvious, lack of exercise, together with a high-grain diet leading to poor circulation of both blood and lymph in the lower limbs, are the predisposing causes.

Signs

The swelling usually involves the pastern, fetlock and either side of the flexor tendons to just below the knee. The leg may be warm to the touch but is usually not painful. When it is pressed with the finger or thumb, a temporary depression is left in the skin, indicating fluid present under the skin.

Lameness is not pronounced, though stiffness when moving may be evident.

Treatment

This involves walking and trotting exercise morning and afternoon, and hot fomentations, followed by cold hosing of the affected leg or legs for 10 minutes, morning and night.

A laxative in the form of a bran mash (see page **95**) should be given; reduce the concentrates in the diet and increase the roughage. When the horse is not in training, reduce the concentrates, particularly grain in the diet. When horses are returned from being out at grass, they should be slowly reintroduced to work and to grain in the diet.

Massage the limbs, and pressure bandage them to keep the swelling down.

Thorough Pin

This condition is a swelling of the tendon sheath near the point of hock. The distension is usually evident on both sides of the hock.

Cause

Hard work, especially in young immature horses.

Signs

The swelling is soft and mobile under the skin; in many cases, however, there is no sign of lameness.

Treatment

Treatment involves rest, cold hosing, and painting with a cooling lotion. Drainage by a veterinary surgeon is sometimes necessary.

Wind Gall

Surrounding a joint or tendon is a capsule or sheath, producing synovial fluid that acts as a lubricant. If the capsule is damaged by concussion or stretching, it produces excess synovial fluid that makes the capsule bulge and forms what is known as a wind gall.

Causes

These may be concussion or hard work that causes overextension or overflexion.

Signs

A soft, round, fluid-filled swelling about 2 cm (¾ in) in diameter most commonly appears on either side of and just above the fetlock joint. Other sites are the flexor tendon sheath above the sesamoid bones, the knee and the hock. The swelling or wind gall is not accompanied by heat, pain or lameness. Wind galls increase in size as the workload increases.

Treatment

This involves an antiphlogestine poultice, cold compresses, drainage by a veterinary surgeon and injection of an anti-inflammatory agent by a veterinary surgeon.

A true wind gall is only a blemish. If it is accompanied by lameness, heat or pain, the area should be thoroughly examined for further problems.

Lice
- *See* Skin Diseases, page **128**

Locking of the Hind Leg
- *See* Leg Injuries and Problems, page **118**

Lockjaw
- *See* Tetanus, page **132**

Mastitis
- *See* Care of the Mare after Foaling, page **149**

Melanoma
- *See* Skin Diseases, page **128**

Meningitis
- *See* Encephalitis, page **103**

Mud Fever
- *See* Foot and Hoof Injuries page **108**

Nail Pricks
- *See* Foot and Hoof Injuries, page **108**

Navicular Disease
- *See* Foot and Hoof Injuries, page **109**

Osselets
- *See* Leg Injuries and Problems, page **119**

Parrot Mouth
- *See* Congenital Peculiarities, page **26**

Patent Urachus
- *See* The Foal, page **151**

Pedal Osteitis
- *See* Foot and Hoof Injuries, page **109**

PENIS & PREPUCE INFECTIONS

The male horse's genitalia are designed anatomically so that the penis is completely enclosed by the prepuce, except when the horse urinates or becomes sexually aroused.

In its moist, warm, dark, waxy environment, with poor air circulation and numerous folds and crevices, the penis is ideally suited for the growth and proliferation of bacteria.

Causes

Poor hygiene is a primary cause of penis infections. If the penis is not cleaned regularly, scale, waxy secretions and debris accumulate in its folds and crevices and also in those of the prepuce. Foreign bodies such as grass seeds may also enter the prepuce while the horse is walking through long grass or herbage.

Signs

These are a creamy discharge from the prepuce, and irritation is indicated by rubbing or frequent dropping out of the penis. When the penis is extended, the surface is covered with heavy, waxy scales; the folds are inflamed and swollen and have an accumulation of pus. Unpleasant odour is associated with the discharge.

Treatment
Place a bucket of warm water, an anti-bacterial soap such as chlorhexidene and a clean towel nearby for use during treatment. Gently put a hand into the prepuce, take hold of the head of the penis and slowly pull it out. When it is fully extended, keep hold of it with the left hand and wash it thoroughly, removing any debris. Rinse well with clean water and dry with a clean towel. If this is not done, any soap left on the penis will act as an irritant, causing the sensitive skin to become inflamed and susceptible to infection. If the area is heavily infected, contact a veterinary surgeon, who will give an antibiotic injection.

Smear a mild antiseptic cream inside the prepuce and around the penis. In fact, about once a month, the penis should be cleaned and coated with this cream, which acts as a lubricant and reduces bacterial contamination.

PERITONITIS

The membrane lining the abdominal cavity and covering the intestine is called the peritoneum. Inflammation of this membrane is known as peritonitis. It was thought that horses were more prone to peritonitis than other animals, but this is not so. Horses have a large surface area of peritoneum so that, when they contract peritonitis, it is difficult to treat and in some cases it can be fatal.

Causes
A common cause is a sharp object such as a broken rail in a fence that may penetrate the abdominal wall when the panic-stricken horse runs into it. Horses are highly strung, some more than others, and panic when something unusual happens, such as a loud clap of thunder in an electrical storm.

Rupture of the stomach or intestines, allowing their contents to spill into the abdominal cavity, usually results in fatal peritonitis.

Signs
These are abdominal discomfort or pain, the horse's reluctance to lie down and tense abdominal muscles. Severe depression and grunting, associated with breathing or when the horse is forced to move, are also signs. Loss of appetite and weight and dehydration are also associated with peritonitis.

Treatment
Call a veterinary surgeon immediately but, while waiting for his arrival, treat the horse as you would if it were suffering from shock (see page **93**).

Many cases of peritonitis may be avoided by eliminating any sharp, protruding objects from the places where horses are stabled, paddocked, or ridden; removing foreign bodies such as baling wire, nails, etc, from the ground where horses graze; providing a systematic worming programme, as bots can cause perforation of the stomach wall.

POISONING

When a horse dies suddenly or is found dead without any obvious sign as to the cause of death, poisoning may be suspected. Poisoning can be accurately identified only by a detailed post mortem and laboratory tests on tissue samples taken from the body.

After the horse has died, the owners are often reluctant to spend money on expensive laboratory tests. Usually they readily accept an opinion that, because it died suddenly and unexpectedly, the horse died from poisoning.

Causes
These can be snakebite, plants, chemicals or insects (obviously geographic locations must be taken into consideration when determining causes of poisoning).

Signs
General signs are refusal of food, depression, dehydration, weight loss and laboured breathing.

Specific signs include swelling. If caused by a snake or insect bite, it is usually found on the legs or the head. Other signs are salivation, diarrhoea, abdominal pain, twitching muscles, hyperexcitability, wobbling, paralysis, convulsions or coma.

Individually or collectively, these signs do not conclusively indicate poisoning. Laboratory analysis of tissue samples taken at the time of post mortem are far more conclusive.

Treatment
Contact a veterinary surgeon immediately. If the poisoning is due to something ingested, give the horse 5 litres (1.3 gal US, 1 gal UK) of mineral oil by mouth while waiting, to hasten removal of the material from the intestine. Don't give the oil if the horse has diarrhoea.

If the horse is hyperexcitable, wobbly or paralysed, place plenty of straw bedding under and around it to help minimise injury. Place the horse in a dark, quiet stable.

Supply water containing electrolytes to prevent dehydration. If shock is setting in, keep the horse well rugged to provide warmth. Check the feed, pasture and water supply. If necessary, change the feed or move the horse to a different pasture.

If the horse has been bitten by a snake, the following steps should be taken quickly but calmly. Kill and keep the snake for identification. Keep the horse as quiet as possible, as movement will stimulate circulation of the poison. Apply a tourniquet above the bite very tightly for 30 minutes, then release it for 2 minutes and reapply. Do not continue with the tourniquet for longer than 3 hours.

Ask the veterinary surgeon to come to the horse. Ice pack and/or cold hose the site of the bite to reduce both the swelling and local circulation and treat the horse for shock (see page **93**).

POLL EVIL

The poll is the prominence behind the ears, indicating where the horse's spine joins the skull. Above and behind the prominence is a fluid-filled sac or bursa. If this becomes inflamed or infected and swollen, the condition is known as poll evil.

Check the headband of the bridle and headstall to see that it fits properly and that it is not causing trauma to the skin in the poll area. Make sure that there is sufficient clearance between the horse's head and roof rafters of the stable.

Causes
These are the same as those given for fistulous withers (*q.v.*). Infection can cause poll evil, as can trauma, such

as the headband of the bridle or headstall rubbing the skin or the horse rearing and hitting the back of its head against a hard object such as a roof rafter. However, in a few cases, there is no observable evidence that infection or trauma is the cause.

Signs
Signs are tenderness around the poll, which may be noticed when putting on the bridle, stiffness in any head movement, or pus discharge in the mane. A well-defined or diffuse, ill-defined swelling may be seen, painful to touch, and as a rule observed only on close inspection of the area.

Treatment
Clip all the hair well away from the swollen area so that any discharge will not mat the hair. Otherwise, treatment is the same as for fistulous withers (*q.v.*).

Proud Flesh
• *See* First Aid, page **92**

Quidding
• *See* Teeth, page **82**

Quittor
• *See* Foot and Hoof Injuries, page **109**

Rain Scald
• *See* Skin Diseases, page **129**

RESPIRATORY PROBLEMS
Broken Wind

This term is often used for horses that are roarers (see Roaring, page **125**). Technically the term refers to horses that have difficulty with expiration, ie, breathing out, especially during and after exercise. Affected horses are of little use for work.

Cause
The specific cause is not known, but it has some relation to chronic bronchitis, allergy to dust in stables, feed and over-exertion.

Signs
In most cases, they appear gradually. Exaggerated and lengthy expiration is the most prominent symptom. Exercise tolerance is poor and the difficulty in breathing is disproportionate to the amount of exercise taken. Over a period of time, respiration is difficult, even at rest, and the horse develops a barrel chest to help compensate. Wheezing associated with a short, shallow cough is evident.

Treatment
Rest in a well-ventilated, dust-free stable is effective, coupled with putting the horse out to pasture in good weather. Dampening the feed to keep the level of dust at a minimum is also necessary. However, in cases where the air sacs in the lungs have ruptured, nothing can be done.

Coughing

A cough is basically a protective mechanism to keep the breathing passages (windpipe and lungs) clear of obstructions, so that air can move in and out freely.

However, excessive coughing irritates and inflames the mucous membrane lining the respiratory tract. Horses in stables or barns are more susceptible to coughs than those in yards or paddocks, mainly because of poor ventilation. Coughing epidemics can be very costly, especially in the racing industry, where they sometimes force horses to rest for months.

Causes
These can be the presence of foreign bodies (chaff, straw, dust) in the atmosphere, bacterial or viral infection, the presence of parasites or allergy.

Signs
All the above causes irritate and inflame the mucous membrane that lines the respiratory tract. When this becomes inflamed, it secretes a copious mucous discharge and swells, setting off a cough in an attempt to expel the source of irritation. The first signs of illness may be lethargy, depressed appetite and watery nasal discharge, followed by heavy purulent discharge and a cough.

Treatment
Rug the horse well. If it has a high temperature and is sweating, a light rug is best. Make the surroundings as draught-free and dust-free as possible.

Rest the horse with minimum exercise, such as a 10-minute walk morning and night. Heavy exercise will aggravate the condition; air rushing in and out of the windpipe irritates the mucous membrane, and exercise will cause the horse's temperature to fluctuate.

A cough elixir can be used to help soothe the throat by being dribbled onto the back of the tongue with a syringe or wiped onto the base of the tongue with a wooden spoon. A nose bag or chaff bag cut to size and hung from the horse's head can be used to give it an inhalation by placing 6 drops of eucalyptus in the nose bag filled with straw.

Call your veterinary surgeon if a heavy nasal discharge is present, if the horse is off its feed and has a temperature, or if it is coughing persistently.

Antibiotics do not arrest viral infections, but in most cases a primary viral infection is accompanied by a secondary bacterial one that will respond readily to antibiotic therapy. Infection sometimes spreads to the lungs, causing pneumonia, which, if not promptly attended to by a veterinary surgeon, may damage the lung tissue sufficiently to render the horse unsound or to cause its death.

Isolate the coughing horse and remove other horses as far away as possible. Coughing is a very efficient method of spreading infection into the atmosphere in minute droplet form. Because of their size and lightness, the droplets can be carried by the wind and spread over a large area. Common areas such as barns, hosing docks, sand rolls and yards act as ideal sites for a coughing horse to spread the disease.

Thoroughly clean feed bins, water buckets, bridles, grooming equipment and the contaminated clothing and hands of attendants.

Pneumonia

This is an infection or inflammation of the lung tissue. It is often seen in foals and in debilitated, stressed, or old horses.

Causes
There are numerous causes of pneumonia, namely

viruses, bacteria, parasites or inhalation of foreign material. A stomach tube being passed incorrectly by an untrained person into the windpipe and fluid, which is poured down the tube, passing directly into the lungs, causes acute pneumonia. If the horse contracts pneumonia in this way, it usually dies or suffers permanent damage to the lung tissue, rendering it useless for riding.

There are many predisposing causes of pneumonia such as travelling, overcrowding, malnutrition and exhaustion, all of which lower the horse's resistance to infection.

Signs

The signs will vary with the suddenness of onset and the volume of lung tissue involved. Generally speaking, the horse will be off its food and lethargic. Respiration is rapid and shallow. Often a cough, nasal discharge and a high temperature are associated with pneumonia. The breath may have a foul odour and, if you place your ear to the chest, moisture may be detected as the horse breathes in and out. The horse will stand in one place, not wanting to move or to lie down. In many cases, the nostrils will be flared.

Treatment

Keep in mind that good nursing is an essential part of any treatment. Consult a veterinary surgeon immediately, because when treatment is delayed or inadequate, 50 per cent of the affected horses either die or suffer from permanent lung damage.

Place the horse in a well ventilated, draught-free stable. Keep its temperature as even as possible by rugging or by removing the rug if the temperature is very high.

Fresh water and nutritious, palatable feed should be available to encourage eating and drinking. Electrolytes in the feed or water are important to prevent dehydration. No exercise should be given for 4 weeks from the time of apparent recovery, otherwise the pneumonia could recur.

Queensland Itch

• *See* Skin Diseases, page **127**

Roaring

This is a very general term that can cover a multitude of respiratory problems.

The condition that most people mean when they mention the term 'roarer', is the peculiar noise, ranging from a whistle to a roar, that some horses make when they breathe in (inspiration). The noise is created by an obstruction to the air flow through the larynx during inspiration. The obstruction is brought about by paralysis of the muscles, usually on the left side of the larynx, causing cartilage on that side to collapse and obstruct.

The degree of noise varies in direct proportion to the degree of paralysis of the laryngeal muscles, which in turn determine the extent of the obstruction to the air flow by the laryngeal cartilage. Most horses only show signs of the noise when galloping fully extended; a minority show signs even at rest.

The obstruction to the air flow has an adverse effect on a horse's ability to perform in events where there is stress on the respiratory system. It is rare in ponies; it occurs most often in horses 16 hands or more in height and aged 3-7 years.

Causes

The primary cause is degeneration of the nerve supplying

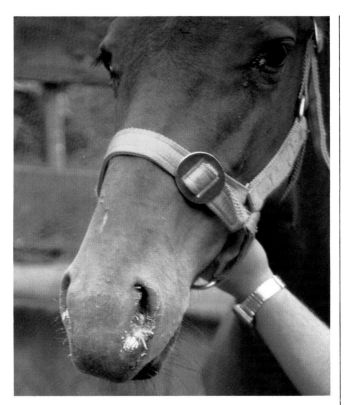

Above: This bilateral nasal discharge has been caused by strangles. Another indication of this disease is swelling of the glands.

the muscles of the larynx. The reasons given for degeneration of the nerve are numerous, and many have not been scientifically substantiated. It is known, however, that roaring is hereditary, though in itself it is not an inherited disease. The size of the horse and its conformation are inherited characteristics that can be causal factors in nerve degeneration. Respiratory viruses and infections can also cause roaring; so can moderate or heavy exercise. In particular, lengthy periods of swimming cause the horse to extend its neck, thus stretching the nerve and causing degeneration.

Signs

The most common sign is a whistle or roaring sound during heavy exercise. The horse's ability to perform is adversely affected because its air supply (oxygen) is markedly reduced.

Treatment

The success of treatment depends on the accuracy of diagnosis; an accurate diagnosis can be made only by a veterinary surgeon after giving the horse a thorough clinical examination. This includes passing up each nostril an instrument known as a rhinolaryngoscope and examining the larynx in detail.

The latest surgical technique is to pull back the collapsed laryngeal cartilage and secure it permanently in its normal position by use of a prosthesis. This technique has an 80-90 per cent success rate, reducing the noise level to normal at all paces.

Strangles

Strangles and upper respiratory *tract* viral infections

are common when many horses, especially young ones, are congregated together. It is a highly contagious, acute disease of young horses, characterised by abscess formation, especially in the submaxillary glands (under the jaw), and inflammation of the upper respiratory tract, with thick, white to yellow nasal discharge.

Causes

The organism causing strangles is a bacteria called *Streptococcus equi*, which can be found in the pus discharge from the nose or from abscesses under the jaw. The bacteria in the pus are fairly resistant to the environment and their presence in the paddocks, feed, or water troughs is a source of infection. They gain entry into the body by ingestion or inhalation.

Outbreaks of strangles occur most commonly when large numbers of horses are kept together. Many of these outbreaks are thought to be initiated by a carrier, ie, an infected horse which appears normal.

Signs

The first symptoms are loss of appetite followed by a slight cough. Within a few days, a bilateral nasal discharge develops, which becomes copious. The lymph nodes of the head and neck may become inflamed and swollen, those under the jaw being first affected. If sinusitis or inflammation of the guttural pouches develops, surgical attention may be necessary. Laryngitis may develop and lead to laryngeal hemiplegia (broken wind), if the horse is being exercised.

Strangles can spread to other parts of the body and localise in areas such as the lungs. If it does, it is referred to as 'bastard strangles'.

Treatment

Call a veterinary surgeon, who will treat the horse with antibiotics and surgically attend to any abscesses if drainage is required. While waiting for the veterinary surgeon to arrive, isolate the horse from any others and provide good general nursing. Early treatment often brings about a quick cure and prevents the spread of the disease to other parts of the body.

Vaccination is used extensively in the treatment of strangles; it was developed because recovery from strangles is usually accompanied by a lasting immunity. Old vaccines caused a tissue reaction ranging from local soreness to a large painful swelling. More recent vaccine has minimal side effects. The initial course involves 3 vaccinations given 2 weeks apart. Effective immunity is reached 2 weeks after the last vaccination.

Viral Respiratory Diseases

Equine Influenza

Also known as Newmarket Cough, Infectious Catarrh of the Upper Respiratory Tract, Infectious Equine Bronchitis.

Causes

This virus belongs to the group of myxoviruses. It is caused by influenza viruses, A-equi-1 and A-equi-2. Immunity develops to the one type only and therefore animals may contract influenza twice in one year. The virus is destroyed by heat, light, formalin, soaps and detergents.

The respiratory viruses are spread by horses coughing droplets of infected mucus which are inhaled by a healthy horse. By having heavy mucus running from the nose, horses may also contaminate the environment. A healthy horse inhales the virus as it grazes. A group of

horses will develop the same symptoms in 1–3 days because of the highly contagious nature of these viruses.

Signs

A readily observed sign of equine influenza is a dry cough, persisting sometimes for 3 weeks.

Initially, the nasal discharge is clear and watery, progressing to thick mucus. A high temperature over a 4-day period often indicates developing pneumonia. Loss of appetite, lethargy and generalised muscular weakness are consistent with viral infections. Foals and older horses or horses under stress, such as those in work or being transported, are more susceptible to viruses and secondary bacterial infections.

Treatment

Rest from work for 3 weeks is important in order to allow the mucous membrane lining the respiratory tract to heal.

Protect the horse from the environment. For instance, rug and stable it from the cold and wind; provide shade in very hot weather.

Make water available at all times and provide a high-quality, nutritous diet.

Contact your veterinary surgeon who, if a secondary bacterial infection is evident, will administer a course of antibiotics and treat the horse according to its symptoms. Isolate the horse from others. Overcrowding should be avoided.

Horses are commonly vaccinated against equine influenza in England, Ireland, Europe and the USA. Stables, including feed bins and water buckets, should be disinfected if contaminated.

Rhinopneumonitis (Equine Viral Abortion)

This was often confused with influenza until the virus was identified as Equine Herpes Virus 1. Rhinopneumonitis occurs in two forms: abortion and respiratory disease (see Viral Abortion, page **143**). It is not as contagious as influenza and causes abortion from 3 weeks to 4 months following a mild respiratory infection.

RIG (CRYPTORCHID)

A rig or cryptorchid is a male horse with one or both testicles undescended. Most foals are born with the testicles descended and present in the scrotum. If one or both have not descended and are not detectable by deep palpation of the groin by the time the horse reaches 2 years of age, it is unlikely that they will descend naturally.

Cause

This condition is inherited.

Signs

The horse exhibits the characteristics of a stallion such as crest on the neck, aggressiveness and sexual interest in mares, but if only one testicle is seen and felt in the scrotum, the horse is obviously a rig. If no testicle is evident, the horse may be a rig or an aggressive gelding. Contact a veterinary surgeon, who will examine the horse rectally. If the horse is a rig, the testicles will be located in the abdomen.

Treatment

With hormone treatment by a veterinary surgeon, the testicle or testicles may descend into the scrotum and develop to normal size.

Another form of treatment is castration. In the case of

a rig, surgery is a more complex procedure, sometimes involving the opening of the abdomen to locate and remove the undescended testicle or testicles.

The fact that this condition is inherited indicates that rigs used for breeding are likely to sire male foals that are also rigs. Breed societies should be aware of the existence of this inherited defect and discourage their members from using horses with one tesicle for breeding. Horses with both testicles undescended are generally considered to be infertile. There is a further possible danger in that a retained testicle in the abdomen may become cancerous as the horse grows older.

Ringbone
- *See* Leg Injuries and Problems, page **119**

Ringworm
- *See* Skin Diseases, page **128**

Roaring
- *See* Respiratory Problems, page **125**

Rope Burn
- *See* Skin Diseases, page **128**

Ruptured Bladder
- *See* The Foal, page **151**

Saddle Sore
- *See* Skin Diseases, page **129**

Sarcoid
- *See* Skin Diseases, page **129**

Seedy Toe
- *See* Foot and Hoof Injuries, page **109**

Septicaemia (Blood Poisoning)
- *See* The Foal, page **152**

Sesamoiditis
- *See* Leg Injuries and Problems, page **120**

Sore Shins
- *See* Leg Injuries and Problems, page **120**

SKIN DISEASES
Lice

Lice infestation is most common in late winter and early spring. There are two kinds, biting and sucking lice. The biting louse is found on the body coat, whereas the sucking louse is found in the long hair of the mane and tail. Lice are light grey in colour and 1 mm–1.5 mm in length.

The lice that infect horses cannot survive on man or other animals. Biting lice can live for 10 days in loose hair shed by the horse.

Causes
Horses are more susceptible to lice infestation if they are in poor condition, if their coat is long, unkempt and dirty and if they are kept in large numbers in a paddock. These horses are at an even higher risk during the infestation period.

Signs
These include severe irritation of the skin, accompanied by rubbing, biting, and scratching. The coat becomes dull and, as some hair falls out, the horse assumes a motley appearance. The long hair of the mane and tail also becomes matted.

Loss of condition can be considerable if infestation is heavy and the lice can be seen under good natural or artifical lighting if the hair is parted.

Treatment
Clip the horse if the body coat is long. Any loose hair should be burned. Spray the horse thoroughly with 0.1 per cent DDT, taking care to avoid the nose, eyes and mouth. The DDT treatment should be repeated 3 weeks later. As an alternative to DDT, pour Tiguvon over the horse.

To prevent lice, keep the skin and coat clean by thorough and regular grooming and isolate any infected horses.

Treat grooming gear that has been used on infected horses with a solution containing 0.1 per cent of DDT.

Brush loose hair from rugs used by infected horses. Collect and burn the hair and expose the rug to sunlight.

Stables and yards should be cleaned of loose hair left by the infected horses. All such loose hair should be burnt.

Melanoma

Melanomas are benign or malignant tumours of the skin occurring more frequently in old, grey horses. Cause is unknown.

Signs
Small 1 cm ($^3/_8$ in) to large (10 cm/4 in or more) dark lumps may be located around the anus or vulva, under the tail and occasionally on or near the eyelids.

Treatment
Depending on the tumour's size, nature, and location and the result of a biopsy, the veterinary surgeon will decide whether or not it should be excised surgically.

Queensland Itch

This disease has been recognised for years as a skin allergy to the bites of a species of sandfly. It is seasonal, occurring during the hot humid months with the highest incidence along coasts.

It is not a contagious disease so that only hypersensitive horses show signs of it.

Signs
These are itching, rubbing and biting, causing hair loss and abrasion of the skin, mainly in the areas of the ears, mane, withers and tail. The skin in long-standing cases becomes thickened, wrinkled and discoloured, with sparse hair cover.

Treatment
The sandflies are most prevalent from 4 o'clock in the afternoon to the early hours of the evening. Prevention can be achieved by insect-proof stabling or by rugging and hooding during these hours of the day. Spraying with insecticidal solutions offers some protection.

Contact a veterinary surgeon for the treatment of allergic skin reaction in some cases and for secondary infection of broken skin, caused by rubbing and biting.

Rain Scald

Some horses when exposed to the environment without shelter or protection develop this skin irritation.

Cause
Long hair on the back and croup mats together with inflammatory fluid that oozes from the skin. Some of the clumps of matted hair fall out but others, if peeled off, leave a raw, bleeding surface.

Treatment
Provide some form of protection from the elements such as a stable, shelter shed, trees or a rug. Wash the affected areas with warm water and an anti-bacterial soap, gently lifting any loose hair and scabs with your finger tips. Dry thoroughly. Groom gently and cautiously in the affected areas with a soft body bush. Apply lanolin to the exposed skin to keep it moist and supple.

Ringworm

Ringworm is a highly contagious fungal infection. It may be spread by more than one type of fungus.

Causes
Ringworm may be spread by man, for example, by the use of contaminated boots, girths, rugs, other tack and grooming gear, or by poor management in the recognition and treatment of the infection.

Direct contact is also a cause. One infected horse infects another in a paddock or in some location where body contact is possible. The disease may also be spread by indirect contact. An infected horse rubs against a fence, thereby depositing the fungi in loose hair that can infect a healthy horse if it rubs in the same place.

Flies, mosquitoes and other biting insects can be responsible for the spread of ringworm.

Signs
The common sites of infection are the head, girth and shoulders, but in some cases the site is more generalised. The lesions begin as a circular area of raised hair from 1–3 cms (⅜–1 in) in diameter. The hair becomes brittle and falls out approximately 10 days after infection. The circular clump of hair can be plucked out, leaving a moist, circular, hairless lesion, sometimes dotted with a few spots of blood.

Treatment
A horse with ringworm is usually regarded as contagious for 3 weeks from the time of infection. Thoroughly wash the infected horse daily for 3–4 minutes in an iodine-based scrub. Gently lift and remove any loose scab or crust when washing. These, along with any loose hair, should be collected and burned. After washing, dab the hairless areas with tincture of iodine.

Isolate the horse from any other non-infected horses and do not use on any healthy horse the tack or grooming gear used on the infected horse. Wipe the tack and soak the grooming gear in anti-fungal wash.

If the hairless areas are increasing in size or number, contact a veterinary surgeon. Hair regrowth may take a month or more after successful treatment.

Rope Burn

This is a common problem, associated with ropes accidentally wrapping around a lower limb.

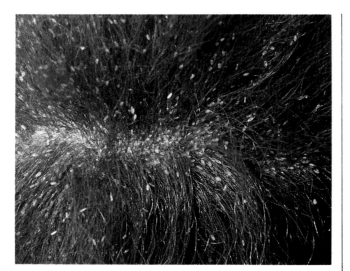

Above: Lice which can be seen sucking amongst the long hair of this horse.

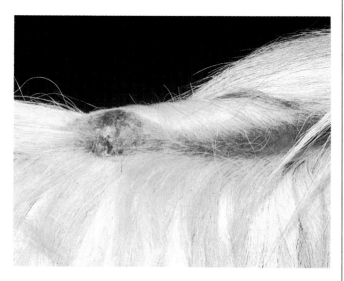

Above: A melanoma, which is a benign or malignant tumour, under the tail.

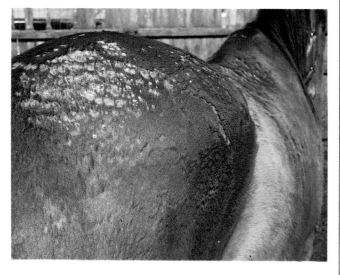

Above: Weatherbeat or rain scald along the back of this horse.

Cause

Negligence is the most common reason for a rope tangling around the limb of a horse. Never restrain a horse with rope in direct contact with the skin. When the rope tightens, the horse will always struggle, no matter how placid its temperament may be. Always use leather hobbles around the legs or, if hobbles are not available, first heavily bandage the leg in the area that the rope will pass over or around.

Signs

The most common site of the rope burn is the back of the pastern. It is interesting to note that in many cases where the hair has been removed and the skin slightly abraded, the large swelling, severe soreness and lameness that then appear are out of proportion to the extent of the abrasion. Rope burns often become infected.

Treatment

Thoroughly clean by washing the area in warm water and soap. Rinse thoroughly with cold water, pat dry and apply a drying agent such as gentian violet if the area is moist or zinc cream if it is dry.

Saddle Sore and Girth Gall

These sores develop because of excessive pressure and/or a frictional rub from the saddle or girth.

Causes

These include pressure brought about by an ill-fitting saddle, such as one with a shallow gullet being used on a horse with a high, narrow wither.

A wrong technique may be used in saddling the horse. Some signs are that the hair is turned back rather than lying flat and smooth, the saddle cloth is wrinkled or the skin under the girth is wrinkled.

Signs

The hair is rubbed off and the skin broken by constant pressure or rubbing, often leaving raw, bleeding sores that vary in size and are slow to heal.

Treatment

Rest the horse from the saddle and girth. If the horse needs exercise to maintain its fitness, this is an opportune time to lunge and swim it.

Check the saddle and girth in relation to the shape of the horse. Also check the technique of saddling.

Apply zinc cream to the sores twice a day until they show signs of drying and healing. If the sores are swollen, hot, oozing and painful, contact the veterinary surgeon. Fistulous withers may develop because of an untreated, infected saddle sore on the withers (see Fistulous Withers, page **106**).

Sarcoid

Sarcoid is a skin tumour located mainly on the head, shoulders and lower limbs, although it may appear anywhere on the body. These tumours have not been known to spread to internal organs, but because of their resistance to treatment or tendency to recur, a veterinary surgeon should be consulted.

Cause

A virus is suspected as the cause of sarcoids in horses and it may gain entry into skin that has been abraded by rubbing or by trauma.

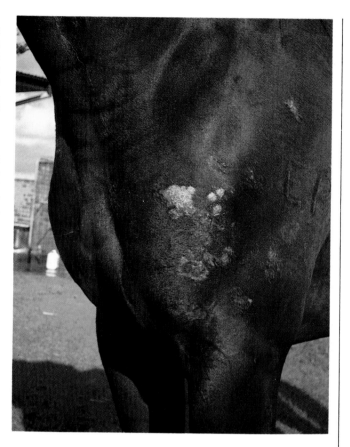

Above: One of the varieties of ringworm found this time on the shoulder.

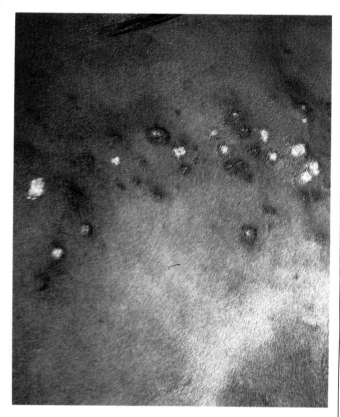

Above: Another type of ringworm and on the neck of the horse.

Signs

There may be one or several sarcoids varying in size from 1–10 cm in diameter. They are wart like in appearance; some have a thick crusty surface, others a raw ulcerated fleshy surface that bleeds freely when touched.

Treatment

If the sarcoid is small (1 cm or ⅜ in), paint it with Podophyllin, taking care not to get it on the normal skin, or severe burning will follow. Often when the sarcoid is painted with Podophyllin, it runs off the surface of the sarcoid onto the skin. As a preventative measure, smear vaseline on the skin around the sarcoid before painting it. Continue applying the paint until the sarcoid has been burned back to the level of the skin.

If the sarcoid recurs or is larger than 1 cm, contact a veterinary surgeon who may cauterise or surgically excise the lesion. Even after surgical excision, the sarcoid can recur. The only answer is further surgical excision, followed by radiation treatment.

Sunburn

Areas particularly around the head and back are susceptible to sunburn.

Causes

A number of cases of sunburn are associated with grazing on certain lush clover pastures that appear to make the skin, especially the non-pigmented areas, hypersensitive to sunlight. Non-pigmented and hairless skin, eg, on the muzzle is more easily burned by the hot sun.

Signs

Hairless, non-pigmented areas such as the nose become red, swollen, and ooze serum. The skin often peels, leaving raw, bleeding areas that are very sensitive to touch. Along the back of the horse, the serum mats with the hair, dries, hardens and peels. After a time the skin becomes dry and wrinkled with little or no hair cover.

Treatment

Provide shade in the form of a stable, shed, or trees. Horses that will not stand in the shade in a paddock should be placed in an enclosed stable. Apply zinc cream to the burned areas. It will provide a barrier against the sun as well as soothing the skin. Where the skin is not peeling, sun-screening preparations are beneficial.

If the horse is grazing on lush clover, remove it from the paddock and hand feed it with oaten hay and a small quantity of grain. If the skin over a large area has been severely burned, contact a veterinary surgeon.

Sweet Itch

This a form of eczema.

Causes

These are not fully understood but the horse develops it in the summer, especially if turned out to grass. Midges are a possible cause.

Signs

Rubbing of affected areas (usually crest, dock and sometimes withers).

Treatment

Keep the horse stabled. Consult a veterinary surgeon.

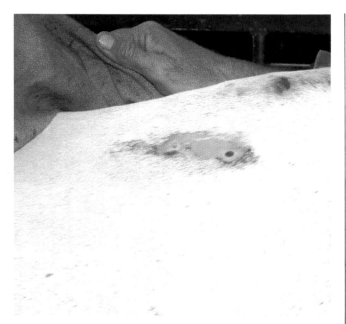

Above: A saddle sore. The saddle has rubbed the hair off a patch under the saddle.

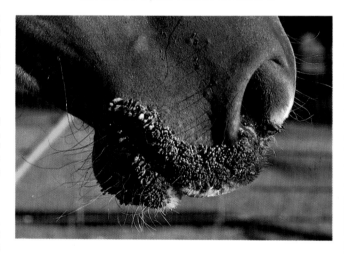

Above: One of the varieties of warts found around the mouth of the horse.

Above: Another variation of warts around and above the nostrils and mouth.

Warbles

The larvae of these flies occasionally live in horses.

Causes
Eggs laid on the horse's coat and maggots which hatch, pass into the skin and migrate through the body to eventually lie under the skin on the back.

Signs
Small bumps with a small hole through which the maggot breathes and eventually emerges.

Treatment
Do not squeeze but leave to emerge. Do not ride if under the saddle. Warm poultices help the maggots to emerge. Derris or Metriphonate can be applied.

Warts

Warts usually occur around the heads of young horses up to 3 years old. They vary greatly in number.

Cause
This is a virus that can be transmitted from one horse to another, probably gaining entry through a cut or abrasion in the skin. Biting flies may be involved.

Signs
The warts may vary in size from 2 mm–20 mm ($\frac{1}{8}$ in to 8 in) and in colour from pink to grey. The common sites are the nose, lips, eyelids and cheeks. The warts are raised with a rough, horny surface.

Treatment
The condition is self-limiting, usually regressing within 3 months. Sometimes the warts can be broken by rubbing, then they bleed and are susceptible to fly strike. In these cases, crude castor oil will eradicate them. The castor oil should be carefully applied to the wart only, not to the surrounding skin.

If warts are a problem, especially on horse studs, fences, stables, head collars and brushes should be thoroughly cleaned with a formalin solution.

Snake Bite
• *See* Poisoning, page **123**

Splints
• *See* Leg Injuries and Problems, page **121**

SPONDYLITIS

Spondylitis is an inflammation of the vertebrae, the bones that make up the spinal column. This condition is fairly common in racing horses, both thoroughbreds and standard breds. The most common site of the inflammation is the lumbar area, between the back and croup. In some horses, primarily hunters, there is involvement of the sacroiliac joint, located where the spine joins the pelvis.

Inflammation of the vertebrae over a long period of time often produces spur formations on the under edge of the vertebrae. These spurs grow towards each other, finally joining together to form a bridge. This is called ankylosing spondylitis. Once the vertebrae have ankylosed, there is a reduction of movement of flexibility in the back accompanied by a reduction in pain.

When a horse is sensitive to touch along the back or tends to half squat when running water is sprayed on the back, some trainers wrongly say that it has kidney trouble. In fact, this is very rare in horses. The cause of pain is much more likely to be spondylitis.

Causes
These include positioning of the saddle too far back; this often occurs with heavy riders. Bucking can also cause spondylitis. The head check on standard breds may be too short; the horse may carry its head high, thereby indirectly putting pressure on the lower back. Too much stress may be placed on the back of a hunter or jumper.

When a horse is galloping and the front legs are extended or stretched well forward, there is a concave effect on the lower spine. As the front and hindlimbs come together, the lower spine forms an arch or convexity. As the horse gallops, the shape of the lower spine changes constantly from concavity to convexity. This action causes inflammation of the surface of the involved vertebrae in the spine.

Signs
If you apply enough pressure to the back of any horse, it will flinch and tend to squat down, but horses with spondylitis will flinch and squat sometimes to the point of sitting like a dog, when only light pressure from the tip of a pen is run down either side of the spine.

When saddled up for riding, some horses will straighten the back and half squat or arch the back as if they are going to buck. Twitching of the tail, restlessness, laying back the ears and inability to stand still indicate pain associated with spondylitis.

Some horses show no signs of spondylitis until the rider mounts, then they half squat and often walk off in that position for half a dozen paces before straightening up.

During exercise, the horse may feel uncoordinated in the hind-quarters or may not be able to stretch out.

After work, when the horse is being hosed down, the running water from the hose played onto its back may make it squat. When you are grooming the horse, the effect of the brush on its back may also cause it to squat. However, always keep in mind that some horses with sensitive skin do not like to be groomed and react in a fashion similar to those with spondylitis.

Treatment
Rest offers immediate relief, but in many cases the symptoms recur on return to work. An alternative to rest is to give the affected horse a different training programme in which there is less pressure on the back.

Make sure the saddle fits the horse properly and is well forward, with plenty of padding underneath. If the horse is being prepared for racing, use a work rider of the lightest weight and instruct him to ride with his weight well forward.

Try to curb any bucking, shying or kicking up of the hindlegs.

Paint the muscles on both sides of the spinal column with a cooling lotion and consult a veterinary surgeon about using an anti-inflammatory agent.

Strangles
• *See* Respiratory Problems, page **125**

Stringhalt
• *See* Leg Injuries and Problems, page **121**

Sunburn
• *See* Skin Diseases, page **130**

Sweet Itch
- *See* Skin Diseases, page **130**

Swollen Legs
- *See* Leg Injuries and Problems, page **121**

TETANUS (LOCKJAW)

This disease affects all domestic animals except the cat, and is found throughout the world. It is common in horses.

Tetanus is a toxaemia or poisoning produced by the bacterial agent *Clostridium tetani*. It is characterised by spasmodic muscular contractions, resulting in death in many cases.

Cause
Clostridium tetani produces a toxin or poison that affects the nervous system. Puncture wounds of the hoof are not infrequently associated with the development of tetanus. The organism lives in the soil and horses' faeces (manure). Tetanus spores persist in the ground for a long time and are resistant to many standard disinfectants, including steam at 100° for 30 minutes to 1 hour. The entry of tetanus is usually via a deep wound. Even then, it may lie dormant for 4 months until conditions are suitable for tetanus spores to multiply and produce toxin.

Symptoms
The poison causes spasm of the muscles, resulting in stiffness and rigidity of the whole body. The third eyelids partially cover the eyes, often misleading the owner into thinking that there is something wrong with them. Muscle spasms of the head make it difficult to

This young horse has suffered from lockjaw (spasms of the head). Death occurs just 2-3 days after the display of symptoms; but the tetanus spores may have lain dormant for up to 4 months until conditions were suitable.

take food into the mouth and chew (this is known as lockjaw). The horse drools a mixture of saliva and food, sometimes misleading the owner into thinking that it is suffering from a mouth complaint. The general stiffness leads to convulsion and death in up to 80 per cent of cases. Death usually occurs 2–3 days after the onset of symptoms.

Treatment
Call a veterinary surgeon immediately. However, supportive therapy by the owner can be almost as important as veterinary treatment.

Place the horse in a quiet, dark stall, with a deep bed of straw. If possible, do not handle it. Remove any objects that could cause injury. Place feed bins and water containers at such a height that the horse does not have to bend down. Feed it bran mashes (see page **95**) to minimise the necessity to chew, as well as to prevent constipation.

Thorough Pin
- *See* Leg Injuries and Problems, page **122**

Thrush
- *See* Foot and Hoof Injuries, page **110**

THYROID GLAND ENLARGEMENT

The thyroid gland is located on either side of the upper section of the windpipe; it is only obvious when enlarged, being firm, oval-shaped and approximately 7 cm by 4 cm. It is not uncommon to find one or both sides of the thyroid gland enlarged in horses in training.

Causes
A deficiency in iodine. Iodine-deficient areas occur in Great Britain, Australia, North and South American and Europe. Horses grazing on the natural pasture and drinking the water in these areas may suffer from an iodine deficiency.

Those on high calcium or linseed meal diets cannot absorb or utilise iodine efficiently.

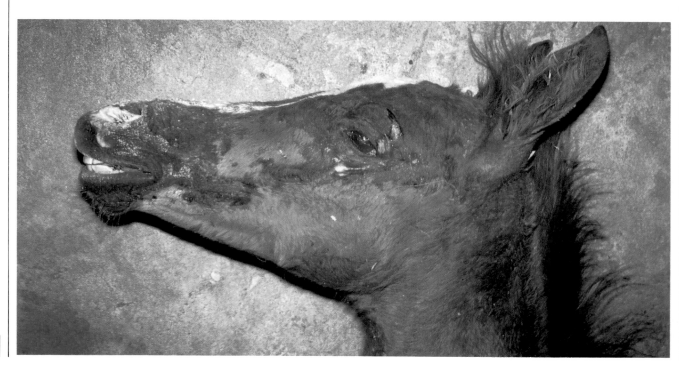

Signs

The signs of thyroid gland enlargement include a loss of condition, general weakness, decreased libido and obesity.

Treatment

A commercially prepared iodised salt or mineral supplement containing iodine fed to the horse can bring about quick remission of the signs of iodine deficiency. However, prolonged dosing or overdosing with iodine can produce a serious illness.

Use it indiscriminately but consult a veterinary surgeon for advice.

VERMINOUS ANEURYSM

An aneurysm is a localised dilation of the wall of an artery, causing the restriction of the blood flow. Aneurysms result from disease or injury.

Verminous aneurysm is the most common form of aneurysm found in the horse.

Cause

The larvae of the red worm *Strongylus vulgaris* migrate into the muscular walls of arteries, particularly the cranial mesenteric artery that supplies the intestine and the major arteries supplying the hindlimbs. The larvae set up inflammation and a fibrous swelling develops. Over a period of time, the fibrous swelling reduces the diameter of the lumen of the artery and restricts the blood flow to the intestine and/or the hindlimbs. In some cases the arterial wall becomes so thickened that the blood supply is cut off.

Signs

In an artery supplying the intestine is partially blocked, recurring bouts of spasmodic colic are the most common symptom (see Colic, page **100**).

In some cases, the arterial wall becomes so thickened that the blood supply is cut off, resulting in necrosis (death) of that portion of the intestine (bowel) supplied by that particular artery. This leads to the eventual death of the horse.

If an artery supplying the hindlimb is small and only partially blocked, the horse may be exercised for lengthy periods before lameness becomes evident. Severe lameness will occur immediately after exercise begins in cases where the lumen of the artery is blocked.

The affected leg will be cool to the touch and show little or no sign of sweating, but the rest of the body may sweat profusely. The horse will show signs of pain and anxiety. Lameness disappears with rest.

Treatment

Once a verminous aneurysm develops, no known treatment will cause it to regress. Only signs caused by the aneurysm can be treated.

Routine and correct worming procedures, especially in the case of young horses, cannot be over-emphasised in preventing the development of verminous aneurysm.

Vices
• *See* Temperament, pages **16** and **17**

Warts
• *See* Skin Diseases, page **131**

Wind Gall
• *See* Leg Injuries and Problems, page **122**

Warbles
• *See* Skin Diseases, page **131**

WOBBLES

This disease is characterised by poor co-ordination and weakness, particularly in the hindquarters. It is seen most commonly in male thoroughbreds, usually before they reach 2 years old.

Causes

It is agreed that narrowing of the canal formed by the vertebrae (bones) in the neck causes damage to the spinal cord, which in turn is responsible for the wobbler syndrome. It is not certain what causes narrowing of the canal.

The disease may be inherited. It occurs 5 times more frequently in males than in females and its incidence in thoroughbreds is far greater than in other breeds. Heavily muscled, well-developed horses appear to be affected more often than others.

Signs

Poor co-ordination, wobbling, weakness, clumsiness and not wanting to lie down or roll are the most serious signs. They may have been present at an earlier age but not recognised because in the first 12 months of life the horses are not so closely observed or handled as they are later.

The severity of signs may vary to include a horse appearing weak in the hindquarters and being poorly co-ordinated when galloping, or displaying drunken, swaying wobbling movements when being walked on a lead. The horse may go down and be unable to get up again.

The condition may remain static or progress from slight wobbling to exaggerated, drunken movements. In this advanced state, you will see the horse crashing into objects and obstacles such as doors and gateways.

The onset of signs may be slow and insidious over a period of months. In other cases, however, signs may appear within 24 hours.

The wobbler is not suitable for use as a performance horse. It is potentially dangerous to the rider and to itself, as it is prone to fall when being ridden at fast gaits.

Treatment

If you suspect your horse is a wobbler, contact a veterinary surgeon, who will conduct detailed tests and take X-rays. These tests will serve either to confirm or dispel your suspicions.

The author has heard of various types of people bringing about miraculous cures. This should not be taken seriously. In these cases, either the horses were not true wobblers to begin with or the 'permanent cure' claims are not genuine.

No treatment has proved effective, although temporary improvement has been observed in some cases after treatment.

Wobblers present their owners with an unhappy situation. Recovery is rare. Their usefulness, in terms of ability to perform, is severely restricted, and potentially wobblers are a source of danger. If they are so badly affected that they cannot fend for themselves in a paddock or are constantly injuring themselves, euthanasia should be considered.

Worms
• *See* Periodic Care, page **78** to **80**

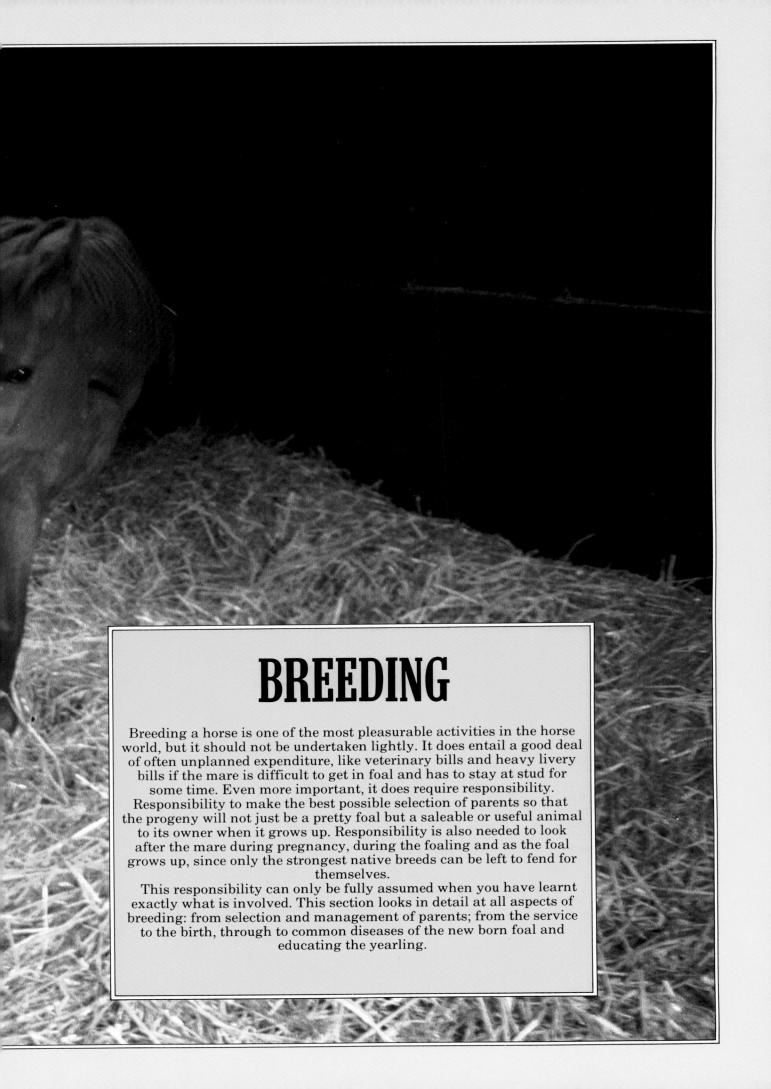

BREEDING

Breeding a horse is one of the most pleasurable activities in the horse world, but it should not be undertaken lightly. It does entail a good deal of often unplanned expenditure, like veterinary bills and heavy livery bills if the mare is difficult to get in foal and has to stay at stud for some time. Even more important, it does require responsibility. Responsibility to make the best possible selection of parents so that the progeny will not just be a pretty foal but a saleable or useful animal to its owner when it grows up. Responsibility is also needed to look after the mare during pregnancy, during the foaling and as the foal grows up, since only the strongest native breeds can be left to fend for themselves.

This responsibility can only be fully assumed when you have learnt exactly what is involved. This section looks in detail at all aspects of breeding: from selection and management of parents; from the service to the birth, through to common diseases of the new born foal and educating the yearling.

THE STALLION

SELECTION

Stud owners base their selection of a stallion on pedigree, performance, conformation, price, and, in some cases, on an intuitive liking for the horse. There is one glaring fault in this method of selection: no assessment of the stallion's fertility has been made.

Determining a stallion's fertility is no simple task. It is an extremely important one and can really be undertaken only by a veterinary surgeon who has the expertise to evaluate the stallion's penis, testicles and ability to serve, as well as having the expertise to collect semen and evaluate it. Even if the evaluation indicates the stallion to be fertile, the only conclusive proof is for it to serve a mare and produce a normal foal.

MANAGEMENT
Stabling

Each stallion should have his own large, well-constructed, well-drained, draught-free stable, if possible with direct access to a paddock. The fence around the paddock should be strong and approximately 1.8 m (6 ft) high with a laneway 3 m (9 ft) wide separating it from surrounding paddocks. This laneway prevents direct body contact with other horses through or over the fence. In this way you can reduce the risk of injury through fighting or playing.

Exercising

It is important for the stallion to be given opportunity for exercise in order to maintain the fitness necessary for an arduous stud season, which means in some cases serving up to 100 mares. Exercise can be provided by allowing the stallion free movement in his paddock, turning him loose in an indoor or enclosed school, or by lungeing or riding him. The personal contact and discipline associated with riding tends to make the stallion more tractable.

Feeding

Most stallions are overfed and under exercised. Founder, impaction colic (constipation) and lack of sexual drive can be directly related to overfeeding. The golden rule is always to give the stallion high quality feed but to regulate the quantity to the workload being undertaken.

During the stud season, depending on the size of the stallion and the number of mares served, up to 12 kg (24 lb) of grain per day can be fed. This can be reduced in the off season to approximately 4 kg (8 lb) of grain per day if the stallion is not being given daily exercise.

The stallion's vitamin A requirement is 2000 to 5000 i.u. per day per 50 kg (100 lb) of body weight, and its vitamin E requirement is 20 i.u. per 50 kg (100 lb) of body weight.

Vaccination

All stallions should be vaccinated annually against tetanus and influenza.

Stallions should have their teeth checked and their feet trimmed regularly. They should also be wormed and botted regularly.

Training

The inexperienced stallion should undergo training before the stud season begins by serving him first with older, quieter and experienced mares that are definitely in season and readily accept the advances of the young stallion. It may take the young, inexperienced stallion half an hour to mount the mare successfuly and this may be achieved only after a number of awkward attempts. Do not rush the stallion in his foreplay with the mare, and familiarise him with the hygiene procedures such as washing his penis after service.

Handling

If possible, the stallion should always be handled by the same person so that horse and handler become accustomed to one another and develop a mutual sense of trust and security.

INFERTILITY

There is no more costly and bitter disappointment than to come face to face with the reality that the stallion, which you so 'carefully' selected, is infertile.

Infertility in the stallion is an extremely complex problem. In its broad sense, it may mean that the horse is unable to produce sperm, or that it can produce sperm which for one reason or another, such as CEM, renders the mare infertile.

Contagious equine metritis (CEM) affects the fertility of stallions without exhibiting any symptoms. CEM does not cause infertility in the stallion, but, by being a carrier, the horse can cause infertility in the mare that it serves. The bacteria live in the folds and crevices of the penis and prepuce. They can be spread from stallion to stallion if the handler touches the penis of an infected stallion then touches the penis of another stallion with contaminated hands, or if the equipment used to wash the infected stallion's penis after service is used again to wash another stallion's penis. Finally, CEM can be spread from the infected stallion to the mare at the time of service or by the handler handling the penis of the stallion and then touching the genitals of the mare with contaminated hands.

Before the start of the stud season, a veterinary surgeon should swab the penis and prepuce of all stallions and teasers on the stud for bacteriological examination. A series of 3 swabs have to be taken at intervals of not less than 2 days apart before a definite diagnosis can be given.

Because of the highly infectious nature of CEM, all stud personnel should handle only the external genitalia of mares and stallions, wearing disposable gloves.

All equipment, such as that used to wash the stallion's penis, should be thoroughly disinfected with chlorhexidine solution after the service.

It is also advisable to consult a veterinary surgeon if there is an infertility problem, as the stallion can be successfully treated with a complex course of antibiotics.

The Role of Nutrition

Overfeeding can lead to fat stallions, some of which become sexually lazy. Fat, overfed stallions may also contract laminitis (founder). Vitamin A deficiency can impair semen production and Vitamin E deficiency can be related to lack of libido and poor sperm quality. However, very little information is available on the relationship between nutrition and fertility in the stallion.

Psychological Problems

Masturbation is not an uncommon problem in stallions and is sometimes reflected in lack of libido and poor quality semen. To prevent masturbation, a stallion ring is fitted onto the flaccid penis, the head of which stops the ring from slipping off. It is important that the ring fits snugly but not too tightly, otherwise the blood circulation to the head of the penis may be impaired, with disastrous results.

Some stallions are selective about the mares they serve. They may reject one mare because of her colour, size, age, or some other factor that is not obvious to the handler and 5 minutes later, they may accept and serve another mare vigorously.

Below: Stallions are more spirited than mares and geldings and need skilled handling.

Genetic Problems

Small testicles that are hard on palpation may be fairly inactive, leading to poor quality semen and lack of libido.

Sometimes a horse may have testicles that have failed to descend (cryptorchidism). This type of horse cannot be used as a stallion because he is sterile.

The monorchid is the horse with only one testicle descended. He should not be used as a stallion, even though he is fertile, because the condition is thought to be hereditary. This recommendation would still apply even if the other testicle, through the use of hormones, could be made to descend and develop.

Hormonal Problems

Lack of libido or sexual drive in old stallions or overused stallions late in the season, or in others for unknown reasons, can be given hormone treatment with varying degrees of success. Prolonged use of hormones may eventually cause a reduction in the size of the testicles, resulting in permanent low libido.

THE MARE

REPRODUCTIVE CYCLE

Mares are seasonal breeders. The length of their heat, season or oestrus cycle can vary from short and intense to long and less intense, from regular to irregular or to no obvious cycle at all.

The mare's heat, season or oestrus period lasts for 5 or 6 days, then for the following 15 days there is no obvious sign of oestrus; a 21-day cycle. In the last 24–48 hours of oestrus, ovulation takes place. The 15-day period, where there is no oestrus, is known as dioestrus.

The regularity of the mare's reproductive cycle is affected by length of daylight hours, nutrition and temperature, as well as by other climatic and environmental factors. During the late autumn and winter months, the mare shows very little or no ovulation activity and subsequently does not exhibit any signs of oestrus behaviour. The mare is then said to be in a state of anoestrus. Spring heralds the increase in daylight hours and in nutrition which cause the hypothalamus to release a hormone stimulating the pituitary gland in the brain, to produce and release two hormones. These are follicle stimulating hormone (FSH), which causes follicle development in the ovaries. As the follicle develops, the mare exhibits signs of oestrus. The luteinising hormone (LH) causes rupture of the mature follicle and release of the egg, with the mare going off heat. If the egg is not fertilised, the mare will remain off heat or in a state of dioestrus for approximately 15 days.

The most important external stimulus to ovarian activity and ovulation is the length of daylight hours.

Oestrus is best determined by the stallion or teaser.

The mare in oestrus is generally attracted towards the stallion and accepts his advances. She does not kick, lower her ears nor attempt to bite. She elevates her tail, urinates and squats slightly to spread her legs, with protrusion of the clitoris.

The veterinary surgeon can help not only in helping to confirm oestrus but also to assess the particular stage of oestrus and time of ovulation. However, he does not replace the role of the teaser or stallion.

Visual examination during heat reveals a change in the colour of the vaginal mucous membrane, relaxation of cervix and labia, increased mucoid secretion from the vagina and oedema of the mucous membrane. These changes become more marked at the time of ovulation.

Rectal examination can determine ovarian activity, such as number of follicles, their shape, size, development and consistency.

The dioestrus phase is characterised by non-acceptance of the stallion or teaser, indicated by such actions as biting, kicking, laying back of ears, trying to get away and squealing. There are corresponding changes in the ovaries, uterus, cervix and vagina which are obvious with rectal and visual examination.

When ovulation occurs, the ruptured follicle collapses and fills with blood to form into the corpus luteum, a hard lump on the ovary that can be palpated about 48 hours after ovulation. The corpus luteum produces a hormone that prepares the lining of the uterus to accept a fertilised egg. If the egg is not fertilised, the corpus luteum will regress and at the end of 14 days will be non-existent as the mare comes in season again.

The mare's gestation period lasts for 342 days on average (it can be 10 days more or less).

Above: This photograph shows a mare in oestrus: she is attracted towards the stallion. She elevates her tail and the clitoris protrudes.

Above: The mare is now squatting slightly to spread her legs. This shows that she is ready to accept the advances of the stallion.

RELATIONSHIP OF OESTRUS, OVARIAN ACTIVITY AND ENVIRONMENTAL FACTORS

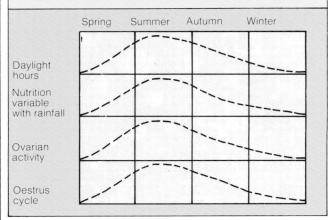

Above: This diagram shows the relationship between ovarian activity and various climatic and environmental factors. In late autumn and winter, there is little ovulation activity and consequently no signs of oestrus behaviour.

INFERTILITY

One of the greatest disappointments that a brood mare owner faces is to hear that his mare has failed to become pregnant or is infertile. About 25 per cent of thoroughbred brood mares do not become pregnant in any one stud season.

Such a state leads us to the question: why is such a large percentage of mares infertile in any season? The answer is that the causes of infertility are numerous and complex and often impossible to track down with certainty. The following factors are generally the causes of infertility, either individually or in various combinations.

Infection

The most common cause of infertility in the mare is infection. Many mares harbour bacteria in the reproductive tract; some are apparently harmless and others are known to be harmful or pathogenic. The latter are known to cause infection of the uterus.

Contagious equine metritis (CEM) is a highly contagious infection of the uterus, caused by bacteria that have been isolated in England, France, Ireland, USA and Australia. CEM can affect stallions without their exhibiting any symptoms.

Mares suspected of being infected should be swabbed by a veterinary surgeon and, if the results are positive, the veterinary surgeon can treat the mare with antibiotics. However, treatment is not always successful.

Most studs require that mares should be swabbed before visiting the stallions, and this will not only identify infected mares but also the symptomless carriers. Consult a veterinary surgeon about this matter, as the swabbing technique is complex. Bacteria can lodge in some areas of the reproductive tract and be absent from other areas. A set of swabs are taken from a number of areas on two separate occasions at different stages of the heat cycle.

Blood testing for CEM is reliable in mares 19–40 days after infection with the CEM bacteria.

All stud personnel should wear disposable gloves when handling the external genitalia of mares and stallions. Any equipment that comes into contact with the genitalia should be thoroughly disinfected with chlorhexidine or a similar solution.

Other bacterial infections of the uterus (metritis) can cause infertility in the mare. Positive identification of infected mares is made by a veterinary surgeon clinically examining the mares' reproductive tracts and by swabbing. Swabs can be taken routinely from every mare when in season or when suspected of being infected. A mare may have contracted bacterial infection if pus discharges from the vagina, she comes on heat earlier than expected, she returns to service for the second or third time or she is old with a poor breeding history.

Following the results of swabbing, an infected mare is treated by a veterinary surgeon with the appropriate antibiotics at the correct stage of the oestrus cycle.

Structural Defects in the Vulva

Windsucking through the vagina can be a common cause of infertility in the mare. It is most commonly seen in mares that have had numerous foals, causing loss of tone in the lips of the vulva, or those with a sunken anus and a vulva that slopes downwards and outwards.

Mares with this problem should have the lips of their vagina stitched together by a veterinary surgeon, allowing sufficient room at the lower end of the vulva for the mare to urinate. Such an operation is called Caslick's operation. Racing fillies with poor conformation of the vulva benefit from this surgical procedure.

Hormonal Imbalance

The normal reproductive cycle of the mare is best determined by the teaser or the stallion. The veterinary surgeon can help to confirm the stages of oestrus.

During the normal breeding season, the mare may not be coming in season regularly, 'showing' obviously to the teaser, or failing to show signs of heat. The mare may be on heat or in season continually or be showing irregular heat cycles.

If any of these factors is obvious, the mare should be examined by a veterinary surgeon to establish whether or not she has a hormonal abnormality. If she has, she may be successfully treated with hormone therapy.

Nutritional Factors

As the mare approaches the stud season, she should be steadily gaining weight. Overfat mares or mares in very poor condition have a greater tendency to suffer infertility problems.

Psychological Problems

The mare may not exhibit signs of oestrus (heat) because she dislikes the colour of the teaser or is in a strange environment. Again, this may be because she is anxious about her newborn foal or is worried about her separation from another mare with which she has a strong relationship. Whatever psychological factors may be causing the mare's infertility, steps may be taken to counteract them once they have been identified.

Strange as it may seem, it is a fact that psychological factors may be the cause of infertility.

SERVING OR MATING

This section is concerned only with hand serving. Today this form of serving is necessary in most cases to minimise the chance of injury or infection to the valuable stallion or mare. If the use of the stallion is restricted to serving those mares that are at the optimum time for becoming pregnant, it is reasonable to assume that the stallion will successfully serve a larger number of mares than would otherwise be the case.

Serving Area

The area should be quiet so that neither stallion nor mare is disturbed prior to or during mating.

The yard or breeding barn should be big enough to allow sufficient separation of the mare from the stallion if the mare violently objects to being served.

The serving area should only be used for that purpose and should be kept clean to minimise infection. It should be close to the stallion yard and to the area where the mares are teased and checked to ascertain if they are in season and ready to be served.

The surface of the serving area should allow the stallion to get plenty of traction when mounting the mare.

Preparing the Mare

The mare is washed with warm, soapy water around the genitalia and rinsed thoroughly with fresh water, as soap is spermicidal. The tail is wrapped and the lips of the vagina are checked to see if they have been stitched together. It is most important to remove any stitches so that the lips are parted, otherwise damage and tearing can occur at the time of service. If the mare has a foal at foot, the foal should be confined in a safe position where the mare can see it and vice versa. The mare is hobbled and is sometimes twitched and held so that there is no possibility of injury to the stallion.

The Service

The stallion is led into the serving yard and allowed to approach the mare while still on the lead. He smells the external genitalia and flanks of the mare, extends his neck, curls the upper lip and nibbles the mare gently on the back and neck.

With his penis erect, the stallion mounts the mare; she tends to squat slightly and moves her tail to one side. After ejaculation, the stallion dismounts with penis still extended. For hygienic reasons, the penis is dipped into a container of diluted Hibiclens or some such preparation and then rinsed in water.

ARTIFICAL INSEMINATION

Artifical insemination has aroused mixed feelings in equine circles. The term refers to a technique whereby semen is collected from the stallion by the use of an artifical vagina and then inseminated into mares that are on season and about to ovulate.

The aim of an artifical insemination programme at any stud is to get the maximum number of mares pregnant in the shortest possible time during the breeding season, subsequently reducing costs and other overheads as well as concentrating the foaling season into a shorter time and breading earlier foals.

The advantages of artifical breeding are many and

Above: A mare being covered by a stallion with one assistant holding her head, and the other controlling the stallion.

varied. Any injuries that might occur to stallion or mare during mating are avoided, and artifical breeding increases the number of mares a stallion can impregnate. A normal ejaculate of semen can be divided into 20 or more doses, each capable of producing pregnancy in a suitable mare. Artifical insemination eliminates the spread of various highly contagious diseases such as contagious equine metritis (CEM), which is spread venereally from stallion to mare or mare to stallion. Careful evaluation of semen by a veterinary surgeon will ensure whether or not it is free from harmful bacteria. It prevents overuse of the stallion, and more effective use can be made of old stallions or stallions that find difficulty in mounting the mare. Artifical insemination also allows for regular evaluation of semen quality by the veterinary surgeon, thus providing opportunity for early diagnosis of fertility problems.

A number of complex procedures must be taken if an artifical insemination programme is to be completed successfully. These include collection, evaluation and preparation of semen, evaluation of the mare's heat cycle and recognition of ovulation, assessment of the mare's health and suitability and the insemination of the mare.

The services of a veterinary surgeon are essential to ensure maximum reproductive efficiency in an artifical breeding programme.

There is a newer and more reliable pregnancy test which is coming into general use, and that is the ultrasound scan (see opposite).

PREGNANCY DIAGNOSIS

There are several reasons why an owner and stud master wish to know as soon as possible whether a mare is pregnant; owner interest and financial return, costs and maximum use of stallion are some. Another very important reason is that, if the mare is not pregnant, she can be examined to see if there is any problem and can be teased and served at the next appropriate time. Of course the owner and stud manager will also be anxious to see if the mare maintains her pregnancy for the full term.

There are three traditional types of pregnancy test. The rectal examination is the most accurate of these three, provided that proper facilities, such as a crush and a good handler, are available. If they are not, for safety reasons the veterinary surgeon may use the blood or the urine test, though these are generally recognised as being less accurate.

Rectal Examination

The degree of accuracy varies with the time at which the test is done. At 30 days after the mare has been served, the rectal examination is about 90 per cent accurate; at 42 days or more, the test should be 100 per cent accurate. To maintain such a percentage accuracy, it is important that both the mare and examiner feel secure, safe and relaxed.

Examination can be carried out by means of a crush. A simple one that suits most breeds and types of horses is 2.5 m long by 1.3 m high and 0.75 m wide (8.2 × 4.2 × 2.4 ft), open at both ends. It is made out of heavy smooth timber. Once the mare is in the crush, rails are secured in front and behind her so that backward and forward movement is prevented and the examiner is protected from being kicked.

The examination of mares over stable doors or while wearing service hobbles is fraught with danger to the veterinary surgeon, making it difficult for him to test the mare accurately.

A well-lubricated, gloved hand is gently eased through the anus into the rectum. Faeces in the rectum are emptied to enable the examiner to palpate the uterus carefully through the wall of the rectum, ascertaining whether the mare is pregnant.

As already stated, it is important for the mare to be handled firmly yet gently so that she feels secure and relaxed while in the crush and during the examination. If she is tense or fidgeting, examination is more difficult as well as being dangerous for the mare.

A small percentage of mares strain vigorously during rectal examination, causing damage to the rectum. This may be as serious as perforation and subsequent peritonitis.

Experience, and the small amount of research work that has been done, seems to support the theory that pregnancy testing by rectal palpation is a negligibly contributing factor to abortion.

The advantages of rectal examination are several. It gives immediate results, it differentiates between a single foal or twins, and if the mare is pregnant, a certificate can be issued 42 days after service. If the mare is not pregnant, the examination can be continued at the same time to try and establish why not. This examination should be 100 per cent accurate after 42 days (allow for human error).

Blood Tests

These are generally carried out by means of the A-Z Test and MIP Test Kit. However, they are useful only between the 40th and 110th days of pregnancy, as in that period the pregnant mare produces a hormone that is found circulating in the bloodstream.

If the test is negative, the result is highly accurate; if positive, the result indicates very accurately that the

Above: A specially constructed pen giving little room for the mares to move and so making it easier for rectal examinations.

mare is pregnant or has been pregnant for 40 days or more but may have aborted before the test was taken. In short, a positive result does not indicate that the mare is still carrying the foal.

Another blood test can be carried out at the 20th day of pregnancy to evaluate progesterone levels. Mares with low levels of progesterone can be accurately evaluated as not being pregnant; mares with high levels are very likely to be pregnant.

Urine Test

This test is useful only from 120–300 days after conception. It is not widely used.

Ultrasonics

Diagnostic ultrasonic is playing an increasingly important role in equine medicine, especially in the examination of the female reproductive tract.

A probe (transducer) is passed per rectum and scanned over the uterus and ovaries. The transducer emits and then receives the echoes from high frequency sound waves. The pattern of the reflection of the echoes depends on the density of the tissues being penetrated. This information appears on a TV monitor or an oscilloscope as a true-to-life, two-dimensional picture (known as real time) of the structures being scanned. The procedure does not harm either the mare or the developing pregnancy.

Pregnancy can be detected as early as 14 days from ovulation. From around 24 days, the developing foal can be seen and from 35 days a heart beat can sometimes be seen.

As well as enabling accurate early diagnosis of pregnancy, this method is especially helpful in the early diagnosis of twins. It is also useful in the diagnosis of some uterine and ovarian diseases.

THE PREGNANT MARE

Management of a pregnant mare is important, and it may include the following.

Stitching

If the mare is known to suck air into the vagina, if she has tears from previous foalings that cause the lips of the vagina to hang open or if her vulva in shape and position is in poor relationship to her anus, she may easily develop infection due to faecal particles, dirt and other foreign material entering the vagina.

Following service by a stallion, mares in this category should have the lips of their vagina (vulva) stitched together by a veterinary surgeon, allowing sufficient room at the lower end of the vulva for the mare to urinate. This is known as Caslick's operation.

Abortion

Some mares continually abort (slip) in the early stages of pregnancy. If the cause is narrowed down to hormone deficiency, the mare may be given a hormone injection to help maintain satisfactory hormone levels.

Teeth

The teeth should be examined once the mare has been certified pregnant, to ensure that she can cope with grazing in the paddock or with hand feeding.

Feet

Hoof trimming is advisable to reduce the risk of lameness, especially in the heavily pregnant mare. If the feet are neglected and become broken and infected, causing the mare to lie down, the pregnancy can become complicated.

Nutrition

The volume of food during the first two-thirds of pregnancy need not be markedly increased. However, it is important to see that ample quality food is available in the last 3 months of pregnancy to satisfy the demands of the rapidly growing foetus. As the 3 months prior to foaling coincide with poorer quality winter pasture, feed often needs to be supplemented. For good foetal development, it is important that there is no nutritional deficiency. A well-balanced vitamin-mineral supplement in addition to good quality pasture, hays and grains is essential.

Worming

The mare should be wormed regularly every 2 months during pregnancy, the final worming taking place 1 month before foaling. It is desirable for the veterinary surgeon to be engaged for the worming programme as some preparations may cause abortion, especially in the last 3 months of pregnancy. Any preparation containing the organo-phosphate compounds should not be used in the last 3 months of pregnancy.

The purpose of a worming programme is to free the mare of any worm burden during pregnancy so that her energies are concentrated on the developing foal in her uterus. A further purpose is to prevent the mare passing on worms to her foal via eggs in her droppings.

Vaccination

Mares should be vaccinated in the last month of pregnancy with tetanus and, in areas where the disease is common, the strangles vaccine.

The tetanus vaccine is extremely helpful if, at the time of birth, the vagina and/or vulva is torn, thus exposing the mare to the danger of tetanus. Furthermore, the immunity developed by the mare is passed onto the foal through the colostrum (see Immediate Care of the Newborn Foal, page **150**) giving the foal immunity to tetanus and strangles for an average period of 6 weeks and in some cases up to 16 weeks after birth.

Exercise

For about the first 6 months of pregnancy, the mare should be given light exercise to maintain her muscle tone and to prevent her from becoming overweight. Overfat mares may have trouble in foaling. In the last 3 months of pregnancy, the mare should be placed in a paddock with plenty of room so that she can exercise naturally at will.

ABORTION

Abortion refers to the abnormal expulsion of a foetus, dead or alive, from first month to the full term of pregnancy.

Abortion cannot be substantiated in the first month or 30 days of pregnancy because it is difficult to diagnose accurately that the mare is pregnant. If the developing embryo dies, it is generally reabsorbed by the mare rather than being expelled.

Above: A mare which has had the lips of the vulva stitched together by a veterinary surgeon following service by a stallion.

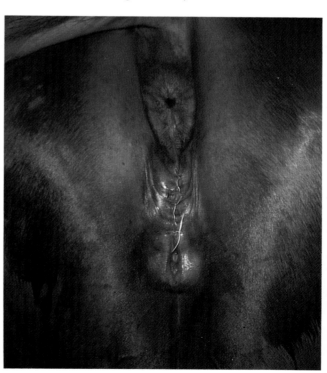

If your mare aborts, other mares in the paddock or yard where the abortion occurred should be moved to an isolated, empty paddock. The mare, the foetus and the foetal membranes should *not* be moved. A veterinary surgeon should be called to do a post mortem and to take tissue samples and a cervical swab from the mare for laboratory examination. The remains of the foal and membranes should be burned or buried. The mare should be isolated, preferably in a stall that can be disinfected at a later date. She should be kept isolated until the results of the laboratory tests are known; generally 2 weeks. The general area where the abortion took place should be disinfected with Hibitane or a similar preparation. Any staff who handle the mare or aborted foetus should thoroughly wash their hands, disinfect their boots and change their clothes before handling other horses, especially pregnant mares.

CAUSES OF ABORTION

Viral Abortion

A virus in the mare may cause abortion, usually in the last half of pregnancy, the birth of stillborn foals, or deaths in the foals within 3 days of birth.

Generally the mare catches the virus and the symptoms evident are those of a cold or respiratory disease. All horses are susceptible to this virus and they spread the disease by coughing, sneezing or leaving deposits of nasal discharge in the environment.

After the initial outbreak, weanlings are most susceptible and could be future carriers. It is therefore advisable to keep weanlings in a paddock some distance away from brood mares. After abortion due to the viral disease, immunity develops naturally.

To prevent viral abortion, run pregnant mares in

small groups to minimise the chance of the disease spreading. Reduce the movement of mares from stud to stud. Mares on known infected properties should be left there. If moved, they should be isolated on arrival at the next property and kept in isolation until they have foaled. Keep weanlings and yearlings as far away from pregnant mares as possible.

Bacterial Abortion

Bacteria are easier to identify than viruses and do not spread as readily. They also respond more quickly to treatment with antibiotics and, provided all necessary steps and precautions are taken, some bacterial abortions can be prevented.

Twinning Abortion

The idea of your mare having twins sounds marvellous but in most instances it is a disaster. Two per cent of abortions in Australian thoroughbreds are due to twinning. Usually one foetus develops more rapidly, progressively assuming the major portion of the blood supply and the other foetus dies. The death of one foetus results in the abortion of both. Abortion is most common between the fifth and ninth months. Mares with a history of producing twins should be examined by a veterinary surgeon when they are in season and before being served in order to evaluate the number and size of follicles on the ovaries. If there are two large follicles of similar size, do not serve the mare until one follicle is distinctly larger and more mature than the other.

Hormonal Abortion

Mares that have a history of aborting which is unrelated to infection or other known causes are suspected of a hormonal imbalance. Judicious use of progesterone helps maintain many of these pregnancies for the full term.

Above: Abortion is a serious problem in breeding. This foetus was aborted about twenty six weeks after conception.

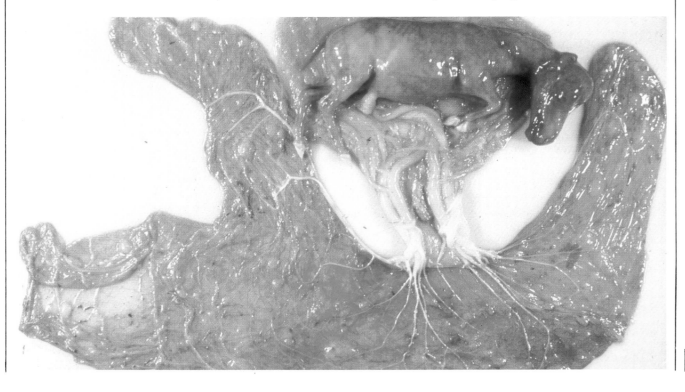

FOALING

An owner witnessing the birth of his first foal may be distressed or disturbed by the mare's strenuous labour or by the sight of the afterbirth dangling from the vulva. However, any such feeling will be minimal if it is kept in mind that these situations are facets of the natural, normal process of birth.

Precautions

Precautions that you should take at least 2 weeks before the anticipated birth of the foal are to inform the veterinary surgeon of the approximate birth time so that he will be available if called, and to provide a suitable environment for the birth; warm comfortable and isolated from the other animals. The best is a disinfected box or stall about 3.5 m (11.5 ft) square, adjacent to a yard. The walls of the box should be free from nails and other dangerous extrusions; the floor should have a deep bed of clean, long straw. If the box is not available, a small, level, grassy paddock is adequate.

Store the necessary equipment to help in the birth near the foaling site. The equipment should include tincture of iodine, cotton wool, clean towelling, two buckets for hot water and disinfectant.

Signs that Mare is going to Foal

Some mares may show all the signs outlined below; others will only show one or two. Some mares have been known to show none of these signs and to go straight into Stage 1 of foaling.

An electronic device, recently developed in Australia, is attached to the mare's head collar, emitting a beep. When the mare lies down to foal, the device is activated by contacting the ground. A receiver in the stud manager's room picks up a signal, alerting him to the fact that the mare is foaling.

Waxing Up
About 50 per cent of mares produce a waxlike secretion on their teats about 2-4 days before foaling.

Bagging Up
The udder will become noticeably larger about 2-6 weeks before foaling. It is often the case that some hours before foaling, mares will be seen to have milk dripping from their teats.

Muscle Shrinkage
This takes place on both sides of the croup and causes grooves to appear, which are more evident in some mares than in others. It usually appears about 7-10 days before foaling.

Irritability
The mare becomes tense or irritable. If she is in a paddock, the mare will often seek a quiet area away from other animals.

NORMAL LABOUR

It should be kept in mind at all times that the mare is an individual and may not follow precisely the normal labour pattern outlined below.

Stage 1

Foaling generally takes place during the night and about 80 per cent of foals are born between 11 pm and 1 am. The first signs of foaling are usually sweating and restless or agitated movements such as pawing the ground, stretching, swishing the tail or lying down and getting up.

No visible straining is evident.

The placenta ruptures and fluid slightly darker than urine gushes from the vagina, whether the mare is lying down or standing up. If she is standing up, the fluid may be mistaken for urine.

Below: One of the signs that the mare is going to foal is bagging-up when the udder enlarges about 2-6 weeks before foaling.

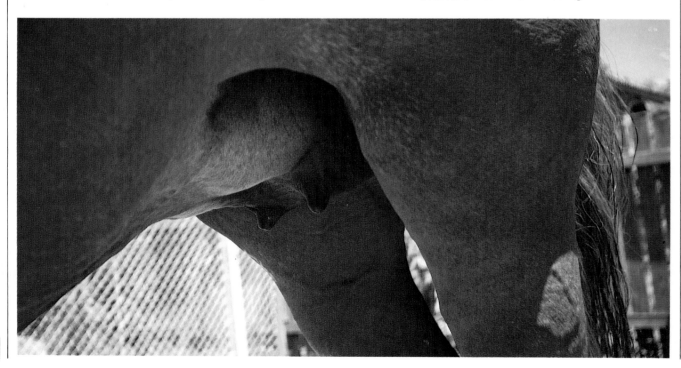

Stage 2

Characteristics of the beginnings of this stage are that the mare lies down, visible straining is evident and the foetal membrane appears. In straining, the mare may change her position from lying on her side with legs fully extended, to sitting.

With straining, the membrane enclosing the foetus, ie, the amnion, appears at the vulva.

The amnion is rather like a bluish-white plastic bag lining the placenta and enveloping the foetus; when ruptured, it discharges about 5 litres (1.3 gal US, 1 gal UK) of yellowish fluid. Not infrequently, the amnion ruptures before appearing at the vulva.

As the amnion appears at the vulva, the foal's front feet also appear, either having pushed through the amnion or being enveloped by it. One front foot leads the other by about 15 cm (6 in).

If the mare is lying down, the soles of the foal's feet should face the mare's feet, and if the mare is standing up, the foal's feet should face the ground. At this point, the mare may stand then lie down again to give a number of powerful expulsive contractions. Between these contractions, she rests for about 3 minutes. Some onlookers become alarmed at this phase, but there is no need to be worried; this is the mare's normal, natural response.

The powerful contractions are generally associated with the appearance of the head through the vulva, resting on the forelegs and followed by the shoulders and chest. The rest of the body follows with comparative ease and the birth is over within 20 minutes or so. The mare and foal take a well-deserved rest for about 30 minutes.

The hindlegs of the foal may remain in the vagina during the rest period but they are dislodged in a natural way by the subsequent movement of the foal and/or mare. The mare's movement is usually to sit up and look at her foal.

If the straining and contractions are excessively long with no appearance of the foal, the advice of the veterinary surgeon should be sought.

Above: This is the start of the foaling. The foal's leading foreleg can be seen surrounded by the amnion and the foot is correctly facing the ground, so it is not a breech birth.

Below: The mare is now lying down, and the two front legs of the foal have now emerged and can be very clearly seen.

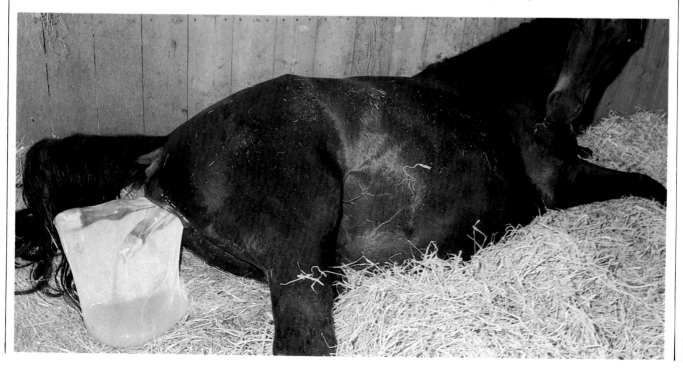

Stage 3

When the head of the foal appears, remove immediately any foetal membrane that may be obstructing the nostrils so that the foal can breathe freely.

The umbilical cord is intact when the foal is born. It is important to allow it to remain thus for as long as possible in order to effect a complete transfer of blood from placenta to foal. The umbilical cord will break naturally about 5–8 cm (2–3 in) from the foal's navel when it struggles to rise, or when the mare gets to its feet.

Thoroughly swab the stump of the cord with tincture of iodine. The stump will dry out and drop off in 2–3 weeks, leaving the foal with a neat navel.

Within about 3 hours after foaling, the mare will expel the placental membrane, or afterbirth as it is commonly called. It is normal for the afterbirth to hang from the mare's vulva for up to about 8 hours.

Spread out the afterbirth on the ground for examination. If it is intact or all there, all is well; if it is not, some of it has probably been left in the mare and veterinary advice should be sought. Never remove the placenta by force.

The foal makes a number of awkward movements to get on its feet and, when reasonably steady on its legs, will seek its first drink within an hour of being born. By about the same time, the mare is on her feet, usually licking and nuzzling the foal and thereby establishing and enjoying her role as mother.

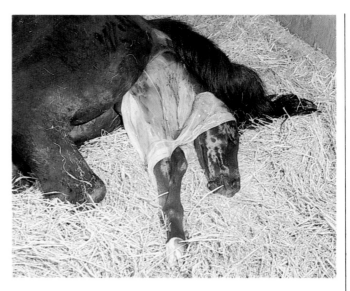

Above: The foal has broken through the water bag and the head as well as the fore limbs can now be seen.

Below: Practically all of the foal's body has now emerged. It is this stage which marks the end of the most strenuous part of the foaling sequence.

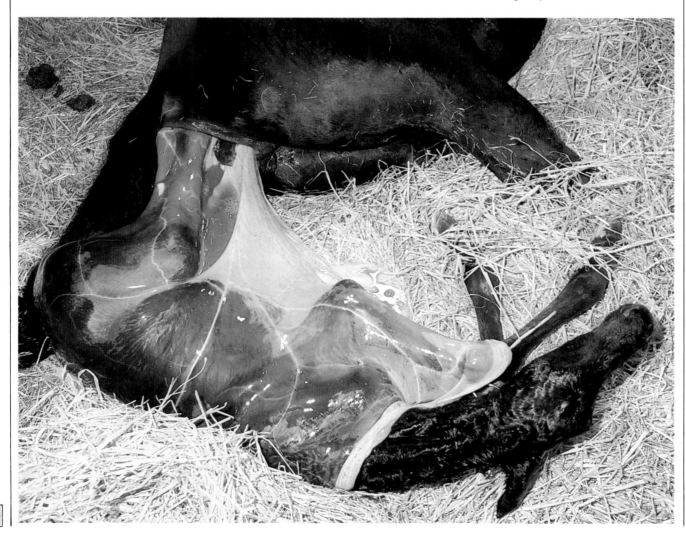

Above: At last, after all the hard work, the first moments of that wonderful encounter between the mare and her newly born foal. Both appear to be in good health.

Below: It is usually considered wisest to leave the mare and foal as quiet as possible after the birth and only rub dry the foal if the weather is very cold or the foal weak.

ABNORMAL LABOUR

The mare's labour usually proceeds without a hitch, but sometimes complications occur. If they do, it is important to recognise them as early as possible and to take quick, knowledgeable action so that any danger to the life of mare and foal is minimised. In such situations, the wisest course to follow is to seek the help of a veterinary surgeon immediately. When complications become apparent, some competent owners and observers assist with the birth and cope successfully. However, there are always some people who do not cope, and who either worsen the complications or create others.

Foal Present at the Vulva

If the competent owner or observer decides to examine the foal presented at the vulva, certain precautions should first be taken. The hands and arms should be scrubbed thoroughly and a surgical glove, if available, should be worn. The area around the mare's anus and vulva should be washed down with a non-irritant antiseptic.

If the presentation is normal, the hand inside the vagina should be able to feel the head (mouth, muzzle and eyes) lying on top of both forelegs. One foreleg is slightly in front of the other; the soles of the forefeet face the ground if the mare is standing up and face the back of her legs if she is lying down.

Whether such examination reveals the normal presentation as just described or an abnormal one, if the foal is not expelled, action must be taken.

If there is normal straining and normal presentation but the foal is not expelled, take hold of both the foal's forelegs and gently but firmly pull downwards and outwards to assist the passage. If there is no change, call the veterinary surgeon.

Sometimes only one leg is presented. However, before you put your hand and arm into the vagina to search for the other leg, make sure that they have been scrubbed with a non-irritant disinfectant and lubricated as it is necessary to prevent tissue damage and infection that endanger the lives of mare and foal.

The foal's elbow may be caught on the brim of the mare's pelvis. In this case, that leg need only be pulled out to bring it almost level with the one in a normal position. This action lifts the foal's elbow over the rim of the pelvis, thus allowing free passage of the foal.

Feel gently inside the vagina for the leg because, if the mucous membrane around the foal is irritated, it can swell rapidly and trap the foal inside it, much as a cork may be trapped inside a bottle. Furthermore, swollen, bruised mucous membrane is very susceptible to infection. The need for a careful and gentle approach in this situation is obvious.

Excessive bulging of the mare's anus may indicate that, instead of emerging through the vaginal opening, the feet of the foal are being pushed upwards towards the rectum by the mare's contractions.

If this push continues, the feet may tear through the wall of the vagina into the rectum. This tearing is called a rectovaginal fistula and in many cases it renders the mare infertile. Put the cleansed hand inside the vagina and guide the foal's feet downward to the vaginal opening.

A veterinary surgeon must be called as quickly as possible in the following cases. Firstly, the forefeet may be presented but the head may be back in the uterus, possibly resting on the flank of the foal. The foal may be lying on its back with the soles of its forefeet and lower

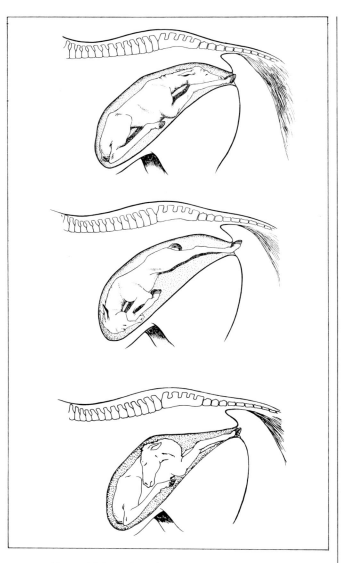

Above: This series of diagrams shows various presentations of the foal at birth. The top diagram shows the correct presentation, the middle is a breach presentation, and the bottom diagram shows another abnormal presentation.

jaw uppermost. It may be doubled upon itself so that the head, forefeet and hindfeet are all presented together. The hindfeet may be presented first with the soles facing upwards. Help should also be summoned if the buttocks and tail of the foal are presented (breech presentation), if the buttocks, tail and points of both hocks are presented or if there are twin foals. Veterinary help is also necessary if the foal is born dead.

No Foal Present at the Vulva

The veterinary surgeon should be called immediately if no foal appears after about 25 minutes of obvious contractions and straining. If there are no obvious contractions and the mare is continually getting up and down and showing signs of pain by kicking, swishing her tail, or looking at her flanks; if, after 15 minutes of obvious contractions and straining, the mare appears to give up and her efforts for the following half hour are weak and less frequent.

INDUCTION OF LABOUR

A relatively new technique in the veterinary field is the induction of labour. This may be recommended for mares that are well overdue or at least 330 days pregnant and are producing milk. The labour should also be induced if a vaginal examination reveals that the mare has a relaxed cervix.

The actual induction of labour is brought about by the intravenous or intramuscular injection of a drug given by a veterinary surgeon.

Supporters of induced labour put forward several reasons to justify its use in some cases. For example, induction ensures that a veterinary surgeon is on duty prior to and during labour, and a time can be selected for the labour that suits both the veterinary surgeon and the owner. After the injection and before the birth, 15–30 minutes elapse, during which the veterinary surgeon can correct any malpresentation. Moreover, a mare with a history of difficult births can receive as much assistance as she needs.

CARE OF THE MARE AFTER FOALING

Cleansing

The mare's tail, vulva, udder and hindlegs should be washed thoroughly after the birth of the foal. Cleansing to get rid of the blood, dirt and discharge collected on the skin and hair not only helps make the mare feel better but also prevents the spread or growth of bacteria that may be harmful to mare or foal. Use an antiseptic non-irritant wash; do not use harsh disinfectants as they may scald the skin, especially in the sensitive udder area. If that happens, the mare may reject the foal when it attempts to suckle. It is also important to wash off the remains of any soap, especially in the udder area, because the taste may inhibit the foal from sucking.

While the mare is being washed, someone should hold the foal in front of her so that she can see it, thus allaying any anxiety she may feel.

Tears, Bruising and Swelling

After the mare has been cleaned, she should be examined for tears, bruising and swelling of the vulva and outer vaginal area. Lift the mare's tail out of the way so that the anus and vulva can be observed without hindrance.

Tears of any length or depth should be attended by a veterinary surgeon who will stitch the wound as well as protecting the mare with tetanus and antibiotic injections.

A tear through the vaginal wall into the rectum, which is called a rectovaginal fistula and is caused by the foal's feet during birth, must be surgically corrected immediately by the veterinary surgeon. If left unattended, the tear will render the mare infertile and possibly lead to infection that will endanger her life.

Swelling and/or bruising is normally present after foaling and usually subsides over 48 hours. If the swelling is excessive and persists for longer or is accompanied by severe bruising, the mare is susceptible to infection, so consult your veterinary surgeon.

Cold hosing of the swollen areas can have a twofold action. Firstly it cleanses the area, and secondly, the massaging effect of the water pressure will disperse and reduce the swelling, whilst the coldness of the water will help to stop the bleeding that causes the bruising.

Vaginal Discharge

The excretion of small amounts of clear, serous discharge, sometimes blood-tinged, is normal up to a week after foaling. However, a constant drip of blood, a bloody brown discharge or pus coming from the vulva is abnormal. The mare should be examined by a veterinary surgeon.

The Udder

Examine both nipples to see that they are normal. Some mares have inverted nipples, making it impossible for the foal to suckle. Express milk from the nipples to make sure that there is a satisfactory flow and to observe the status of the milk.

The udder may be larger on one side than the other because the foal suckles constantly from one nipple, or there may be an infection of the udder on one side (mastitis). If the udder is infected on one or both sides, it is very painful to touch as well as being hot, swollen, hard and sometimes lumpy. It may be difficult to express milk, which may be thick and discoloured. In acute cases, the mare will have a high temperature.

When treating the mare for mastitis remove the foal from her, apply hot and cold foments, manually milk the mare and call a veterinary surgeon who will treat her with antibiotics.

The Afterbirth

The afterbirth (placental membranes) may be expelled from the mare before she gets to her feet after foaling. On average, it is expelled within 3 hours after foaling, although it may hang from the mare's vulva for up to 8 hours. If there is risk of the mare treading on the membranes and tearing them with her hind feet, it is best to tie the membrane in a knot so that it is not dragging on the ground.

If the membranes have not come away from the mare after 8 hours, contact the veterinary surgeon. The afterbirth may be easily removed by manually pulling on it with firm, even tension. If it is not removed in this way, the use of a drug will be necessary to aid in separation of the afterbirth from its attachments in the uterus. Other drugs are used to prevent laminitis (foal founder).

If the afterbirth has been expelled normally, it is very important to lay out the membranes on the ground to check that they have all been expelled. Sometimes a small portion of the afterbirth is retained in the uterus, leading to serious complications such as infection and founder.

Foal Heat

Eighty per cent of mares come on heat 9–12 days after foaling. This heat is as fertile as any other. A veterinary surgeon should be consulted and asked to examine the mare at the beginning of the foal heat period to see if it is advisable for her to be served. The veterinary surgeon might advise against her being served because of infection, tears, severe bruising or retained foetal membrane. He will advise against serving if the foal has been stillborn.

THE FOAL

The Premature Foal

Premature foals are born before they are fully developed in the mother's uterus. Foals born after spending less than 330 days in the uterus are classified as premature.

Since the premature foal is not fully developed, it experiences greater difffculty in coping with the external environment than does the normal foal.

Some premature foals can stand and suckle (usually 2-3 weeks premature) and some cannot (usually 5 weeks or more premature). Sparse body hair covering, such as in the mane and tail, is evident in many premature foals.

Whether or not your premature foal can stand and suckle, it is advisable for you to call a veterinary surgeon and at the same time to provide the foal with warmth and rest.

When the veterinary surgeon arrives, he will probably give the foal an injection of antibiotics. If your foal is unable to walk and suckle, he will most likely give it an intravenous fluid and electrolyte drip and then pass a stomach tube and secure it permanently in position. The actual feeding of colostrum through the tube can be done by the owner, stud groom or breeder. The stomach tube is left in position so that the feeding can be continued until the foal can stand and shows signs of suckling.

Above: This foal is premature and consequently it is not fully developed and is unable to stand.

Immediate Care of the Newborn Foal

A close watch should be kept on the foal; what to do and when to do it will be determined primarily by the foal's needs. Nevertheless, the following guidelines may be accepted as basic to the immediate care of the newborn foal.

As soon as the foal is born, check to see that it is breathing. If necessary, clear away any placental membrane or mucus that may be blocking the nostrils. If the foal is not breathing, it should be given oxygen therapy by means of a resuscitator or mouth-to-nose resuscitation as quickly as possible. Someone can be directed to apply firm pressure to the foal's chest with both hands, then to release it sharply and pause before repeating the cycle at the rate of 10 presses per minute. In each cycle, the press takes about 4 seconds and the release 2 seconds. The foal's head should be lower than the rest of the body, thus allowing the blood to flow more freely to the brain.

Allow the umbilical cord to break naturally when the mare moves away from the foal or when the foal first attempts to stand. Premature breaking of the umbilical cord by any person assisting at the birth may deprive the foal of its maximum blood supply, thus starving the brain of oxygen, with consequent brain damage.

Usually the stump of the umbilical cord is about 3-5 cm (1-2 in) long. It should be liberally swabbed with tincture of iodine and in 2-3 weeks it will wither and drop off.

The foal is born with whitish, gelatinous pads in the soles of the feet. These usually break out before or during the foal's first efforts to stand, and may be observed in the birth area.

If the foal does not suckle the mare – and do not mistake mouthing of the teats for sucking – this failure may be caused by weakness or deformity in the foal, by the mare being cranky or by some other factor. Normally the foal suckles within minutes of finding its way to its mother's flank. If it has not suckled within 2-3 hours, it should be guided close to the teats and the index finger placed in its mouth. When the foal starts suckling the finger, its mouth should be transferred to the mother's

Above: The umbilical cord here is still unbroken; it should be allowed to break naturally.

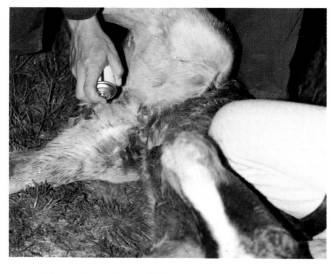

Above: Once the umbilical cord has been cut, it can be sprayed with an aerosol antibiotic.

teat close by. If this ploy is not successful, leave the foal for another 2-3 hours and, if it has not suckled by then, hand feed it by milking the mare, placing the milk in a baby's bottle and, again using the index finger as a guide, teach the foal to suck. When it does, transfer it to the nipple on the bottle. At the next feeding time, try to transfer the foal from the bottle to the mare's teats.

Colostrum is the name given to the first milk that the mare produces. It is very thick, bright yellow to orange in colour and gives the foal immunity against infection in its early days of life. Colostrum is only produced by the mare for about the first 24 hours after its foal is born and the foal can only absorb the antibodies from it for about the first 36 hours of life. Colostrum has high vitamin content and food value and guards against constipation. The foal must drink it in those early hours of life, either from its mother or from some other source. Colostrum keeps indefinitely in deep freeze so breeders are able to store an emergency supply. Stocks can be built up by milking about 600 ml (1 milk bottle) from mares that have just foaled and have an ample supply.

Meconium, a thick, dark and tarlike product of the foal's first bowel motion, should be seen on the ground where the foal has been. It is usually passed within 2-3 hours of birth but may be passed later. If it is not passed, constipation will beset the foal, with accompanying straining to no avail, lethargy and disinclination to suckle. Constipation can develop into a very serious condition if not arrested; an enema should be administered within 12 hours after the birth if the meconium is not passed. If, after the foal has first suckled the mare, it passes a soft yellow-brown motion, do not fear at this stage that it has diarrhoea.

Diseases and Problems of the Young or Newborn Foal

Isoimmune Haemolytic Jaundice
Isoimmune haemolytic jaundice is the most common form of jaundice found in the newborn foal. It can be compared to the Rh disease in human babies. It is due to a clash between the antibodies in the mare's colostrum and the red blood cells of the foal. The end result is destruction of the foal's red blood cells and, if the disease is not arrested, death will occur. Keep in mind that a foal with this form of jaundice is not born with it; only when it ingests the antibodies from its mother's colostrum may it be subject to this disease.

Signs are fairly obvious. In 12-36 hours after it first suckles, the foal becomes sluggish, dull, weak, no longer suckles and wants to lie down. Breathing is rapid and shallow (panting), especially after exercise. During the first 24 hours, the gums and membrane around the eye are pale, but after that time, when the condition worsens, the pallor changes to varying shades of yellow. After 24 hours too, the urine becomes dark brown in colour.

Foals with advanced jaundice may be found in a state of collapse and coma.

Once you suspect jaundice, call a veterinary surgeon immediately. In the meantime, if your foal is less than 48 hours old, you can help by preventing the foal from suckling the mare either by muzzling the foal or removing it. In either case, the mare should be milked out hourly and the milk discarded; the foal should be fed with colostrum by a foster mother, baby's bottle or stomach tube. After the foal is 48 hours old, it should be allowed to return to its mother to suckle normally. The veterinary surgeon treats mild cases of jaundice with antibiotics, while severe cases require a blood transfusion.

Isoimmune haemolytic jaundice may be prevented by simply giving the pregnant mare a blood test before the foal is born. If the test proves positive, no milk from that mare should be given to its foal for the first 48 hours after birth. During that period, the young foal should be fed with colostrum that has been obtained from a foster mother or has been held in deep freeze to meet an emergency such as this.

If a mare has a history of producing foals with isoimmune haemolytic jaundice, it is advisable to send her to a different yet compatible stallion.

Umbilical Hernia
This congenital defect is a swelling in the region of the navel; it may be up to 5 cm (2 in) in diameter. It is caused by fatty tissue or the intestine passing through a hole in the muscles of the abdominal wall and pressing against the skin.

Many small umbilical hernias close up and disappear over a period of 12 months. Nevertheless, it is wise to ask a veterinary surgeon to evaluate the hernia and to recommend whether it should be corrected surgically.

If the hernia opening in the muscular wall of the abdomen is large enough, a loop of the intestine may become twisted in it and strangle itself, cutting off the blood supply to that portion of the intestine and necessitating emergency surgery to save the foal's life.

Patent Urachus
This is a relatively common condition where urine drips from the stump of the navel cord. The flow increases when the foal strains to urinate. Often there is a wet patch around the umbilical stump.

Clean the area thoroughly and cauterise the navel stump daily with a solution containing 10 per cent iodine or silver nitrate until the drip ceases. Antibiotic cover for 5 days should be administered.

Ruptured Bladder
This problem may be due to pressure on a full bladder at the time of foaling or to incomplete closure of the bladder during intrauterine development. The foal appears normal for 12-24 hours after birth but then shows signs of depression, particularly 12-24 hours later. It strains repeatedly to urinate with very little or no urine being passed. The straining can resemble that of a constipated foal, but should not be confused with it.

Contact a veterinary surgeon immediately.

Atresia Ani
There is no opening at the site of the anus. The foal cannot pass a motion, shows signs of constipation, becomes colicy and its abdomen swells. This condition can be corrected surgically.

Diarrhoea
Diarrhoea, more commonly known as scouring, often causes death if unchecked, particularly in the first 2 days of a foal's life. Diarrhoea may be caused by septicaemia and gastroenteritis. In cases of infection, the temperature rises, colic may be present, the motion is fluid and putrid and the foal is lethargic and lacks appetite. Call the veterinary surgeon immediately. Once the causative organisms have been identified, appropriate drugs can be administered.

If the foal is a greedy drinker and the mare is a good milker, diarrhoea often results. The cure is to restrain the foal from drinking too much by milking the mare. Remember that the young foal drinks about every half hour but has a relatively small stomach, so the guiding principle for its intake should be 'a little often'.

Foals that ingest the mare's faeces are often subject to diarrhoea. Immediate removal of the mare's droppings is the best form of control.

The mare comes on heat 9–12 days after foaling and the heat period lasts for 3–5 days. During this period, the foal may have diarrhoea but the condition ends when the mare goes off heat and usually no harm is done.

Good general nursing contributes significantly to the foal's recovery from diarrhoea. It is advisable to observe the following precedures. Keep the foal warm and protected from the elements, and provide it with clean water and electrolytes to prevent dehydration. Isolate the foal from any other foals or weanlings, disinfect the stable or box in which the foal is housed and decrease the foal's milk intake by regularly milking out the mare.

Constipation

The most common cause of constipation in the young foal is blockage of the bowel by meconium, the thick, dark tarlike faeces present in the lower bowels at the time of birth. The condition is seen more frequently in colts than in fillies.

In most cases, symptoms of constipation become most obvious 12–18 hours after birth. Straining with restlessness and tail cocked are warning signs. With more frequent straining, there is less suckling which may cease if the pain continues. With no relief, the abdominal pains become more severe, the foal gets up and down, lies flat out, rolls on its back, crouches, throws itself to the ground and thrashes about violently. Ultimately, the foal may go into a state of shock. Veterinary help must be at hand if the foal is to be saved.

Unless you observe the foal's first motion, it is wise to adopt the routine of giving all foals that have not passed their meconium an enema within 12 hours of birth. Again, if a foal has passed its first motion but later shows signs of straining with no motion, it is advisable to administer an enema. An enema may consist of about 300 ml (10 fl oz) of warm, mild soapy water or about 300 ml of paraffin oil. A human disposable enema pack is also effective.

In administering an enema, take care not to damage the lining of the rectum and anus. The problem of constipation might be worsened by swelling of the rectum and anus, thereby reducing the diameter of the opening through which the foal has to pass its motion.

Leg Deformities

The particular cause of a limb deformity is difficult to isolate; it may be a single one or the combination of several. Generally the causes may be classified as nutritional, malpositioning of the foal in the mare's uterus, inherited genetic abnormalities or injury.

Whatever the cause, it is essential to treat the deformity as soon as possible to remedy it and, failing that, to stabilise it and prevent it from worsening.

It is always wise to check the nutritional status of mare and foal. If necessary, supplement their diet with a vitamin and mineral supplement rich in calcium. A foal may suffer from the deformity of contracted tendons.

Confine it to a stable or box to reduce movement to a minimum. There should be a deep bed of straw to prevent abrasion to the skin and to act as a cushion and support for the legs.

The veterinary surgeon should be called as soon as possible after the condition has been recognised. The usual treatment is to apply a brace to the back of the leg; this is released about every 2 hours to allow circulation to the skin to resume. After 1 or 2 days, the brace need no longer be used, as in normal cases the tendons have stretched to the point where they allow the sole of the

foot to touch the ground. Once the sole of the foot comes in normal contact with the ground, the movement of the foal and the weight-bearing effect on the tendons will ensure that the legs assume normal conformation.

In many cases, a foal's flexor tendons are so weak that they allow the back of the fetlock to touch the ground; the foal walks on it rather than on the sole of the foot.

Strict confinement to a stable with a deep bed of straw hastens recovery. Some cases require a light fibreglass cast to support the fetlock for a few days.

Young foals are often known to suffer from medical deviation of the knee (knock knees). Confinement to the stable, combined with hoof trimming, is a successful form of treatment for most cases. The outside edge of the hoof should be kept trimmed by rasping it repeatedly until the leg is straightened.

Cases that fail to respond to this kind of treatment should be referred to the veterinary surgeon. A metal staple may have to be inserted surgically on the inside of the knee to correct the problem.

Infections and Infectious Diseases

In the case of infection, the old adage applies: prevention is better than cure. With this in mind, stud masters should avoid overuse of their foaling yard, and take care to see that the mare and foal are kept in a clean environment. They should see that the foal's umbilical cord is liberally swabbed with tincture of iodine at birth, and check that the foal has had its colostrum intake shortly after birth.

Septicaemia

This is often known as blood poisoning which is circulation of bacteria in large numbers in the bloodstream.

Bacteria can enter the foal's bloodstream in a number of ways. Before birth, bacteria can pass from the mare's bloodstream across the placenta to the foal's bloodstream. The umbilical cord is also a common source of infection. Bacteria enters the foal's bloodstream by ascending the stump of the umbilical cord.

Skin wounds, however slight, provide a means for the penetration of bacteria. Contaminated food, milk or foreign bodies, if taken into the mouth and swallowed, are a source of infection. A foal sniffing around, particularly on the ground, can inhale bacteria. Keep the environment of the mare and foal clean.

Symptoms of septicaemia are that the foal is very depressed, shows signs of weakness, fails to suckle, breathes rapidly, has a harsh coat and a temperature that is too high or too low. Contact a veterinary surgeon immediately, and while waiting for his arrival, keep the foal confined, warm and quiet.

Pneumonia

This can be referred to as rattles because of the rattling sound in the chest that accompanies breathing. It is an infectious disease of young foals, occurring in most countries. This problem appears to localise itself to certain studs in any one area, suggesting that it may be due to a particular kind of management.

The bacterium known as *Corynebacterium equi* is the causative agent. It enters the foal's body via the stump of the umbilical cord, via the placenta while the foal is in the uterus, or via migrating roundworm larvae. In some cases it is unknown how the bacteria enter the living tissue of the foal.

Symptoms of pneumonia are coughing, especially when moving, and a loud nose (rattles) due to moisture in the lungs, accompanied by laboured breathing often stimulated by handling. The foal has a harsh coat and an elevated temperature.

Call the veterinary surgeon. In the meantime, keep the foal confined, warm, and well nourished.

Pneumonia can be controlled, but an order of priorities needs to be established. Such a programme in order of priority might be to establish a routine of giving antibiotics at birth if the disease is common on the stud. Isolate infected foals, clean yards and boxes regularly, establish a well-organised worming procedure and maintain a good nutrition programme.

Joint Ill

This is an arthritic condition caused by a generalised infection (septicaemia) localising itself in one or more joints of the newborn foal. Symptoms are lameness and stiffness in movement, temperature rise and heat, pain and swelling in the affected joint or joints.

Call a veterinary surgeon. While awaiting his arrival, confine foal and mare to a clean box or yard where warmth and rest are available. Check the mare's milk supply to see that the foal is adequately fed.

Make sure the mare is thoroughly clean around the vulva, udder and legs. Wash with an antiseptic non-irritant wash and apply supportive bandages to the affected joint or joints of the foal. Hot foment or poultice the affected joint or joints with antiphlogestine.

To control joint ill, wash the mare thoroughly after foaling and make sure the foal is given adequate colostrum. Apply tincture of iodine on the stub of the umbilical cord of the newborn foal. Alternate the foaling paddocks every 2 years and control parasites.

The Orphan Foal

The category of orphan foal includes not only the foal whose mother died during birth or shortly after, but also the foal whose mother, for one reason or another, has no milk or cannot nurse her offspring.

Because of the strong emotional ties that develop between orphan foal and handler, the foal is often mismanaged to the point of being spoilt, and it subsequently grows into a mischievous, difficult weanling. The foal should be handled gently but firmly and, in order to develop into a well-disciplined horse with a good temperament, its education must begin at birth.

Bottle Feeding

The foal should be fed every 3 hours, day and night, for the 1st week of life. Thereafter, the frequency of the feeds should be decreased and the amount increased, so that at 4 weeks old, the foal is fed 4 times a day.

The foal should be given at least 1200 ml (4.05 fl oz) of colostrum ie, 2 full milk bottles, as soon as possible after birth. It loses the ability to absorb colostrum from its intestines after it is about 36 hours old.

At each 3-hourly feed, the foal should receive 600 ml (20.2 fl oz) of milk substitute, and this amount can be varied according to individual demand.

Substitute milk can be made up according to this formula: 300 ml (10 fl oz) cow's milk, 300 ml warm, boiled water, 5 ml (teaspoon) lime water and 1 teaspoon Glucodin. An alternative formula is 300 ml evaporated or powdered milk, 300 ml water and 1 teaspoon Glucodin.

Foals have the ability to suck naturally, but if the foal rejects the teat on the bottle, place your index finger in its mouth. If it still does not suck, move the index finger against the roof of the mouth and tongue. Slowly replace the index finger by the teat on the bottle.

The disadvantage of bottle feeding is that it is time-consuming (cleaning the bottle and teat and holding the bottle while the foal is feeding) and consequently costly as far as labour is concerned.

Foster Mother

In many cases, a foster mother is not readily available when urgently required. Some mares are good foster mothers but others will not readily accept the orphan foal and may even reject it. Mares that become a little fractious and unwilling in this situation can be calmed by the use of a twitch or tranquilliser. It is wise to introduce the orphan foal to the mother with some caution so that no harm is done.

Bucket Feeding

Apart from the foster mare, this is the best form of feeding becasue it is easier and less time-consuming than any other and very effective.

At the outset a little more time and patience are needed to encourage the foal to feed from the bucket. Isolate it for a number of hours in a warm, safe environment until it wants some attention as well as being hungry. Pour the milk into a plastic bucket with a wide opening so that the foal will not balk at putting its head into it; as the foal suckles naturally from its mother with its head up, the biggest problem in getting it to drink from a bucket is persuading it to suck with its head down. Firstly, make it suck on your index finger with its head up, much as it does when suckling from the mare's teats, then gradually direct its head downwards, the foal still sucking on the index finger, until its mouth is down in the milk in the bucket. Withdraw the finger; with luck the foal will continue sucking. If it doesn't suck after the first attempt, go through the same procedure again. Patience!

The milk prepared from a formula should be placed in the bucket, kept at room temperature (though cold milk is quite suitable) and be made freely available to the foal, in which case it will not overdrink. Change the milk and clean the bucket thoroughly twice a day.

Hang the bucket in a secure position at a height convenient for the foal to drink at will.

Dry Feeding

Once the foal is drinking readily from the bucket and is several days old, set up another bucket similar in shape and position and put into it about two handfuls of a readily digestible milk-based, pelleted food.

Encourage the foal to eat the pellets by placing a few in the mouth and again directing the head to the bucket. Once the foal accepts the pellets by eating them readily, make them freely available at all times.

When the foal is eating about 1 kg (2 lb) of the milk-based pellets per day, a grain-based pellet should be gradually substituted.

At 4 weeks of age, the foal can be weaned completely off the prepared milk formulae and fed dry pellets and good quality grains as well as limited quantities of hay.

Stomach Tube

If the foal is very weak and unable to stand, a stomach tube can be passed, preferably by a veterinary surgeon, and secured permanently in position. The owner or stud groom can connect a funnel to the tube and pour the necessary nutritional requirements down the tube every 3 hours. This procedure should be continued until the foal is strong enough to stand and suckle.

Medication

Even if orphan foals have received colostrum, they should be given a course of antibiotics by the veterinary surgeon as soon after birth as possible.

YOUNGSTOCK

HANDLING THE FOAL

Patient handling establishes respect and trust and will pay dividends in the future. Foals coming in at night can have daily handling sessions of 5–14 minutes. Those at grass can be left until they are weaned.

The basic concept in handling a foal is that it will stop struggling and resisting as soon as it realizes a human being is more powerful, that it can't get away and that there is no need to get away, because no harm is intended. In this way, it will learn that it can trust its handlers.

One of the first tasks is to fit a head collar. This is most easily accomplished in a stable. One person approaches the foal from the nearside, putting a left arm around the foal's chest and holding the tail at the root with the right arm. While the foal is being securely held, a second person puts on the head collar. If the foal is not weaned, a helper is needed to hold the mare.

The foal can be taught to lead by being pushed from behind – never pull it by the head collar. In the first few lessons, put a stable rubber around the foal's neck (this is soft and won't hurt) while holding the hindquarters with the other hand. This can be used to push the foal forward. The mare is led in front of the foal, which will encourage it to follow. Gradually, over a period of days, the pushing will become less necessary and the foal can be led more from the stable rubber. Eventually, as it relaxes, it can be led off the headcollar.

The other vital aspect of handling is getting the foal used to its feet being picked up. It's important to take care of the feet, and they should be regularly cleaned out with a hoof pick. From about 2 months of age, regular trimming is advisable. If there are any deformities of the feet, corrections can often be made by the farrier. Success is more likely when the bone is still soft.

WEANING

Weaning can be a traumatic experience for the foal, but it need not be so if the foal is prepared for it whenever the opportunity presents itself in the days following birth.

The mare and foal should be wormed when the foal is 6 weeks old, and every 6 weeks thereafter. When the mare is brought in from the paddock, this is an ideal opportunity to familiarise the foal with gates, laneways, yards and the presence of people.

While the foals are running on the mares in the paddock, they should be fed with high-quality grains and hay to improve their growth rate and to teach them to eat concentrates, so that on weaning there is no sudden change in diet. Sudden changes in diet in foals, or for that matter in all horses, can make them refuse to eat or can upset their intestinal functions, possibly causing diarrhoea or constipation. All this adds up to a setback that a young foal can ill afford.

Generally, a foal is weaned at approximately 5 months old but this can vary with the condition of the mare, the foal and/or the environment.

There are two main methods of weaning. The first is the more artificial, but it is safer and easier to manage, and is practiced at most studs. If the mare has been given grain (such as oats), this is cut down to reduce her milk production. Mares out at grass are brought in (at least at night) 7–10 days before weaning so the foal can learn to eat grain and hay. Feed mare and foal from separate containers.

Put them in a stable that is thickly bedded. For the last few days do not muck them out. The mare's smell will remain in the box. The mare is led out quickly and taken far enough away to ensure that neither the mare nor the foal will hear each other's whinnies.

The foal is happier if left with other youngsters. It can then be turned out to grass with them after 2 or 3 days. This sudden separation is very stressful for the foal, and at this time it may lose weight and become particularly liable to picking up nervous habits, such as weaving, cirb biting and walking the box.

The alternative, more-natural method is to turn a group of mares and foals out in a paddock and keep them together for several weeks so social bonds develop. To start weaning, two mares are taken out and their foals left. The youngsters don't usually become so upset because they have the herd to return to. After 2 or 3 days, two further mares are taken away; the process continues until only the foals remain. If the foals are stabled at night, the weaning is done when they are first turned out in the morning. In the evenings, pairs of weanlings are put in a stable together.

The mares must dry off, and their milk production must stop. Less grain helps this. It is inadvisable to touch the udder, and the mares should only be milked if they are very full, because milking encourages further milk production.

Feeding

Diet is an important part of healthy growth. The first major growth period occurs directly after foaling. In the first month, the foal's height increases by about 30 per cent. The second growth period is from 6–9 months, when most foals are weaned. The third is after puberty. Good feed is vital to maximize growth and to ensure healthy development of the best possible individual.

The important factor is to keep the youngstock in good condition – not too thin or too fat. Overweight can have as serious an effect on bone development as under-nourishment. Overfeeding leads to limb troubles (too much weight to carry), and underfeeding restricts growth, so it is important that a balance between the two is reached.

The amount of feed to give depends on the type of youngstock. Native ponies need very little, while throughbreds need a good deal. Also important are the quality and quantity of the grass (in winter its nourishment value falls), the time spent in the stable and the future use of the youngstock. Those that need to mature quickly, such as racehorses and show stock, should be given more grain.

The important factor, whatever the quantity given, is that the food is good quality. Particularly important is the hay, which if musty and dusty can easily cause wind problems with the lungs in the future.

Although the quantity of hard feed varies, a typical diet for a freshly weaned riding-horse foal would be 2.25 kg (5 lb) of crushed oats, and 0.5 kg (1 lb) bran. It is very important that youngstock eat sufficient calcium and phosphorus, so give supplements containing these. Small amounts of linseed (once or twice weekly), carrots, cod liver oil (daily in one feed) and sugar beet can be added.

Handling the Weanling

With the weanling tied up or being held, run your hands all over the body. Don't pat the weanling, as this can frighten it; just rub the hand over the body and down the back of the legs, picking up the feet. While doing all this, talk to the weanling. Once it allows its feet to be picked up and held, the feet should be trimmed and rasped and any obvious problems corrected.

Soon after weaning, the weanling should be wormed, vaccinated and, where appropriate, branded.

BRANDING

Identification of a horse is based on colour, age, sex, markings and brands. It is possible to find two horses that are so alike that the only way to distinguish them positively is by the brands. The brand fulfils the same purpose as a registration number plate on a car.

Branding is not a requirement in the UK, but it is used by some breeds such as the Exmoor, and most of the Continental warm-bloods are branded. Lip tatooing is the general form of branding in the USA for thoroughbreds. In Australia, one of the requirements for a horse to be accepted into the Australian Stud Book is that it be properly branded and that the brand used has been registered with the appropriate authority. The brand must be permanent, clearly read and in the correct form and position.

Branding is best done during the weaning process prior to the mare being separated from the foal.

In order to ensure that no two horses carry the same combination of brands and numbers, and that the meaning of the numerals is quite clear, the brands and numerals are required to be placed in a particular position on the horse. In some countries they are placed on the near shoulder or on the rump; in others they are placed on the off shoulder. In many countries, the breeder's or owner's identifying brand is used on the near (left) shoulder. The brand on the off (right) shoulder consists of distinguishing numerals comprising the reference number over the last figure of the season of foaling. For example, 1 over 1 means the first foal dropped on the stud for the 1981 season; 2 over 1 means the second foal dropped for the 1981 season.

Fire Branding

The area in which the brand is to be applied is clipped of excess hair and washed free of dirt with a non-inflammable solution such as Zephiran or Hibitane. The head of the branding iron should be clean and flat. Leave the head in the fire until it is red-hot.

The weanling or adult horse should be in an enclosed area and held up against the wall or fence to restrict its movement when the brand is applied. A nose twitch is of great value to assist in restraining the horse. A hand covering the eye will prevent the horse seeing the approaching brand and thus eliminate flinching.

The red-hot brand need only be applied for a few seconds. If the brand is not red-hot, it must be held on the skin for longer, thus increasing the risk of movement and smudging. In addition, the burn may be too shallow, resulting in a brand that fades over a period of time and is eventually unable to be seen. Application of an antibiotic spray to the burn will minimise the possibility of infection.

Freeze Branding

This form of branding is relatively painless. It utilises intense cold, resulting in the growth of unpigmented white hair. A good freeze brand is permanent and can be read from a distance of about 40 m (45 yards): very useful for paddock identification. Preparation of the site is the

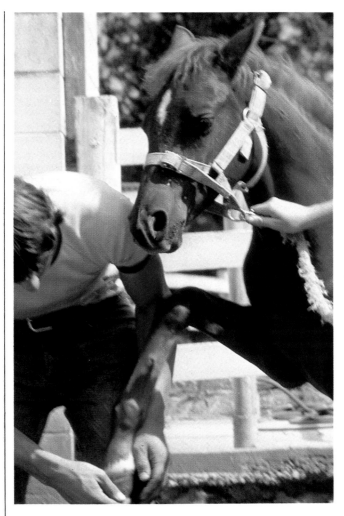

Above: An important aspect of handling is teaching the young horse to have his feet picked up. This is the correct procedure for picking up the weanling's feet.

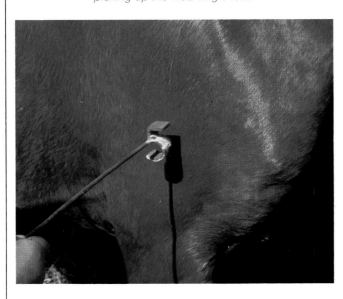

Above: Some breeds are fire branded and this red hot iron is poised over the horse's shoulder before being held on the skin for a few seconds.

same as for fire branding except that the skin should be wiped over with methylated spirits.

The head of the branding iron is made of copper because it is a better conductor than other metals. To chill the brands, place the head in a container of crushed dry ice and methylated spirits. It takes about 20 minutes for the heads of the brands to be chilled sufficiently. Rechilling of the brands takes about 2 minutes.

The weanling or horse is restrained in the same way as for fire branding. The brand is applied with firm pressure to the skin for 25 seconds. There is little or no reaction, apart from some muscle tremor. With grey horses the brand should be left in contact with the skin for 35 seconds. Several months pass before the white hair grows completely over the branded area.

The chances of infection are less with freeze branding than with fire branding, and the former is recommended.

EDUCATING THE YEARLING

The weanling stays in the paddock for 10–12 months, playing, exercising, growing and developing into a yearling. It then needs further education, whether it is intended to be a child's pony and companion or a top-class racehorse.

To begin its programme of further education, the yearling is brought in from the paddock and housed in a stable. The basic procedures that it has already been taught as a weanling: putting on a head collar, leading, typing up and handling, are all revised and consolidated. In teaching the yearling further basic disciplines, the processes of repetition and letting the yearling know that you are pleased each time it performs well by giving it a kind word of praise such as 'good girl' and a gentle stroke or brush on the near side of the neck, are essential in a good training programme. Rewarding actions reinforce that form of behaviour and are more likely to ensure success next time. Success or near-success, reinforcement with rewards and repetition (but not to the point where trainer and horse are tired) are thus the elements behind a good training or education programme.

In the further education of the yearling, the following activities may be included in the programme.

Catching the Yearling in the Stable

When it is brought in from the paddock, leave the head collar on the yearling. If it is difficult to catch, a strap can be left hanging from the head collar; one can more readily grasp this than the collar.

The other alternative is to have a stick about a metre (3 ft) long with a blunt wire hook on the end to enable one to hook onto the ring in the head collar just under the jaw. The lead is then secured.

When you are walking into the stable, a well-mannered yearling should face you as you approach. However, sometimes a vice can develop; every time you approach the yearling, it turns its hindquarters towards you. You run a real risk of being kicked if you continue to make your approach. The use of a whip to flick the yearling below the hocks will soon have the horse facing you as you approach it.

Handling

In handling a yearling, start with your hand on the neck, giving it a soft brush with the back of the hand, then work the hand along and towards the section you wish to examine. Always keep your hand in contact with the yearling from the neck, along and down, so that it knows through its sense of touch where you are at all times.

Lifting the Near (left) Side Foreleg

Standing beside the leg facing the hindquarters, put your left hand on the yearling's neck on the near side. Give the neck a soft brush or two, then run your hand down to the elbow and down the back of the leg to the pastern. Roll your hand around to the front of the pastern and left the leg.

Lifting the Near (left) Side Hindleg

Run your left hand from the yearling's neck along to the hip and keep it there. At this point you are standing in front of and to the side of the hindleg facing towards the yearling's rear. From where your left hand is on the hip, run your right hand down the back of the leg until it reaches the pastern, at which point you can lift the leg and pull it forward.

The reason for keeping your left hand on the hip is that it enables you to push yourself away from the yearling if it kicks. When you push yourself away, you also tend to push the yearling away and off balance.

If the yearling resents the hindlimb being touched, a lead can be looped around the pastern and used to pull the leg forward; the lead is then released. This procedure is repeated until the yearling no longer resents its leg being touched and lifted. The same procedure for lifting the legs on the other (off) side should be practised.

Hoof Cleaning and Dressing

Associated with the education of the yearling to cooperate in lifting its legs is getting the yearling used to the routines of cleaning and dressing its hooves. See the section on hoof care (pages **70** and **71**).

Grooming

In the early stages of handling the yearling, use a very soft brush to groom the coat lightly, not so much to get the dirt out of the coat as to familiarise the yearling with the touch of the brush. Start in the area of the neck and slowly progress over a number of days until eventually the yearling quietly accepts a light brush all over.

Rugs

These are not needed by most youngstock but thoroughbreds which are being prepared for sales or show horses for in-hand classes can benefit from wearing them. This training should be done in the stable. Enlist the aid of an assistant to hold the yearling's head while you approach from the near side and slowly lay a rolled up light horse rug over the withers. Holding the end of the rug with the left hand, unroll it with the right. Fasten the front strap and check the rug for size, making certain it sits evenly on the yearling's back. Slowly fasten the leg straps. If you take the precaution of seeing that the straps are the same length and are crossed between the legs, the rug will not slip to one side.

Maturity of the Yearling

Once the yearling is familiar with and adept at its education activities, it can be turned out in the paddock and allowed to mature further.

Some yearlings, particularly thoroughbreds, are broken in during the winter but most well-muscled, well-grown yearlings are skeletally immature. You may have a horse in which the flesh (muscle) is willing but the skeleton (bones and associated ligaments, tendons and connective tissue) is weak. Many horses are not skeletally mature until they are about 4½ years old.

Many yearlings and 2-year-olds have open epiphyseal lines that cannot be seen by looking at the knees, and are not related to the term 'open knees'. Typically, during its growth, a long bone possesses a long middle part known as the shaft or diaphysis and two ends, each known as an epiphysis.

During development, the epiphysis is not fused with the diaphysis but is actually separated from it by the epiphyseal line, which in the growing stage is said to be open. At maturity, the epiphyseal line disappears; it is said to be closed, and the epiphyses fuse with the diaphysis. The only way to evaluate the state of the epiphyseal line is by X-ray.

The areas normally evaluated by the veterinary surgeon are the knees and hocks, as the epiphyseal lines in these areas are the last to close. X-rays taken approximately 2½ cm (1 in) above the knee will reveal to what extent the epiphyseal line has closed.

The degree of closure of the epiphyseal line in the X-rayed area will indicate the general maturity or immaturity of the whole skeleton, as well as the degree of development in the local area.

Horses with closed epiphyseal lines are usually ready to be broken in, educated and worked; horses with partially closed epiphyseal lines may be broken in, educated, then spelled to allow maturation to take place.

Horses with open epiphyseal lines should be turned out to grass, otherwise the stresses of breaking in and education could cause epiphysitis, sore shins, splints, fractures, poor development and chronic lameness, leading to unsoundness.

Before the yearling goes out to grass, a blood count should be taken to evaluate calcium and phosphorus levels so that the diet can be adjusted to correct any imbalance that may alter or slow down epiphyseal closure.

Drugs may be used in selected cases with the beneficial effect of helping to close the epiphysis and of speeding up the maturation of the yearling's skeleton without any detrimental effects.

There are normal closure times for each epiphyseal line. These times will vary with different breeds of horses, nutritional levels and certain diseases.

CASTRATION

This is a surgical procedure whereby both testicles are removed. A castrated horse is referred to as a gelding.

Age for Castration

There is no definite age at which a horse should be castrated, though the majority are 'done' between 1 and 2 years of age. A stallion at 6 years of age or a weanling of 6 months can be castrated without any complications.

The testicles have usually descended into the scrotum at birth, but in some cases they do not full descend until 10–15 months of age. If after 15 months, a testicle or the testicles have not descended, the horse is referred to as a monorchid, rig or cryptorchid.

Around 2 years of age is a good time for castration because the horse has had time to develop its physical characteristics, personality and temperament; the owner has also been able to evaluate the horse's potential ability.

Reasons for Castration

The colt may be trained for racing or some other activity that requires concentration and his mind to be on the job. He may, however, exhibit traits of aggression such as biting, kicking and waywardness. He may perhaps show too much sexual interest in fillies and mares by trying to mount them or by attracting their attention with such acts as rearing and squealing. Again, the colt may be continually masturbating which may cause weight loss and poor performance and all efforts to cure him may have been useless. In all these cases and in others, castration appears to be the answer to the problem.

Many colts around 2 years of age develop accentuated male characteristics, such as an overdeveloped crest on the neck or excessive general muscular development. They may be unbalanced by being top-heavy; their body is not in proportion to and appears too heavy for their legs. This type of horse is liable to break down due to excessive weight on the legs. Castration usually solves this problem.

If the horse has poor conformation, is a monorchid, rig or cryptorchid or has any other undesirable inheritable characteristic, he should be castrated to prevent the genes being passed on to the next generation.

In some cases, the colt may be balanced in conformation, of good even temperament and genetically sound, but the fences are not high or strong enough to hold it when there is an attractive group of mares in the next paddock. Colts on average reach sexual maturity at 16 months old. Yards with fences of solid construction about 1.8 m (6 ft) high are necessary if the colt is going to be contained. Geldings and mares can be run together, whereas colts or stallions should be each in a separate yard or paddock, appropriately fenced.

Colts with disease involving the testicle such as a tumour or inguinal or scrotal hernia should be castrated.

The Surgical Procedure of Castration

Taking into account the current value placed on horses and the many complications that can be encountered, castration should be performed only by a registered veterinary surgeon, even in those countries where there is no law to enforce this.

The surgery can be done with the horse standing up or with it recumbent under a general anaesthetic. The form of surgery adopted depends on such factors as the horse's temperament, breed, age, position of the testicles, capability of the assistant and whether or not there is sufficient room to give a general anaesthetic.

In the normal castration procedure, where both testicles have descended into the scrotum, the operation is comparatively straightforward and uncomplicated when carried out by a veterinary surgeon. However, in the case of the rig, the surgery may involve complex procedures, such as opening the abdomen to locate and remove the undescended testicle or testicles.

157

INDEX

ACKNOWLEDGEMENTS

The author wishes particularly to thank the following: Ray Joyce; Greg Farrell of Mulawa Arabian Stud, New South Wales; Peter Pond; Australian Thoroughbreds Magazine Pty Ltd; Jean Hawcroft; Pony Club Association of New South Wales; Colin Vickery; Dennis O'Brien; New South Wales Department of Agriculture; Jim Kennard; Tina Wommelsdorf; Paul Silver; Lyn and Roly Green.

The consultant and editor would like to thank the following: Russell Christie B.V.M.S., M.R.C.O.S. for his contribution; Isobel McLean for preparing the index; Jane Perring for her kind permission to take the photographs on pages 50-51 and 54-55 at her stables with Sarah and Wilf Purver and Willow, the horse.

Photographs: Ansett 38; APL 38 (top left), 67 (top); Australian Jockey Club Sydney 10; Vicki Cannon 150; John Charlton Saddlery 46; Ethnor Veterinary Pharmaceutical Manufacturers 79; Jeremy Finnis 50-51, 54-55; Dr W. Hartley, University of Sydney 143; Jan Hawcroft 30, 32-33, 89, 94-95; Ted Hawcroft 105, 130; Kit Houghton 1, 3, 4-5, 47, 55 (bottom left), 67 (bottom), 73, 80, 85, 96, 145, 146-147; Bonny Lestikow 104, 125, 138, 155; S. Neville 10; Reuben Rose, University of Sydney 67, 119, 128; Mike Roberts endpapers, 8-9, 28-29, 56-57, 75, 134-135, 140.

Artwork: John Francis 6, 20-21, 24; Jan Hawcroft 7, 19, 81; Jeffrey Smith 104; Glenn Steward, J.M. & A. 11, 12, 13, 14, 17, 40-41, 43, 44-45, 49, 52-53, 66, 69, 70, 88, 100, 148; Eric Tenney 24 (bottom).